Contents

Acknowledgments	vii
A Short History of Recipes 1-2-3	1
Introduction	3

Part 1: Morning   **13**

Room Service	15
Two-Bowl Breakfast	18
French Triptych	21
Old World–New World	25
Breakfast in Cairo	27
The Cook	30
¡Buenos Dias!	33
Little Morning Meal	36
Breakfast for Fannie Farmer	38
Fried Red Tomatoes	41
Postcard from Portofino	45
Morning Light, Southern Exposure	48
At the King David	51
Holiday Morning	54
Bread-and-Breakfast	57

Part 2: Noon   **61**

Summer in the City	64
Vegetarian Sampler	67
Cool Spaghetti	71
The First Cherries	74
A Poem for the Table	79
An Accidental Guest	82
Lunch for Picasso	85
How to Eat a Mussel	89
Homage to Jean-Georges	93
Mod Cod	98

At the Niçois Table 102

Lunch on the Fourth of July 106

Pan-Asian Primer 110

Sunday "Dinner" 114

Med-Rim Mosaic 118

Afternoon Fiesta! 122

Lunch with Chinese Flavors 126

Autumn Picnic 130

In Honor of James Beard 133

More Tex Than Mex 137

■ ■ ■

Part 3: Night **141**

Supper from the Antipasto Table 145

Dinner on the Right Bank 150

A Dinner of Shrimp and Salmon 155

Where France and Italy Meet 160

Dinner for Mr. Loble 165

In the Italian Kitchen 169

Spring Dinner for Friends 173

A Great Fish Dinner 177

An Imagined Dinner for Julia 181

Hungry Guests 185

Café Caribe 190

An Ode to Spain 193

A Middle Eastern Affair 197

Homage to Lutetia 201

One Duck, Two Courses 206

My 15-Ingredient Thanksgiving Feast 210

Midwinter Magic 216

A Traipse Through Italy 221

Cucina Casalinga 225

Unexpected Pleasures 230

For My Husband's Birthday 234

On Easter 239

The "Seven Species" Dinner 244

Israel's Mediterranean Cuisine 249

Food and Friends 254

A Dinner of Aromatics 258

Dinner for a Doge 261

A Wonderful Autumn Dinner 266

La Bonne Table 270

Father's Day Dinner 275

A Dinner for Epicurus 279

Keeping Company 284

English-Style Holiday Dinner 289

■ ■ ■

Part 4: More Magical Menus **295**

■ ■ ■

Part 5: Menus from the Healthy Kitchen **301**

Index 307

Acknowledgments

To my nurturing coterie: Audrey Appleby, Dale Bellisfield, Amy Berkowitz, Fern Berman, Marcy Blum, Barbara Cohen, Susy Davidson, Cara De Silva, Francesco de'Rogati, Ann Feld, Ben and Phyllis Feder, Phyllis Glaser, Dalia Carmel Goldstein, Rona Jaffe, Reuben Katz, Carol Levy, Dr. Judy Nelson, Steve North, Rachel Rose, Arthur Schwartz, Ann Stewart, Marc Summers, Robin Zucker.

To my creative team: Sally-Jo O'Brien for her diligent retesting of recipes; Mariann Sauvion and Grady Best for their uncanny touch in making my food look "just right" for the photographer's lens both in *Recipes 1-2-3* and this, its sequel; Tom Eckerle, photographer magnifico, for expressing simplicity so beautifully;

Helen Kimmel, M.S., R.D., for her nutrition wisdom; Laura Lehrman, John Ochse, and Renato Biribin for their computer wizardry; Fern Berman for her media savvy and counsel; Jennifer Josephy for being my editor.

To my wine guru: Judy Rundel Sheldon, who collaborated with me on "Grapenotes."

To Dunnewood Vineyards and Swissrose International, special thanks.

To my precious family: Marion Gold, Bill Gold, Dr. Leon and Gail Gold, Jeremy Whiteman, and Anne Whiteman, whom we miss with all our hearts.

To my Michael: who has the power to go where no one else can find me.

Ancient Greece Amphicles, a chef of ancient Greece known for his sophisticated restraint in cooking, opposed the cover-up of natural flavors and excessive use of spices. A precursor of *Recipes 1-2-3*, he would cook red mullet in a grape leaf and lark in a vine leaf. (See Sardines Baked in Grape Leaves, Tomato Reduction, page 83.)

Fourth Century, B.C. Archestratus, Greek poet and gastronome, reflected on his favorite 1-2-3 recipes, from a sow's abdomen cooked in oil and sprinkled with cumin, to conger eel boiled in brine and wrapped in herbs.

1654 Nicholas de Bonnefons, a valet in the court of Louis XIV, wrote a work entitled *Les Delices de la Campagne,* in which he advocated, above all, simplicity: "Let a cabbage soup be entirely cabbage . . . and may what I say about soup be a law applied to everything that is eaten." He advanced the idea of "well-matched flavors," such as mackerel with green fennel. (See Pavé of Cod, *Herbes de Provence,* page 162.)

Late 1800s Annette Boutiscut, aka Mère Poulard, made the ultimate 1-2-3 recipe: The famous puffy omelette of the eponymous restaurant in Mont St. Michel is still made with eggs, butter, and cream and cooked dramatically over an open fire.

Early 1900s The august chef Escoffier, "King of Chefs and Chef of Kings," proclaimed "Faites simple" (keep it simple), although three may not be the precise number of ingredients he had in mind.

1920s French novelist Colette, famous for her simple Chicken *à la Cendre* (in ashes), denounced the innovations of French cuisine in the early part of the twentieth century — where the indiscriminate excess of ingredients became a trend. She said, "It seems that we are a long way removed from the discreet combinations of flavors, thought out at length, that were once the basis of French gourmandise."

1930s Curnonsky, the "Prince of Gastronomes" (so dubbed in 1927), said, "In cooking, as in all the arts, simplicity is the sign of perfection." He also surmised that "cuisine is when things taste like themselves." True to the notion of *Recipes 1-2-3*, he spoke of maximizing the inherent essence of ingredients — *droit en goût* — with unadulterated flavors.

1940s Albert Einstein declared, "Everything should be made as simple as possible, but no simpler."

1954 Architect Mies van der Rohe proclaimed "less is more" (and all hell broke loose).

1957 "Natural foods without embellishment taste wonderfully if they are well cooked," said the internationally celebrated gastronome James Beard.

Early 1970s The advent of nouvelle cuisine advocated a simpler and more natural approach to cooking and presentation of food.

1996 *Recipes 1-2-3* was published and won the James Beard Book Award as the best general cookbook.

1997 The first three-ingredient recipe by a four-star chef appeared in the *New York Times:* Jean-Georges Vongerichten's Sassafras Chicken (June 17, 1997).

1998 *Recipes 1-2-3 Menu Cookbook* was published.

Introduction

Life is about to get easier. Based on one of the most tantalizing culinary promises ever made — fabulous food using only three ingredients — *Recipes 1-2-3 Menu Cookbook* is designed to streamline complex lives in stylish good taste.

Recipes 1-2-3 helped launch a new movement in cooking: It stressed paring down the elements in a dish in order to achieve depth and flavor based on three superb ingredients, perfectly cooked. Its sequel, the *Menu Cookbook,* helps home cooks orchestrate *entire meals* in the same accessible "less-is-more" style of culinary harmony.

Many readers have shared with me their delight in this new approach to cooking — not only do the short ingredient lists save valuable time at the grocery store, but they leave more time for the true pleasures of cooking.

Research tells us that many home cooks aren't comfortable composing a menu. Perhaps they have an idea for a main course, but they're at a loss to harmonize starters, side dishes, and desserts. In approaching each of the menus in this book, I relied on principles that have guided me through more than twenty years as a "menu maker": the idea of a menu or, as a colleague once called it, "the mind of the menu"; the integration of flavors; the composition of each dish; the process of sequencing individual dishes into artful meals.

No fewer than six ingredients, nor more than fifteen, compose each menu, enabling you to assemble a three-course dinner for eight and still slip through your supermarket's express line. This is an enduring promise of *Recipes 1-2-3,* and by now a sign of our times.

In addition, my menus are organized to satisfy many of the cooking, eating, and entertaining pleasures of the day:

• *Breakfast in bed?* Surprise with Souffléed Ricotta

Terrine (see page 37) and Tiny Melons Filled with Raspberries and Framboise (see page 37) (menu = six ingredients).

• *Entertaining a VIP during the week?* Dazzle with Spinach and Smoked Salmon Terrine Lutecè (see page 202), Cornish Hens with Tarragon Rice (see page 203), Belgian Endive and Blue Cheese Gratin (see page 204), followed by classic Crème Brûlée (see page 205) (menu = twelve ingredients).

• *Having friends for lunch on Saturday?* Why not serve Tomato-Mascarpone Soup, Basil Chiffonade (see page 72); "Pasta @ Noon" (see page 72); and sumptuous Marsala-Poached Pears, Crushed Amaretti (see page 73) (menu = nine ingredients)?

Over 260 recipes reflect the new world tapestry of food and ingredients: *Fesenjune:* Chicken Breasts in Walnut and Pomegranate Sauce; Polenta "Lasagne" with Smoked Mozzarella; Moroccan Chicken with Preserved Lemons and Green Olives; Red-Cooked Garlic Spareribs with Cilantro; Skirt Steak with *Salsa Verde*, Raw and Roasted Garlic; Bombay Leg of Lamb with Yogurt and Lime; *arepas* for breakfast; *Limoncello* Zabaglione for dessert.

And, yes, each with only three ingredients.

Like the minimalist movement in art, which reacted to the excesses of abstract expressionism, today the culinary trend is away from the excess and pretense that characterized cooking in the last decade. "We're aiming for simplicity," says the great French chef Joël Robuchon. "We've moved toward a cuisine where the original flavor of the natural product is the most important element in the dish."

The *Menu Cookbook* builds on this approach, for it relates not only to the simplification of a recipe, but to creating an entire meal that, as the minimalist movement in art, finds fulfillment in the carefully crafted purity of simple forms.

About the Menus

Great menus are narratives, tales that make us hunger. My goals are emotive (to tell a story, such as "Lunch for Picasso" or "An Imagined Dinner for Julia"); psychological (to create anticipation, to excite, and, ultimately, to satisfy); and physiological (to consider elements of flavor, texture, and weight; the pleasant sensory irritations of certain spices; the overall balance of taste components, including sour, salty, bitter, and sweet; and the all-encompassing aspects of aroma and bouquet).

At the heart of this book's menus lies the power of simplicity. Beginning with impeccable ingredients, the harmony among courses must connect the cook's intention with the interest of the diner. Flavors should advance in a graceful progression of lighter foods to heavier (the "weight" of a dish), culminating in notes of sweetness we call dessert.

All of my menus are complete, yet many break the clichéd expression of a traditional meal. Not every menu includes bread, nor is every main course laden with both a starch and a vegetable. Certainly you may add your favorite bread to any meal or try your hand at yeasty focaccia (see page 148) or whole wheat pita (see page 246).

Cook your way through this book using the menus as presented, or create your own menu magic based on the 1-2-3 recipes listed by category in the index. I've done some mixing and matching for you in Part 4, "More Magical Menus," based on seasons, holidays, and other inspirations.

Menus have always been for me a delicious kind of poetry, indelibly fixing a pleasurable moment in time. For after the meal is over, the menu remains.

"Grapenotes"

If good menus are to have balance and completeness, then wine selection is a key part of their success. What one drinks can integrate all of a menu's elements and enhances a meal in both physiological and emotional ways.

Often a wine can emphasize desirable flavors in a particular recipe — where, unexpectedly, the herbal notes in a merlot bring out the rosemary essence of a lamb dish, for example.

Conversely, specific dishes can enhance desirable qualities in the wine. Fleshy black olives, for example, can intensify the *terroir*, or "earthiness," of a cabernet or Bordeaux.

Breaking the rules of traditional food and wine pairings can add another level of interest to any menu: a lightish pinot noir (red) pairs beautifully with "Osso Buco" of Salmon (see page 157), whereas a dry Gewürztraminer (white) is an unexpected pleasure with Seared Salmon Steak with Cornichon Vinaigrette (see page 108). It is the preparation of the dish that gives the predominant flavor cue. A dry Spanish *rosado* harmonizes the components of Steamed Mussels *Crema di Salsa* (see page 91); crémant sparkling wine makes

scrambled eggs and asparagus (see page 23) cause for celebration.

In order to tie each menu together, I've included, where appropriate, a "Grapenote," a suggestion of what wine (or occasional beer, cocktail, liqueur, and so on) will endow a meal with a satisfying sense of completeness. My choices cover a broad spectrum of place, taste, and price; they come from the United States, Chile, Spain, Portugal, France, Italy, Israel, Greece, South Africa, and Australia and reflect both new and classical styles of vinification.

If "wine is bottled poetry," as Robert Louis Stevenson once said, then it is taste, not price or geography, that makes it so. The wine selections for dinner in this book range from seven dollars to twenty dollars a bottle, with a few exceptions in either direction, while all those recommended for lunch are under ten dollars.

A true minimalist, of course, might drink only different styles of champagne.

Nutritionally Speaking

After working closely with nutrition guru Helen Kimmel, M.S., R.D., it is always a kick to realize that so many of these dishes are healthful — one of the serendipitous benefits of limiting recipes to three ingredients. In Part 5, "Menus from the Healthy Kitchen," you will find lists of fat-free, low-fat, and low-calorie recipes, including nineteen fat-free desserts and twelve menus composed of "good-for-you" food.

More delightful still: Many recipes using cream,

butter, cheese, and eggs click into one of the above categories. Imagine Belgian Endive and Blue Cheese Gratin (see page 204) being low cal! So if you're accustomed to turning the page when you see "forbidden" foods — think twice.

Ingredients

As my husband so cogently puts it: "I eat very simply. I only want the best."

The same goes for the ingredients you choose as the building blocks for the recipes in this book. They must be of the highest quality, because when you cook with just three ingredients each one assumes critical importance.

Ingredients should taste like themselves and nothing else. Think of their inherent qualities, as did the food writer Patience Gray, who, when describing perfection in olive oil, said, "It should naturally taste of olives."

Know your ingredients. Taste them and respect them, for they are basic to the success of every dish. Coaxing complex flavors from a simple combination of excellent ingredients is this book's objective. Substituting ingredients or quality undoes its goal. In Pot-au-Feu: Chicken, Beef Shin, and Leeks (see page 182), it is beef shin and not any other cut that will imbue the consommé with deeply flavorful and gelatinous distinction. Over-the-hill or inferior domestic Gorgonzola cheese will ruin the considered harmony in Gorgonzola-Grappa Rib Steak (see page 276). A sweet, yielding cantaloupe whose perfume breathes through its webbed rind is fundamental to the plea-sure of my Tequila Melon (see page 140), balanced with tequila and sugar, salt, and pepper.

Only great chocolate (such as Valrhona or Callebaut) can make Chocolate Climax (see page 283) worthy of its name.

You need to get as close as possible to the source of your food . . . to the farmer's market where you can sample produce and talk to the growers; to a great fish store that has built up trust and where whole fish, and not just precut parts, are on display; to specialty shops where cheeses are impeccable and packaged goods are carefully stored. Pick summer herbs from your own window box, and bring in hardy ones like thyme, rosemary, and sage to winter on a sunny sill.

When in doubt be willing to spend a bit more for the best raw materials available. Good taste is not for sale, but good flavor is!

An important note: As in *Recipes 1-2-3*, salt, pepper, and water are "free" ingredients. They are fundaments to all cooking and as such are not counted as ingredients in the recipes.

Essential Utensils

I make the most of a minimum of equipment: a few very large Le Creuset casseroles with covers, heavy nonstick skillets in several sizes, a big stainless-steel pasta pot, a six-cup enamel saucepan and cover, and a newly acquired cast-iron grill pan.

Thanks to cousin Ann Stewart, of New London, Connecticut, I've resurrected my blender, since she reported that's what her friends use most. ("After all," she says, "who can make a daiquiri in a food processor!'') A blender seems easier to clean and whirls, whips, and frappés unlike any processor. So now I use both, along with my KitchenAid mixer.

Scissors abut my knives on a magnetic rack, and a kitchen scale is as important as measuring cups and spoons.

Kitchen life would be unthinkable without my well-worn garlic press, an old-fashioned corkscrew, and a variety of stainless-steel mixing bowls.

Retrograde acquisitions include a potato ricer, bought at a flea market. How did I live without one, or without a food mill (a present from my mother-in-law — small but mighty, with a great sense of family tradition)?

Separate pepper mills contain whole black and whole white peppercorns. An antique saltcellar holds coarse (kosher) salt in a container wide enough to get my hand in.

A large eight-inch coarse-mesh sieve, a six-inch fine-mesh version, slotted spoons, ladles and tongs, and a classic box grater hang on an old-fashioned Peg-Board behind our side-by-side stoves.

A dozen glass custard cups are so helpful, as are a half-dozen sizes of soufflé dishes — perfect for cooking, fashionable for serving.

My global kitchen is also home to a small French *mandoline,* a Chinese cleaver, an Italian Mouli grater, an ancient colander from Turkey, and an ultrasharp, rectangular Japanese knife that's become my all-purpose cutting implement.

Most essential is my husband, who meticulously hones my knives on a diamond-studded sharpening stone.

Reduction Theory

When you're cooking with just a few ingredients, it is imperative to maximize flavors. Many of the following recipes rely on the principle of reduction, which simply means the simmering or boiling of a liquid until most of the water has evaporated.

This evaporation results in an intensity of flavor much more dramatic than that of the original product. For example, when you cook tomato juice down to a glaze, its clean, sparkling acidity makes it preferable to canned tomato paste. (See Baked Eggs Splendido, page 46, and Sardines Baked in Grape Leaves, Tomato Reduction, page 83.)

Reducing chicken stock to a gelatinous syrup creates a flavorful binder for *tubetti* pasta and diced zucchini (see page 84); this gel adds flavor to the dish and eliminates the need for added fat.

Wine, stock, and fruit and vegetable juices lend themselves beautifully to reductions. And they're fun to make.

How about simmering prune juice to a thick "chocolaty" sludge and drizzling it over coffee ice cream strewn with slightly bitter toasted almonds (see page 84)?

It's as easy as 1-2-3 ingredients.

The Minimalist Pantry

In addition to the dry goods specified in some of the recipes, the minimalist pantry includes regular table salt, kosher salt, and coarse French sea salt; whole black peppercorns and butcher-grind black pepper; whole white peppercorns; extra-virgin olive oil and good-quality everyday olive oil; balsamic, sherry, white-wine, and apple-cider vinegars.

Also included are a few of my favorite things, always ready and waiting to be used in a 1-2-3 recipe: Garlic Oil, Chili Oil, Rosemary Oil, Salt-Preserved Lemons, Tapenade, Vanilla Sugar, and Ginger Sugar (see the following recipes).

GARLIC OIL

8 medium to large cloves garlic
1 cup good-quality olive oil
1 California bay leaf

Peel the garlic and place in a small, heavy nonreactive saucepan. Add the oil. Cook gently over low heat for 5 minutes, or until bubbles form on top. Turn off the heat. Add the bay leaf and ¼ teaspoon whole black peppercorns. Let steep and allow to cool completely.

Remove the bay leaf. Put oil in a jar with a tight-fitting lid. The Garlic Oil will be good for up to 2 weeks in the refrigerator.

Makes 1 cup

CHILI OIL

1 cup good-quality olive oil
1 tablespoon chili flakes

Place olive oil and chili flakes in a small saucepan. Add ½ teaspoon salt. Bring just to a boil. Lower heat and simmer 5 minutes. Allow to cool completely. Put oil in a jar with a tight-fitting lid. Store in a cool, dark place for up to 2 months.

Makes 1 cup

ROSEMARY OIL

1 large bunch fresh rosemary
1 cup good-quality olive oil

Separate the rosemary leaves from the stems. Pack a ¼-cup measure tightly with rosemary leaves. Wash and dry well. Bring a small saucepan of water to a boil. Place rosemary in boiling water and cook for 30 seconds. Drain in sieve under cold water. Dry with paper towels. Place rosemary in blender or food processor with olive oil. Process until rosemary is finely chopped. Transfer contents to a bowl or to a jar with a lid. Let sit for 3 hours, stirring frequently or shaking the jar.

Strain the oil through a paper coffee filter or a fine-mesh sieve. Place in a jar, adding a few rosemary branches if desired. Store tightly covered in the refrigerator for up to 2 weeks.

Makes 1 cup

SALT-PRESERVED LEMONS

7 thin-skinned lemons

Wash the lemons. Cut 6 of them vertically into 4 wedges *without* cutting all the way through, so that the pieces are still joined together.

Place in a jar large enough to hold lemons and layer them with kosher salt, making sure the lemons are completely covered with salt. Add the juice of another lemon or moisten salt with 2 tablespoons of water. Cover tightly and let sit in a cool, dark place for 2 weeks before using. These preserved lemons will keep up to 3 months.

Remove salt before using by running under cool water and patting dry.

Makes 6 preserved lemons

TAPENADE

2 cups pitted oil-cured black olives
2-ounce can anchovies with capers
¼ cup extra-virgin olive oil

Put the olives and anchovies with capers in a food processor or blender. With the motor running, slowly add the oil until the tapenade is smooth, adding more oil if necessary. Add freshly ground black pepper to taste.

Cover and store in refrigerator for up to 3 months.

Makes 1¼ cups

VANILLA SUGAR

4 cups sugar
2 moist vanilla beans

Place sugar in a medium bowl.

Place vanilla beans on a cutting board. Cut beans in half lengthwise. With the tip of a small knife, scrape out the seeds and add to the sugar, using your fingers to incorporate vanilla seeds thoroughly into the sugar.

Place in a container. Stick scraped vanilla beans into sugar. Cover tightly. Lasts indefinitely.

Makes 4 cups

GINGER SUGAR

2 cups sugar
4 teaspoons good-quality ground ginger

Place sugar and ginger in a small bowl. Mix together, using a spoon, so that ginger is evenly distributed throughout sugar.

Store in a tightly covered container. Lasts indefinitely.

Makes 2 cups

1

Morning

■ ■ ■
BREAKFAST

First and Main Courses

Poached Eggs with Lime Hollandaise

Smoked Salmon Quesadillas

Irish Oatmeal with Buttermilk and Poppy Seeds

Home-Cured Gravlax

Asparagus and Eggs Georges Blanc

Mamaliga: *Rumanian Cornmeal Porridge*

Labaneh *in Olive Oil with Cucumbers*

Ful Mudammas *with Lemon*

Country-Style Ham and Eggs, Redeye Gravy

Arepas *with Butter and* Queso Blanco

Souffléed Ricotta Terrine

Buttermilk Eggs in Tomato Shells

Canadian Bacon and Dill Tostadas

Frittata with Pancetta and Mint

Baked Eggs Splendido

Buttermilk Grits Soufflé

Pickled Fresh Salmon

Scrambled Eggs and Onions

Panettone French Toast, Thick Cut

Fruits, Breads, and Beverages

Fresh Strawberries, Gingered Yogurt

Spicy Stewed Red Plums

Almond "Toast"

Oranges and Strawberries en Gelée

Raspberry "Borscht"

Feta Cheese–Olives–Grilled Pita

Egyptian Carrot Jam

Warm Buttermilk Biscuits

Candied Tomatoes

Quince-Glazed Fresh Fruit Kabobs

Breakfast Chocolate

Tiny Melons Filled with Raspberries and Framboise

Two-Melon Soup

Warm Cheese Scones

Fried Red Tomatoes

Fresh Figs, Bitter Orange Mascarpone

Bel Paese and Prosciutto Bruschetta

Morning Granita: Grapefruit-Campari

Peaches Flamed in Southern Comfort

Mangoes, Prunes, and Pomegranates

Warm Pear and Cranberry Compote,

Cranberry Syrup

Café Cantata

Halvah and Golden Raisin Turnovers

Chocolate-Raspberry Turnovers

Almond Milk with Orzata *and Coffee Ice Cubes*

■ ■ ■

Room Service

Poached Eggs with Lime Hollandaise

Smoked Salmon Quesadillas

Fresh Strawberries, Gingered Yogurt

9 ingredients

One of life's great pleasures comes when you're most expecting it: room service.

At New York's estimable Mark Hotel, it is especially celebratory.

Dressed in fluffy robes and velvet slippers, after morning rituals, the two of us sit on the love seat in our sunny, terraced room and wait.

But never too long at the Mark.

The hollandaise is always ethereal, the poached eggs hot and properly runny. Quesadillas filled with silken smoked salmon are perfect with rosé champagne.

Ripe strawberries fill cut-crystal bowls, while silver cups brim with ambrosial yogurt and ginger marmalade, to sweeten the berries and intensify their flavor.

The butler returns with double espressos and wishes us happy anniversary. Year after year in suite 1410.

GRAPENOTE

Celebrate with a superb and aptly named rosé champagne: Billecart-Salmon brut rosé NV from France or Iron Horse brut rosé from California.

POACHED EGGS WITH LIME HOLLANDAISE

1½ sticks (¾ cup) unsalted butter
2 large limes
11 extra-large eggs

To clarify butter: Place butter in top half of double boiler over hot water. Heat until butter just melts. Remove top with butter from the hot water and let stand 10 minutes. Skim white foam from the surface, using a large spoon. When the whey has separated and sunk to the bottom, carefully pour off clear yellow liquid into a bowl. You will have approximately ½ cup clarified butter. This can be done ahead of time and rewarmed.

Grate the zest from 1 lime, and squeeze both limes to get 3 tablespoons or more of juice. Set aside.

To make hollandaise: Separate 3 eggs and discard the whites. Whisk the yolks and 1 tablespoon water in top of a double boiler over simmering water. Whisk until very fluffy using a wire whisk. Add clarified butter that has been warmed. Whisk constantly to incorporate; this will take about 4 minutes. Add the grated lime zest and whisk in 2 to 3 tablespoons fresh lime juice (or more to taste). Add salt and pinch of finely ground white pepper. Keep warm. Makes approximately ⅞ cup.

To poach eggs: In a 12-inch nonstick skillet, add cool water to the depth of 1 inch. Add 1 teaspoon salt and bring to a boil, then lower to a simmer. Break remaining 8 eggs, one at a time, into a saucer and slip them into simmering water. Cook eggs until whites are firm and yolks are of desired doneness, about 3 minutes. Remove eggs with slotted spoon and drain on paper towels.

To serve, place 2 hot poached eggs on each of four large plates and top each with 2 tablespoons lime hollandaise. Serve immediately.

Optional garnish: Serve with a thin slice or wedge of lime.

Serves 4

SMOKED SALMON QUESADILLAS

8 8-inch flour tortillas
6 ounces (approximately 12 tablespoons) whipped cream cheese and chives
½ pound good-quality smoked salmon

Preheat oven to 200°.

Place 4 tortillas on a flat surface. Spread each with 3 tablespoons whipped cream cheese to completely cover tortilla.

Cut smoked salmon into 1-inch strips and scatter 2 ounces on top of each tortilla. Add a grinding of black pepper.

Top each with one of the remaining tortillas, pressing down tightly.

Heat 2 large nonstick skillets. Place 1 quesadilla in each skillet. Heat each side for 1 minute until golden, pressing down with a spatula. Repeat process.

Place quesadillas on baking sheet and keep warm in oven until ready to serve. Cut each into quarters.

Serves 4

FRESH STRAWBERRIES, GINGERED YOGURT

2 pints very ripe large strawberries
1½ cups plain yogurt, chilled
4 tablespoons ginger marmalade*

Wash strawberries and remove stems from all but 4, which you will reserve as garnish. Pat dry. Cut de-stemmed berries in half and refrigerate until ready to serve.

In a small bowl mix yogurt and marmalade. You will have 1¾ cups gingered yogurt. Cover and refrigerate if not using immediately.

To serve, divide berries evenly into flat soup plates. Spoon gingered yogurt over berries.

Make fan shapes from 4 remaining berries with stems by cutting thin slices lengthwise, and pressing down to fan out.

Serves 4

* Use a premium brand, such as Tiptree or Crabtree & Evelyn.

■ ■ ■

Two-Bowl Breakfast

Irish Oatmeal with Buttermilk and Poppy Seeds

Spicy Stewed Red Plums

Almond "Toast"

9 ingredients

Some things are better eaten than talked about. This is especially true in the morning.

You might consider making lots of spicy stewed plums at the very end of their season and freezing them in order to extend the unique harmony of this menu.

In the dead of winter, try instead Fruit Salad Vino Cotto (see page 81), also served in a bowl.

IRISH OATMEAL WITH BUTTERMILK AND POPPY SEEDS

1 cup Irish steel-cut oatmeal*
2 teaspoons poppy seeds
1 cup buttermilk

In a medium saucepan, bring 4 cups water and ¼ teaspoon salt to a boil.

Stir in oatmeal and cook over high heat for 5 minutes. Lower heat to medium and cook for 30 minutes, stirring occasionally, until oatmeal is smooth and thick, but not mushy.

Stir in 1½ teaspoons poppy seeds and additional salt and freshly ground black pepper to taste, if desired. The success of this dish is a balance of acidity, salt, and the earthiness of the oatmeal. Divide evenly among 4 bowls. Pour buttermilk over oatmeal and sprinkle with remaining poppy seeds.

Serve immediately.

Serves 4

* McCann's, if possible, or any whole-grain (but not rolled) oatmeal.

SPICY STEWED RED PLUMS

12 ripe red plums
6 tablespoons light brown sugar
2 cinnamon sticks

Wash and dry plums. Cut 6 plums in half and remove the pits. Cut the remaining plums in quarters, also removing pits.

In a medium saucepan, put 2 cups cold water, plums, sugar, cinnamon sticks, ¼ teaspoon whole black peppercorns, a grinding of black pepper from the pepper mill, and a pinch of salt. Bring to a boil.

Reduce heat to medium-low. Cover pot and cook for 15 minutes. Uncover pot and cook 15 minutes longer.

Let cool. Refrigerate until very cold.

Serves 4

ALMOND "TOAST"

4 ³⁄₄-inch-thick slices brioche loaf or challah bread
4 tablespoons sweetened condensed milk
¹⁄₂ cup sliced almonds, with skins

Preheat oven to 375°.

Place bread on a baking sheet. Spread 1 tablespoon sweetened condensed milk over the surface of each slice of bread. Make sure the bread is thoroughly coated.

Completely coat each slice of bread with 2 tablespoons sliced almonds.

Bake for 15 to 18 minutes, until bread is crisped, almonds are golden brown, and the condensed milk has lightly caramelized.

Let cool 5 minutes before serving. Toast should still be warm.

Serves 4

French Triptych

Home-Cured Gravlax

Asparagus and Eggs Georges Blanc

Oranges and Strawberries en Gelée

9 ingredients

1. I first had classic gravlax, not in Sweden, but in Reims, the soul of the Champagne region of France, at the three-star hotel and restaurant Boyer Les Crayères. Clean, silken, dilled ecstasy.

2. I've always been delighted by the intelligent whimsy of three-star chef Georges Blanc of Vonnas, in Burgundy. It was his idea to treat simple asparagus stalks in different ways in the same dish;

it was my idea to fold them into soft-scrambled eggs sauced with nutty beurre noisette.

3. Fresh fruit jewels in a smooth "lake" of aspic was inspired by the insouciant chef of Leon de Lyons . . . in Lyons.

There's lots of culinary intrigue and a wonderful sequence of flavors from nine ingredients!

GRAPENOTE

Delightful with Georges Blanc's own crémant sparkling wine, Brut d'Azenay. Or pop the cork of the Willem Crémant d'Alsace; or from the Loire, Bouvet Saumur Brut Saphir.

HOME-CURED GRAVLAX

2½-pound side of salmon ⃰
¼ cup granulated sugar
1½ cups chopped fresh dill, stems included

Remove all small bones from the salmon with tweezers. Pat dry. Rub salmon flesh with ¼ cup kosher salt, 1 tablespoon butcher-grind black pepper, sugar, and chopped dill. Cover with plastic wrap. Weight down with a baking sheet topped with a couple of cans or other heavy object. Refrigerate 48 to 72 hours. Pour off liquid daily, rewrapping salmon and weighting down each time. Before serving, scrape off dill and seasonings. Slice on the bias as if it were smoked salmon. Use a long, sharp narrow knife at a 30° angle and lift thin gravlax slices off the skin.

Serves 8

 ⃰ Or use a 2½-pound piece of salmon cut from the thick side of a larger fish.

ASPARAGUS AND EGGS GEORGES BLANC

1 pound medium-thick fresh asparagus stalks
7 tablespoons unsalted butter
10 extra-large eggs

Cut top 2 inches of asparagus tips off stalks. Cut tips into very fine julienne. Blanch in boiling water for 1 minute. Plunge into bowl of ice water, then drain well, and reserve.

Cut tough bottoms from stalks with a sharp knife. Using a vegetable peeler, scrape stalks until you have reached the white interior (there should be no dark green left). Cut white stalks into ¼-inch rounds. Boil in salted water until tender, about 6 minutes. Drain in colander under cold running water. Pat dry and reserve.

Break eggs into a large bowl and beat well with wire whisk. Butter the top of a double boiler with 1 tablespoon butter. Add eggs and cook over medium-low heat so that water is just below a boil, stirring constantly with wooden spoon. You want the eggs to be very creamy, almost like a sauce. Lower heat if eggs thicken too quickly. Gradually add small bits of butter to eggs (approximately 3 tablespoons) as they begin to thicken. Add cooked asparagus stalks.

Continue cooking and stirring until eggs are cooked through but still soft and creamy, about 5 minutes. Add salt and freshly ground white pepper to taste.

Meanwhile, melt 3 tablespoons butter in a small nonstick skillet and cook over medium-high heat until butter turns a hazelnut color.

To serve, put hot eggs in center of large plate. Surround with blanched asparagus tips and pour hot beurre noisette over top of eggs.

Serves 4

ORANGES AND STRAWBERRIES *EN GELÉE*

12 juice oranges
12 large strawberries
1 envelope unflavored gelatin

Remove the skin of 4 oranges with a small sharp knife, being careful to remove all the white pith. Cut along membranes to release orange segments.

Wash strawberries, remove stems, and cut berries lengthwise into ⅛-inch-thick slices.

Arrange orange segments and strawberry slices artfully in 4 shallow soup plates.

Squeeze as many of remaining oranges as needed to get 2 cups juice. Put juice in a small saucepan.

Sprinkle gelatin over ¼ cup cold water in a small bowl. Let dissolve 1 minute. Heat orange juice. Add gelatin and over low heat stir until dissolved, about 1 minute.

Let cool slightly. Pour approximately ½ cup juice-gelatin mixture into each bowl of fruit until fruit is submerged.

Chill in refrigerator for several hours until orange juice is completely jelled.

Serves 4

THE FOLLOWING PHOTOGRAPHS DEPICT:

Spicy Stewed Red Plums (page 19) with Almond "Toast" (page 20)

Frittata with Pancetta and Mint (page 43); Fried Red Tomatoes (page 43)

Panettone French Toast (page 55) with Warm Pear and Cranberry Compote, Cranberry Syrup (page 56)

Country-Style Ham and Eggs, Redeye Gravy (page 31); Candied Tomatoes (page 32)

Arepas (page 35) with Quince-Glazed Fruit Kabob (page 34)

Asparagus and Eggs Georges Blanc (page 23); Home-Cured Gravlax (page 22)

Souffléed Ricotta Terrine (page 37) with Tiny Melons Filled with Raspberries and Framboise (page 37)

Old World–New World

Mamaliga: *Rumanian Cornmeal Porridge*

Raspberry "Borscht"

6 ingredients

Mamaliga *is the great national dish of Rumania, a kind of thick cornmeal mush that appears at practically every meal.*

When served with white cheese and butter, it becomes Jewish soul food, particularly satisfying for breakfast.

From that part of the world also come chilled fruit soups and borscht. Here's a hybrid form, providing a refreshingly tart and sweetly spiced fillip to the morning meal.

MAMALIGA: RUMANIAN CORNMEAL PORRIDGE

2 cups stone-ground yellow cornmeal
8 tablespoons unsalted butter
½ pound pot cheese, farmer cheese, or Brinza cheese*

Bring 8 cups cold water plus ½ tablespoon salt to a boil in a medium-size pot.

Slowly add cornmeal, letting it slip through your fingers, stirring constantly with a wire whisk.

Reduce heat to medium-low and continue to whisk for 5 minutes. Add 2 tablespoons of the butter. Continue to cook for 15 to 20 minutes. The porridge is finished when it begins to come away from the sides of the pan and is very thick and smooth.

Melt the remaining 6 tablespoons butter in a small saucepan over low heat. Do not let butter brown.

Pour hot cornmeal into 4 or more large flat bowls or onto large dinner plates. Thinly slice or crumble cheese on top of the cornmeal and then drizzle butter over the top.

Pass the pepper mill and serve immediately.

Serves 4 or more (makes 6 cups)

* You may also use Rumanian kashkaval or a mild feta.

RASPBERRY "BORSCHT"

2¼ cups buttermilk
10 ounces frozen raspberries in syrup, at room temperature
1 teaspoon pumpkin pie spice

In the bowl of a food processor, put 2 cups buttermilk, raspberries with syrup, pinch of salt, and ½ teaspoon pumpkin pie spice.

Process until very smooth. Chill for 2 hours, or until very cold.

Divide soup evenly among 4 flat bowls. Drizzle 1 tablespoon buttermilk over each and sprinkle with a little of the remaining pumpkin pie spice.

Serves 4 (makes 3 cups)

■ ■ ■

Breakfast in Cairo

Labaneh *in Olive Oil with Cucumbers*

Ful Mudammas *with Lemon*

Feta Cheese – Olives – Grilled Pita

Egyptian Carrot Jam

12 ingredients

In the early morning hours, the streets of the cities in the Nile Valley are filled with people lined up in front of vendors selling tempting ful mudammas from earthenware pots.
HABEEB SALLOUM AND JAMES PETERS,
From the Land of Figs and Olives, 1995

From the president to the man in the smoky café, everyone in Egypt eats ful *in the morning. These little brown favas, hot and steamy, have fed this nation since antiquity.*

Once upon a time, I had a remarkably genteel Egyptian roommate (from Monofia, where Anwar Sadat was born) and many Egyptian friends. We ate ful *every morning and breakfasts such as these. Sometimes we soaked and cooked these nourishing legumes overnight, or we would use them from* cans purchased from a local Middle Eastern shop. We made our own labaneh (thickened yogurt) suspended in olive oil, then mixed it with crispy cucumbers.

Salty feta and sweet carrot jam (a recipe from my roommate's mother), lusty ful *with lemon, and olives and charred pita bread held briefly over an open flame were a frequent morning menu. Sometimes we would sip hot mint tea, strongly perfumed and sweet. Other times we would drink thick black coffee scented with cardamom. Often we would discuss the lyrical works of Naguib Mafouz, the great Egyptian writer who found parables and metaphors in chronicles of everyday life and won the 1988 Nobel Prize for Literature. He, too, ate* ful *every morning.*

LABANEH IN OLIVE OIL WITH CUCUMBERS

2 cups plain yogurt
Extra-virgin olive oil
4 kirby cucumbers *

Line a large, coarse-mesh sieve with several layers of cheesecloth.

Put yogurt in sieve and let drain for 48 hours in the refrigerator. Roll drained yogurt "cheese" into 10 to 12 1-inch balls between the palms of your hands. Place on a tray and put in refrigerator overnight. Put cheese balls in a jar with olive oil to cover. Add 1 tea-spoon whole black peppercorns. Cover and refrigerate until ready to use.

When serving, remove cheese from oil, drain most of the oil, and mash. Peel cucumbers, seed, and dice in-to ¼-inch cubes. Stir into *labaneh* and drizzle with oil.

Serves 4 or more

* If unavailable, use half of a hothouse cucumber.

FUL MUDAMMAS WITH LEMON

2 20-ounce cans ful mudammas *
3 tablespoons olive oil, plus more for serving
3 tablespoons fresh lemon juice, plus several lemons for serving

Drain beans in a colander and wash thoroughly. Place in a medium saucepan with cool water just to cover. Add ½ teaspoon salt.

Bring to a boil and lower heat immediately. Let simmer 20 minutes.

Drain beans, saving several tablespoons cooking liquid. Place beans in a bowl and mash a quarter of them lightly.

Add reserved cooking liquid, olive oil, lemon juice, and salt and pepper to taste.

Serve while hot with a cruet of olive oil and some lemons, cut in half.

Serves 4

* Available in all Middle Eastern food stores.

FETA CHEESE–OLIVES–GRILLED PITA

8 ounces feta cheese,* in 1 piece
¼ pound unpitted oil-cured black olives
4 pita breads

Cut feta cheese into ¼-inch-thick slices. Arrange on a platter.

Surround cheese with olives.

Heat the pita breads briefly over an open gas fire using tongs. Toast pita on both sides, turning as you go. You want the pita to get a bit charred. Cut in half. Serve warm.

Serves 4

* If you can find a goat's milk feta from Israel, that would be great. Or use a pungent feta cheese from Greece or Bulgaria.

EGYPTIAN CARROT JAM

2 pounds carrots
6 cups sugar
½ cup fresh lemon juice

Peel carrots and grate on large holes of box grater or use shredding disk of food processor. You will have about 6 cups.

In large, heavy pot, put 2 cups water, sugar, lemon juice, and carrots. Bring to a boil over high heat. Reduce heat and cook over medium heat for 1 to 1½ hours, or until syrup has thickened.

Remove from heat and cool. Sterilize 4 8-ounce jelly jars in boiling water and dry thoroughly. Fill with preserves, seal, and store in refrigerator. Keeps for months.

Makes 2 pints

■ ■ ■

The Cook

Warm Buttermilk Biscuits

Country-Style Ham and Eggs, Redeye Gravy

Candied Tomatoes

9 ingredients

It was nearly 5 A.M., and the sun was rising as slowly as Miss Candy was flouring her cutting board.

Folks would be expecting hot flaky biscuits in just a short while, and Miss Candy was so far behind in her chores that she mistakenly put buttermilk in her biscuit dough. When the first guests arrived shortly after 6 A.M., she spilled coffee on *their ham steaks and rubbed her red eyes in disbelief.*

Instead of putting sugar in the vast pot of iced tea, she poured it into the simmering stewed tomatoes, and they slowly crystallized into shiny ornaments.

Miss Candy left at 7 A.M. and sighed, "Tomorrow is another day."

WARM BUTTERMILK BISCUITS

3 cups self-rising flour
8 tablespoons unsalted butter, slightly softened
1 cup buttermilk, at room temperature

Preheat oven to 350°.

Place flour in a large bowl. Cut butter into the flour and use your fingers to mix together.

Pour buttermilk into flour mixture all at once, and mix quickly, but lightly, until dough just comes together.

Turn out on a well-floured board and fold dough over a few times.

Roll out with a floured rolling pin to a thickness of ¾ inch. Cut out circles with a 2-inch biscuit cutter.

Place on a lightly buttered baking sheet and bake for 15 to 20 minutes, until tops are golden.

Makes 12 to 14 biscuits

COUNTRY-STYLE HAM AND EGGS, REDEYE GRAVY

2 large ham steaks with bone (about 10 ounces each)
½ cup or more freshly brewed black coffee
4 extra-large eggs

Trim fat from ham steaks. Cut fat in small dice, and reserve.

Heat 2 large nonstick skillets, or cast-iron skillets if you happen to have them.

Place ham steaks in hot skillets and brown well, about 2 minutes, on both sides. Make sure to press down hard with spatula to keep ham from curling.

Remove ham to warm platter and cut each steak in half.

Deglaze pans with coffee and cook, scraping up browned bits. Cook over high heat until sauce reduces a little and pour over ham. Cover with foil to keep warm.

In one of the skillets, melt the ham fat, then quickly fry eggs until desired firmness and serve 1 egg atop each piece of ham.

Pass the pepper mill.

Serves 4

CANDIED TOMATOES

2 pounds (8) ripe medium tomatoes
1 cup sugar
2 large cinnamon sticks

In a saucepan big enough to accommodate tomatoes in one layer, put 2 cups water, sugar, and pinch of salt. Bring to a boil.

Add tomatoes and cinnamon sticks.

Cook over low heat for 45 to 50 minutes, turning tomatoes once or twice. Remove tomatoes with slotted spoon and place in a large bowl. Tomatoes should still retain most of their shape.

Reduce liquid over high heat to half its volume, approximately ¾ cup. It will be syrupy and thick.

Pour the liquid over tomatoes. Let tomatoes cool. You can reheat them, or serve them at room temperature, or even slightly chilled.

Serves 4 or more

■ ■ ■

¡Buenos Dias!

Quince-Glazed Fresh Fruit Kabobs

Arepas *with Butter and* Queso Blanco

Breakfast Chocolate

9 ingredients

Maria Palacios-Hardes is the sweetheart of our partner, Dennis Sweeney. She hails from Cali and eats arepas *for breakfast.*

The staff of life for many in Colombia and Venezuela, this dense corn-bread "cake" is one inch thick, cooked on a griddle, and split like a primitive English muffin. "It's delicioso *with plenty of melted butter and* queso blanco, *or mild white cheese," says Maria.*

Sometimes she longs for Cali, not the world's most tranquil place, where her mother presides over the large family farm with a shotgun. But it's Señora Palacios's thick hot chocolate, not buckshot, with which she confronts most visitors.

Maria, too, is invincible. She owns a large bus company in New York and drives handicapped children to school.

It's hard to do special things for Maria because she's always doing them for everyone else.

So I dedicate this breakfast to her.

QUINCE-GLAZED FRESH FRUIT KABOBS

16 large ripe strawberries
2 large ripe bananas
⅓ cup quince jelly *

You will need 4 10-inch bamboo or metal skewers.
Preheat broiler.

Remove stems from 12 strawberries, keeping 4 intact. Peel bananas and cut each into 8 1-inch slices.

Thread 4 skewers alternately with a chunk of banana, then a strawberry, ending with a strawberry with a green stem.

Heat jelly in a small saucepan over low heat until it melts and is the consistency of honey.

Using a pastry brush, glaze the fruit with the melted jelly, making sure to cover all the fruit lightly.

Place on a baking sheet and broil 30 seconds on each side, until the fruit just begins to lightly brown. Let cool slightly before serving.

Serves 4

* Smucker's makes a particularly delicious one, or you may substitute apple jelly.

AREPAS WITH BUTTER AND *QUESO BLANCO*

2 ¼ cups white cornmeal
4 tablespoons unsalted butter, plus more for serving
½ pound queso blanco, Manchego, or white cheddar cheese

Preheat oven to 350°.

Bring 3½ cups water and ½ tablespoon salt to a rapid boil in a medium pot. Lower heat to medium and slowly stir in cornmeal. It will thicken rapidly.

When all cornmeal is added, turn off heat. Transfer to bowl of electric mixer and knead, using paddle, 5 minutes, or until glossy.

Dampen hands with water. Form dough into 8 balls. Flatten to 1-inch-thick cakes.

Melt 4 tablespoons butter in large skillet. Cook each cake over medium-high heat until golden-brown crust forms, about 5 minutes on each side.

Place on baking sheet. Bake 20 minutes in oven, turning twice. A thick crust will form.

Serve sliced white cheese on top, or split and put cheese in center. Serve hot.

Optional garnish: Serve with additional butter.

Serves 4

BREAKFAST CHOCOLATE

3 cups milk
5 tablespoons Vanilla Sugar (see page 11)
6 ounces good-quality unsweetened chocolate, at room temperature

In a large saucepan, bring milk to just below a boil. Add sugar and mix until sugar dissolves, about 1 minute, being careful not to let milk boil.

Grate chocolate on large holes of box grater and slowly add to milk. Cook over low heat for several minutes until the chocolate has melted, stirring often. The hot chocolate should be smooth and thick.

Serve immediately.

Serves 4

Little Morning Meal

Souffléed Ricotta Terrine
Tiny Melons Filled with Raspberries and Framboise

6 ingredients

My advice: Serve both components of this menu on a single large plate, for I want you to consider the sensual sweet-acid trickles of raspberry essence against the silky neutrality of the soufflé.

In France, this lovely wake-up call would be called frichti, *colloquial for a light meal or snack served at home (from the German word* Frühstück, *"breakfast").*

The soufflé, not dissimilar to a cake called tourteau fromage, is addictive and when cold tastes like cheesecake, only more gossamer.

Cavaillons are tiny, hand-size melons sporadically imported from France. If they are unavailable, choose a lovely Galia from Israel, or cut a wedge from a superripe honeydew or cantaloupe.

GRAPENOTE

For a special occasion, splash framboise into a glass of bubbly for a Kir Imperial.

SOUFFLÉED RICOTTA TERRINE

2 15-ounce containers whole-milk ricotta cheese
6 extra-large eggs
⅔ cup Vanilla Sugar (see page 11)

Preheat oven to 350°.

Place ricotta cheese in a fine-mesh sieve over a bowl. Let drain 20 minutes to release any liquid.

Beat eggs lightly in bowl of an electric mixer. Add drained ricotta and sugar and blend well. Beat on medium speed for 1 minute, until very smooth.

Spray a 2-quart glass loaf pan with vegetable spray. Pour in ricotta mixture.

Bake 60 to 70 minutes, until golden brown and puffed. Remove from oven, let cool slightly before serving, then cut into thick slices. This is also delicious at room temperature.

Serves 6

TINY MELONS FILLED WITH RASPBERRIES AND FRAMBOISE

3 small hand-size ripe Cavaillon or Galia melons*
3 cups ripe raspberries
5 tablespoons framboise liqueur or raspberry eau-de-vie

Cut melons in half and remove seeds. Cut a little slice off bottom of melon halves so they won't wobble.

Wash berries and dry. Place in a medium bowl.

Add framboise or raspberry eau-de-vie and toss gently.

Fill melon halves with raspberries.

Serves 6

* If these melons are unavailable, use a wedge from a ripe cantaloupe or honeydew melon.

Breakfast for Fannie Farmer

Buttermilk Eggs in Tomato Shells

Canadian Bacon and Dill Tostadas

Two-Melon Soup

9 ingredients

Marion Cunningham, famous for rejuvenating The Fannie Farmer Cookbook, *is also America's champion of breakfast.*

In addition to writing the charming best-seller The Breakfast Book, *she created, with Chef John Hudspeth, what many considered the country's ultimate breakfast restaurant. At the antique-filled Bridge Creek in Berkeley (where else?), I had the best of all breakfasts: Heavenly Hots, so aptly named, were cloudlike, almost flourless pancakes;* velvety eggs baked in buttermilk; silken melon soup; and juice freshly squeezed from exotic blood oranges.

Thanks to Marion, America's morning dishes were endowed with the respect generally reserved for dinner.

Once dubbed "the Temple of Oat-Cuisine," Bridge Creek sadly is closed but longingly remembered.

BUTTERMILK EGGS IN TOMATO SHELLS

4 medium-large ripe tomatoes (5 to 6 ounces each)
½ cup buttermilk
4 extra-large eggs

Preheat oven to 350°.

Cut a very thin slice from bottom of each tomato so that it won't wobble. Do not cut into the liquid part of the tomato.

Cut a ½-inch slice off tops of tomatoes and scoop out seeds and pulp from cavity, leaving the shell of the tomato intact and being careful not to penetrate the bottom.

Sprinkle insides of tomatoes with salt and freshly ground pepper. Put ½ tablespoon buttermilk in bottom of each shell.

Fill each shell with a raw egg, which will come almost to the top of tomato. Carefully spoon 1 tablespoon buttermilk on top of each. Sprinkle with salt.

Place in shallow baking dish and bake 25 minutes, or until eggs are set but not overcooked.

Serves 4

CANADIAN BACON AND DILL TOSTADAS

4 8-inch flour tortillas
16 thin slices (about 8 ounces) Canadian bacon
8 ounces dill Havarti cheese

Preheat oven to 400°.

Place tortillas on 2 baking sheets. Place 4 slices Canadian bacon on each tortilla, leaving a ½-inch border. Add a liberal grinding of black pepper.

Grate cheese on large holes of box grater. Distribute evenly over Canadian bacon, leaving a ½-inch border.

Bake for 5 minutes, until cheese begins to melt, then place under broiler until lightly browned. Remove from oven.

Let sit 2 to 3 minutes before serving. Serve whole or cut into quarters.

Serves 4

TWO-MELON SOUP

1 small ripe cantaloupe (about 2 pounds)
½ cup Lillet *
1 small ripe honeydew (about 2¼ pounds)

Remove rind from cantaloupe with a sharp knife. Cut in half and remove seeds. Cut cantaloupe into chunks and place in food processor. Puree with 6 tablespoons Lillet and a pinch of salt until very smooth. Transfer to a clean container or pitcher and chill until very cold.

Repeat process with honeydew melon, adding 2 tablespoons Lillet and a pinch of salt to a clean food processor bowl. Puree until very smooth, and chill several hours until very cold.

To serve, using pitchers or ladles, pour 2 melon purees at the same time into a flat soup plate, keeping each puree separate. They will come together in the middle. Serve immediately.

Serves 4 (makes approximately 2½ cups of each flavor)

---

* Lillet is a French apéritif from the Bordeaux area, now available in a red version. Use the original golden version for this recipe or Dubonnet blanc.

Fried Red Tomatoes

Warm Cheese Scones

Frittata with Pancetta and Mint

Fried Red Tomatoes

Fresh Figs, Bitter Orange Mascarpone

12 ingredients

This is breakfast American style, with strong Italian accents. Its Technicolor menu provides exciting taste sensations: salty pancetta against the verve of mint; acid-sweet tomatoes softened in a crunchy cornmeal crust; ripe figs and rich mascarpone with a counterpoint of bitter citrus.

WARM CHEESE SCONES

6 ounces Italian fontina or Swiss cheese
⅓ cup sun-dried tomatoes in oil
*2½ cups or more well-packed biscuit mix, * plus more for dusting*

Remove rind from cheese. Grate cheese on large holes of box grater. You will have about 1¾ cups. Set aside.

Preheat oven to 400°.

Drain oil from sun-dried tomatoes, reserving 2 tablespoons oil. Pat tomatoes dry and finely chop.

In a large bowl, put 2½ cups biscuit mix, half the grated cheese, chopped sun-dried tomatoes, 2 table-spoons reserved oil, ½ cup cold water, and pinch of salt.

Mix well with hands, adding more biscuit mix if

* Use a brand such as Bisquick.

dough is too wet or sticky or more water if too dry. Turn onto surface dusted with biscuit mix. Knead 15 to 20 times. Roll with rolling pin into 10-inch circle that is ½ inch thick. With sharp knife, cut into 8 pie-shaped triangles.

Mound reserved cheese evenly on top of each scone. Place on ungreased baking sheet. Bake 15 to 17 min-utes, or until golden. Let sit 5 minutes before serving.

Makes 8 scones

FRITTATA WITH PANCETTA AND MINT

4 ounces pancetta, in ¼-inch-thick slices
10 extra-large eggs
1 large bunch fresh mint, leaves only

Cut pancetta into ¼-inch dice. Put in a 10-inch oven-proof nonstick skillet and cook over low heat for 8 minutes, until pancetta begins to get crisp, but not brown, and fat is rendered.

In the bowl of electric mixer, put eggs, 3 tablespoons cold water, ¼ teaspoon salt, and freshly ground black pepper. Beat well.

Pour beaten eggs into hot pan with pancetta. Add ½ cup packed mint leaves. Over low heat, stir briefly with wooden spoon and then let eggs cook slowly, without stirring.

After 1 minute, cover frittata and cook until almost firm, about 7 minutes. Meanwhile, preheat broiler.

Place under broiler for 30 seconds to 1 minute, until firm. Let cool for 3 or 4 minutes, then cut into wedges.

Serves 4

FRIED RED TOMATOES

4 medium firm ripe red tomatoes
1 cup stone-ground yellow cornmeal
Corn oil for frying

Slice off top and bottom ends of tomatoes. Cut each tomato into 3 slices.

Place cornmeal on a flat plate. Dredge both sides of each slice of tomato in cornmeal. Make sure slices are thickly coated (sides will not get coated).

Heat ¼ inch of oil in a large nonstick skillet, then add tomatoes in one layer. Cook over medium heat for two minutes on each side until crisp and golden brown. Do not overcook, as you want tomatoes to retain their shape.

Sprinkle generously with salt and freshly ground black pepper. Serve 3 slices per person.

Serves 4

FRESH FIGS, BITTER ORANGE MASCARPONE

12 small ripe purple figs
3 ounces mascarpone or cream cheese, at room temperature
2 tablespoons bitter orange marmalade

Wash figs gently and dry carefully with paper towels.

In a small bowl, mix together mascarpone or cream cheese with marmalade. Cream together with a fork or wooden spoon until very well blended.

Slicing down from the stem end, cut figs in quarters, but stop halfway down each fig.

Stuff each opening with 2 teaspoons filling. Place on platter and refrigerate, standing up, until ready to serve.

Serves 4

■ ■ ■

Postcard from Portofino

Baked Eggs Splendido

Bel Paese and Prosciutto Bruschetta

Morning Granita: Grapefruit-Campari

9 ingredients

July 1972

Dearest Ma,

A whirlwind tour: Rome, Florence, Milan, San Remo, Viareggio. What an incredible first trip abroad. Of course you know how much attention you get when you're nineteen and your traveling companion looks like Grace Kelly.

But in Portofino . . .

Amy H. and I are staying in this budget pensione shadowed by the opulence and majesty of the Hotel Splendido up the hill.

One morning, I yank Amy H. out of bed and say, "Let's have breakfast at the Splendido. It's the only thing we can afford and I'm just dying to see it and say we've been!"

We're sitting on the palatial patio having the only thing we can afford: a delicious open-face sandwich of Bel Paese and prosciutto, and a slushy ice made from grapefruit and Campari. We share it!

The waiter comes over to me, not with the check, but with the phone. He says it's for me. A Marcello Mastroianni voice says he's peering at our table from behind the curtain in the ristorante. I say, "Oh, you must want my friend, the blond." He says no. Can you believe it?

After espresso with Pepe, who works in the hotel, we pack our bags and move in for the rest of the week.

Arrivederci, Mama!
R.

BAKED EGGS SPLENDIDO

1¾ cups tomato juice
1 large bunch fresh basil
4 extra-large eggs

Put tomato juice in a small saucepan. Bring to a boil. Lower heat to medium and cook until reduced to 1 cup, about 20 minutes.

When ready to serve, put reduced tomato juice in a 10-inch, nonstick skillet.

Bring to a boil, then lower heat. Cut enough basil leaves into chiffonade so that you have a scant ½ cup: Stack basil leaves and roll them like small cigars; holding a roll firmly, cut crosswise into ⅛-inch strips.

Sprinkle basil over reduced juice and break 4 or more eggs into sauce. Let cook over medium heat until whites just begin to set, about 2 minutes.

Cover pan and cook over very low heat until yolks are cooked to desired doneness.

Garnish with fresh basil sprigs and serve immediately.

Serves 4

BEL PAESE AND PROSCIUTTO *BRUSCHETTA*

8 slices good-quality Italian bread, cut on a diagonal
4 ounces thinly sliced prosciutto
8 ounces thinly sliced Bel Paese cheese

Preheat oven to 400°.

Toast bread slices on each side until they begin to crisp. This can be easily done by placing bread on a baking sheet in a 400° oven for 5 minutes or longer, turning once. Or toast in a toaster until golden.

Cover each slice of toast with prosciutto, then add a slice of cheese on top of prosciutto.

Place *bruschetta* on a baking sheet and bake just until cheese melts, about 3 minutes. Serve warm.

Serves 4

MORNING GRANITA: GRAPEFRUIT-CAMPARI

½ cup sugar
3 cups freshly squeezed grapefruit juice
3 tablespoons Campari, plus more for drizzling

Make a simple syrup by placing sugar in a small saucepan with ½ cup water. Bring to a boil, lower heat to medium and cook until sugar is dissolved. Remove from heat and let cool.

Combine grapefruit juice, simple syrup, and Campari. Pour into a 13-by-9-inch baking pan and freeze for 4 hours, scraping with a fork every 30 minutes to break up ice crystals.

Divide evenly into 4 wineglasses and drizzle with additional Campari.

Optional garnish: You can dip rims of wineglasses into Campari, then into additional sugar so that rims are sugar coated. Let harden a few minutes, then fill glasses with granita.

Serves 4

■ ■ ■

Morning Light, Southern Exposure

Buttermilk Grits Soufflé

Peaches Flamed in Southern Comfort

6 ingredients

MORNING VERSE

Bits of grits in buttermilk
Hot and steamy, smooth as silk
Followed by peaches in bourbon flambé
An odd sort of morning but boozy bouquet.

(This breakfast has fewer calories than a
New York bagel with cream cheese.)

BUTTERMILK GRITS SOUFFLÉ ✗

1 cup quick-cooking grits
1½ cups buttermilk
4 extra-large eggs

Preheat the oven to 375°.

Bring 2 cups water and 1 teaspoon salt to a boil in a medium pot.

Slowly add grits, stirring constantly. Lower heat to a simmer and cook while stirring, for 5 minutes, until grits are thick and smooth.

Remove from heat. Add 1 cup buttermilk and stir until very smooth.

Separate egg yolks from egg whites. Add yolks to grits and buttermilk and stir until ingredients are thoroughly incorporated. Add freshly ground black pepper and stir.

Beat egg whites with a pinch of salt in bowl of electric mixer until stiff.

Fold whites into grits mixture. Spray a 2-quart soufflé dish with vegetable spray. Carefully pour grits mixture into dish.

Bake for 40 to 45 minutes, until golden brown and puffy.

Serve hot directly from casserole. Using a cake knife, cut into large wedges. Pour 2 tablespoons buttermilk over each portion. Pass the pepper mill.

Serves 4 or more

PEACHES FLAMED IN SOUTHERN COMFORT

1 pound (5 or 6) small ripe peaches
3 tablespoons unsalted whipped butter
4 tablespoons Southern Comfort

Wash peaches and dry well.

Cut peaches in half and carefully remove pits. Cut each peach half in half.

In a large nonstick skillet, melt butter over medium heat. Add quartered peaches and raise heat to medium-high. Cook for 2 minutes, stirring with wooden spoon.

Add 3 tablespoons Southern Comfort and continue to cook over medium-high heat for 1 minute. Peaches will begin to caramelize. (Do not overcook, or butter sauce will break.)

Before serving, add remaining tablespoon Southern Comfort to pan and light with match. Flames will die out quickly. Serve immediately.

Serves 4

■ ■ ■

At the King David

Pickled Fresh Salmon

Scrambled Eggs and Onions

Mangoes, Prunes, and Pomegranates

9 ingredients

As the sun rises over the Temple Mount and casts its rays on the golden dome, three thousand years of history shine before your eyes in Jerusalem. It's enough to make a girl hungry.

At the historic and magnificent King David Hotel, one expects even breakfast to be divinely inspired.

Your choice is breakfast Jewish style or Israeli style. The latter means eating salads and vege-tables, tomatoes and fresh white cheese, yogurt and hard-boiled eggs, all of which are especially luxurious on the Sabbath, when no cooking is allowed.

During the week, I choose Jewish style, reveling in copious amounts of pickled fresh salmon, soft-scrambled eggs with onions, and a lovely fruit compote.

Either way, it makes lunch seem improbable.

PICKLED FRESH SALMON

4 8-ounce salmon steaks
6 tablespoons distilled white vinegar
4 teaspoons pickling spices

Place salmon steaks in 2 large nonstick skillets. To each pan, add 1 cup water, 3 tablespoons vinegar, 2 teaspoons pickling spices, and 2 teaspoons kosher salt.

Cover each with a round of waxed paper. Bring just to a boil. Lower heat. Cook gently over medium heat for 4 to 5 minutes, until fish begins to lose its transparency. Turn over and cook 2 to 3 minutes. Be careful not to overcook. Discard waxed paper.

With a spatula, remove fish to a shallow casserole.

Strain liquid through a fine-mesh sieve directly over fish. Cool, then refrigerate until cold.

Remove from liquid before serving. Salmon will keep up to 4 days refrigerated. Serve 1 salmon steak per person. Or remove skin and center bone and cut in half.

Serves 4 or 8

SCRAMBLED EGGS AND ONIONS

1 large yellow onion
2½ tablespoons unsalted butter
8 extra-large eggs

Peel onion. Cut into very small dice. You will have approximately 1½ cups diced onion.

Melt butter in a large nonstick skillet. Do not let brown. Add onions. Cook over low heat until onions are very soft, but not brown. This will take approximately 10 to 15 minutes.

Beat eggs well in the bowl of an electric mixer with 3 tablespoons water, ½ teaspoon salt, and freshly ground black pepper.

Add beaten eggs to cooked onions in pan and continue to cook over low heat until eggs just begin to set. Scramble eggs with wooden spoon and continue to cook until desired doneness, about 5 or 6 minutes; they should still be a little runny, as they will continue to cook.

Serve immediately.

Serves 4

MANGOES, PRUNES, AND POMEGRANATES

24 extra-large prunes
1 large ripe mango, chilled
1 pomegranate

Place prunes in medium pot with water to cover by ¼ inch. Bring to a boil. Lower heat and cover pot. Simmer 15 minutes. Let prunes cool in liquid, then refrigerate until very cold. The longer the prunes sit, the thicker the liquid will become.

When ready to serve, peel mango and cut into ½-inch chunks. Drain prunes, reserving liquid. Mix prunes with mango and distribute evenly among 4 flat soup plates.

Cut pomegranate in half and scoop out seeds. Scatter 2 tablespoons, or more, pomegranate seeds on top of compote. Spoon several tablespoons of prune liquid around fruit.

Serves 4

Holiday Morning

Panettone French Toast, Thick Cut

Warm Pear and Cranberry Compote, Cranberry Syrup

Café Cantata

9 ingredients

Deck the halls.

Set the mood: Bach's Christmas Oratorio.

Serve the food.

Change the record: Bach's "Coffee Cantata."

Shovel the walk.

PANETTONE FRENCH TOAST, THICK CUT

*1 small imported panettone (17.6 ounces or 500 grams) ***
6 extra-large eggs
6 tablespoons unsalted butter

Preheat oven to 350°.

Stand panettone upright. Cut thin slices of crust from opposite sides of cylindrical shape and discard both slices. Then, from top to bottom, cut the remainder into six slices of equal thickness. Place on baking sheet and bake 5 minutes so that panettone is lightly toasted and slightly dried out.

Meanwhile, beat eggs with 3 tablespoons water in bowl of electric mixer until light and fluffy.

Place panettone in a shallow casserole and cover with beaten eggs. Let sit 10 minutes, turning once or twice, so that bread is soaked.

Heat 2 large nonstick skillets. Melt 2 tablespoons butter in each. Add 2 slices of panettone to each pan. Cook over medium-high heat for 5 minutes on each side, until golden. Place on a baking sheet. Repeat process, adding more butter as you go along. When all the panettone is cooked and placed on baking sheet, place in oven for 8 to 10 minutes, until golden brown and puffy.

Cut in half and serve 3 pieces per person. Serve immediately. Pass extra butter, if desired.

Serves 4

* Panettone is a cylindrical, slightly sweet, raisin-studded bread from Italy. There are several good brands available in most specialty-food stores and often in supermarkets.

WARM PEAR AND CRANBERRY COMPOTE, CRANBERRY SYRUP

1 cup sugar
2 large firm Comice pears
2 cups (6 ounces) cranberries

Bring 2 cups water plus 1 cup sugar to a boil in a medium pot.

Peel pears and cut into 8 wedges. Remove any seeds. Add with cranberries to boiling sugar syrup.

Lower heat and cook 20 minutes, until pears are tender but still retain their shape. Remove pears and cranberries with slotted spoon and place in a clean medium pot.

Meanwhile, continue to cook cranberry syrup over medium-high heat until syrup is reduced to ¾ cup. Syrup should be thick and the consistency of honey.

Gently reheat pear-cranberry compote. Spoon cranberry syrup over compote (and also over Panettone French Toast—see the preceding recipe).

Serves 4

CAFÉ CANTATA

*6 tablespoons Tuaca liqueur **
3 cups freshly brewed hot strong coffee
½ cup heavy cream, whipped

Place 1½ tablespoons liqueur in each of 4 large sturdy wineglasses. Add ¾ cup hot coffee to each and stir well.

Top with lightly whipped cream.

Serves 4

* Tuaca, orange-vanilla liqueur, is intensely delicious in this coffee preparation. It comes from Tuscany and dates from the Renaissance. Tuaca is available in most liquor stores. You may substitute Grand Marnier.

■ ■ ■

Bread-and-Breakfast

Halvah and Golden Raisin Turnovers

Chocolate-Raspberry Turnovers

Almond Milk with **Orzata** *and Coffee Ice Cubes*

9 ingredients

Everyone's fantasy.

You can open up your own bed-and-breakfast with the following amazing array of breads-for-breakfast, and with very little cash.

If all else fails, a platter of warm halvah-and-golden-raisin-filled turnovers alongside a pitcher of cold "almond milk" is enough to guarantee a major loan from the bank.

Let me know what happens.

Almond "Toast" (see page 20)

Warm Buttermilk Biscuits (see page 31)

Warm Cheese Scones (see page 42)

Whole Wheat Pita Bread (see page 246)

Homemade Focaccia (see page 148)

HALVAH AND GOLDEN RAISIN TURNOVERS

1 sheet frozen puff pastry (8¾ ounces)
2 ounces (⅓ cup packed) pistachio halvah
4 tablespoons golden raisins

Preheat oven to 400°.

Thaw pastry for 20 to 30 minutes at room temperature so that it is pliable but still cool to the touch.

Crumble halvah between your fingers. Chop raisins and add to halvah. You will have approximately ½ cup packed halvah-raisin filling.

Roll pastry to make a 9-by-13½-inch rectangle. Cut into 6 4½-inch squares.

Place 1 heaping tablespoon halvah-raisin mixture in center of each square. Fold over to make a triangular turnover. Brush edges with water and crimp together tightly, then trim edges with a sharp knife.

Place on a baking sheet and bake 10 minutes, or until puffed and golden brown. Let cool.

Makes 6 turnovers

CHOCOLATE-RASPBERRY TURNOVERS

1 sheet frozen puff pastry (8¾ ounces)
6 teaspoons good-quality raspberry jam
6 tablespoons grated semisweet chocolate

Preheat oven to 400°.

Thaw pastry for 20 to 30 minutes at room temperature so that it is pliable but still cool to the touch.

Roll pastry to make a 9-by-13½-inch rectangle. Cut into 6 4½-inch squares.

Place 1 teaspoon jam in center of each square. Place 1 tablespoon grated chocolate over jam.

Fold pastry over to make a triangular turnover.

Brush edges with water and crimp together tightly, then trim edges with a sharp knife.

Place on a baking sheet and bake 10 minutes, or until puffed and golden brown. Let cool.

Optional garnish: Melt additional chocolate and drizzle over cooled turnovers. Let cool again so chocolate hardens.

Makes 6 turnovers

ALMOND MILK WITH *ORZATA* AND COFFEE ICE CUBES

3 cups freshly brewed strong coffee, cooled
4 cups whole milk, chilled
4 tablespoons orzata *(almond syrup)* *

Put cool coffee into 2 ice-cube trays to make 24 ice cubes. Place in freezer for several hours until solid.

For each drink, put 1 cup milk in a large wineglass. Add 1 tablespoon *orzata* to each glass and stir well.

Add 6 coffee ice cubes to each and serve immediately.

Serves 4

* Available at specialty-food stores, especially those featuring Italian imports. Also known as orgeat.

2

Noon

■ ■ ■
LUNCH

First Courses

Salade de Tomates *with Verjus*

*Japanese Eggplants with Roasted Garlic
and Sun-Dried Tomatoes*

Tomato-Mascarpone Soup, Basil Chiffonade

Roasted Pepper "Sandwiches"

Salad of Watercress, Orange, and Chorizo

Roquefort Mousse and Celery Crudités

Roasted Red Onion and Feta Salad

Sweet Corn Soup with Scallion Butter

Tiny Clams with Wasabi and Pickled Ginger

Yellow Pea Soup with Dill

Warm Feta Cheese and Cherry Tomato Compote

Chilled Green Bean Soup, Sour Cream Dollop

Immune Soup

Oysters with "Malted" Mignonette

Jalapeño and Pepperoni Tortilla Flat

Main Courses

Spinach Fettuccine with Ricotta and Parmesan

Polenta "Lasagne" with Smoked Mozzarella

"Pasta @ Noon"

Pithiviers of Smoked Ham and Port Salut

Lemony Tuna Salad, Tuna-Tahina Dressing

Sardines Baked in Grape Leaves, Tomato Reduction

Bay Scallops with Parsley Puree

Steamed Mussels Crema di Salsa

Sea Bass Steamed in Lettuce, Rosemary Oil

Crispy Cod with Potato Flakes

Gougonettes *of Turbot in Chickpea Flour*

Seared Salmon Steak with Cornichon Vinaigrette

Pan-Grilled Swordfish, Pepper-Lime Sauce

*Chicken Roulades with Roasted Peppers
and* Soppressata

*Moroccan Chicken with Preserved Lemons
and Green Olives*

Chicken Chipotle with Red Onions

Chili-Cooked Garlic Spareribs with Cilantro

Mustard-Molasses Lamb Riblets

Skillet Chopped Steak with Scallions and Soy

Skirt Steak with Salsa Verde, *Raw and Roasted Garlic*

Side Dishes

Blasted Green Beans with Niçoise Olives

Mâche and Granny Smith Salad, Apple Vinaigrette

Sweet Pepper Green Beans

Tubetti *with Zucchini*

Tomatoes Provençale

Country Garlic Bread

Potato Silk

Courgettes with Basil

*Celery Salad with French Black Olives
and Truffle Oil*

Horseradish Potato Salad

Jasmine Rice and Poppy Seeds

Dutch Noodles with Aged Gouda
Pilaf Baked in Lavash
Tostones: *Fried Plantains and Fresh Lime*
Rice with Water Chestnuts and Sesame Oil
Cabbage "Cream" Slaw
Lemon Yellow Beans
Cremini *Mushrooms, Sherry-Pepper Cream*
Sour Cream Mashed Potatoes
with Skillet-Roasted Corn

Desserts

Purple Plums with Mascarpone and Brown Sugar
Amaretto Granita
Marsala-Poached Pears, Crushed Amaretti
Fresh Cherry Soup
Brown Sugar Shortbread
Fruit Salad Vino Cotto
Coffee Ice Cream with Toasted Almonds, Prune Syrup
Poached Oranges in Lemon Syrup, Citrus Granita
Pink Grapefruit Sherbet, Pink Grapefruit Syrup
Almond Water Ice with Fresh Cherry Salad,
Cherry Syrup
Watermelon Granita with Chocolate "Seeds"
Polenta with Sugar and Oranges
Red, White, and Blueberries
Pineapple Flan
Gingersnap Baked Apples
Vanilla Bean Ice Cream with Orange-Flower Water
and Pistachios

Margarita Sorbet, Sugared Raspberries
Lychee Sorbet and Almond Cookie Dessert
Warm Apple Kissel, Apple Chips
Old-Fashioned Rice Pudding
Tequila Melon

Summer in the City

Salade de Tomates *with* **Verjus**

Spinach Fettuccine with Ricotta and Parmesan

Purple Plums with Mascarpone and Brown Sugar

9 ingredients

Tomatoes are with us all year, but a true tomato is transitory; to grasp its essence, you need a super-ripe one plucked after mid-August, for only then does its balance of sugar, acidity, and juiciness proclaim: Summer.

French writer Madeleine Kamman inspired this menu's facile tomato salad enhanced with verjus, the slightly sour juice of unripe grapes, which adds an unidentifiable acidity.

Verjus, used in French and Italian cooking since the Middle Ages, is now available from California, where this unfermented "must" is known as a wine-friendly alternative to vinegar.

Keeping it simple is a good idea during summer in the city. And so this menu requires nothing more than a plate, a pot, and a pan.

GRAPENOTE

A hot summer's day — and this menu — call for a crisp, bright white: sauvignon blanc. The one from Corbett Canyon is a great value; the one from Stoneleigh, a great find.

SALADE DE TOMATES WITH VERJUS

6 large very ripe beefsteak tomatoes (8 ounces each)
4 tablespoons finely minced shallots
*½ cup verjus ***

Bring large pot of water to boil. Cut a small X in bottom of each tomato and plunge in boiling water for 1 minute. Remove tomatoes, and peel, saving skin. Let cool. Cut tomatoes into ¼-inch thick slices. Arrange on platter. Squeeze shallots in paper towel to remove bitter juices.

Sprinkle tomato slices with shallots, a pinch of sea salt, butcher-grind black pepper, and *verjus*. Let stand 20 to 30 minutes at room temperature. Garnish with tomato skin, shaped into a rose.

Serves 6

* A good brand is Fusion Napa Valley Verjus.

SPINACH FETTUCCINE WITH RICOTTA AND PARMESAN

18 ounces fresh spinach fettuccine
2 15-ounce containers part-skim ricotta cheese, at room temperature
2 cups freshly grated best-quality Parmesan cheese

Bring a large pot of salted water to a boil.

Add pasta and cook 5 minutes, or until pasta is just tender (do not overcook). Drain pasta in colander, saving ½ cup of the cooking water.

Transfer pasta to a ceramic bowl. Add ricotta cheese, salt, and lots of freshly ground black pepper. Toss gently, adding some of the cooking water to moisten.

Sprinkle all of the Parmesan cheese over the pasta. Serve immediately.

Serves 6 or more

PURPLE PLUMS WITH MASCARPONE AND BROWN SUGAR

9 ripe purple plums
6 tablespoons mascarpone
6 tablespoons dark brown sugar

Preheat broiler.

Wash plums and dry well. Cut in half and remove pits.

Place plum halves, cut sides up, in a shallow baking pan. Place 1 teaspoon mascarpone in center of each plum.

Sprinkle 1 teaspoon brown sugar on each. Broil for 30 seconds to 1 minute, just until sugar melts. Remove plums with a metal spatula and place on platter. Cool to room temperature before serving. Can be made 1 hour before serving.

Serves 6

Vegetarian Sampler

Japanese Eggplants with Roasted Garlic
and Sun-Dried Tomatoes
Polenta "Lasagne" with Smoked Mozzarella
Blasted Green Beans with Niçoise Olives
Amaretto Granita
12 ingredients

In the patchwork quilt of American cookery, someone should embroider GIVE PEAS A CHANCE.

"Vegetables aren't really about nutrition. They're about power. Parents have it. Kids want it, and the struggle is usually engaged at the table" (Richard Atcheson, quoted in *The Great Food Almanac, by Irena Chalmers, 1994). This menu is designed to make everyone happy — especially any ovo-lacto vegetarians who might be stopping by for lunch.*

Japanese eggplants, long and slender, are each perfect for a single serving. Their blotterlike texture soaks up delicious flavors, but my cooking method reduces the quantity of oil usually required.

Meatless goes mainstream with my multilayered casserole: cushions of polenta, instead of sheets of pasta, stacked between layers of tomatoes and smoked cheese.

Blast-baking, at five hundred degrees, evaporates moisture and intensifies the flavor of green beans, and olives as well, for they emerge looking like Raisinets, with pits, and are equally addictive.

GRAPENOTE

Smoked and roasted flavors call for a lighter-style Côtes du Rhône like Jaboulet's Parallèle 45 or a flavorful *sangiovese* from Santa Cristina.

JAPANESE EGGPLANTS WITH ROASTED GARLIC AND SUN-DRIED TOMATOES

4 long slender Japanese eggplants
10 pieces sun-dried tomatoes in oil
20 thin slices fresh garlic

Preheat oven to 375°.

Cut 5 slits across the width of each eggplant approximately 1 inch apart. Cut sun-dried tomatoes in half, reserving oil. Slip a piece of sun-dried tomato and slice of garlic into each slit.

Place eggplants on foil. Drizzle with a little sun-dried tomato oil. Sprinkle with kosher salt and freshly ground black pepper. Fold foil to enclose eggplants in a sealed package. Put on baking sheet and bake 40 minutes, or until eggplants are soft.

Serve hot or at room temperature.

Serves 4

POLENTA "LASAGNE" WITH SMOKED MOZZARELLA ✗

12 ounces smoked mozzarella cheese
2 cups stone-ground yellow cornmeal
28-ounce can whole tomatoes in puree

Cut a third of the cheese into small pieces. Cut remainder into slices.

In large, heavy saucepan, bring 7 cups water to a boil. Add 2 teaspoons salt, ⅛ teaspoon freshly ground white pepper, and cornmeal in a slow, steady stream. Stir briskly with a wooden spoon until smooth. Break up lumps with back of spoon. Lower heat to medium.

Stir constantly until polenta begins to pull away from the sides of pan. After 20 minutes, add the small pieces of cheese and stir until melted. Continue stirring for another 15 minutes, until polenta is very thick.

Spray an 11-by-14-inch baking pan with nonstick vegetable spray. Pour hot polenta into pan to make an even layer. Let cool at least 2 hours at room temperature. Polenta will harden.

Preheat broiler. Cut polenta, in pan, into 12 squares. Put under broiler for 3 minutes, or until tops are lightly browned and crisp. Remove from broiler.

Preheat oven to 350°.

Meanwhile, puree tomatoes with their liquid in a food processor until fairly smooth. Put in a small heavy saucepan with lots of freshly ground black pepper. Bring to a boil, lower heat, and simmer 5 minutes. Set aside.

To assemble, put 6 pieces of polenta, touching, side by side in a 10-by-10-inch or 9-by-11-inch casserole. Spoon on half the tomato sauce to cover. Cover tomato sauce with half the cheese slices. Top with another layer of polenta, sauce, and cheese.

Bake for 10 to 15 minutes. Serve hot.

Serves 6 or more

BLASTED GREEN BEANS WITH NIÇOISE OLIVES

1 pound tender green beans
3 tablespoons olive oil
½ cup unpitted small black olives, preferably niçoise

Preheat oven to 500°.

Remove strings from green beans. This is a *must* when roasting them. Then trim ends with a small sharp knife. Wash beans in colander and dry well with paper towels.

Place green beans in shallow baking pan. Drizzle with 2 tablespoons olive oil and mix well to coat. Add olives. Sprinkle with salt and freshly ground black pepper.

Place pan in oven. Roast 6 minutes. Shake pan to turn beans. Roast another 5 to 6 minutes. Beans will be slightly wrinkled with a few brown patches.

Serve immediately on platter, drizzled with additional tablespoon of oil.

Also delicious served cold as a salad.

Serves 4

AMARETTO GRANITA

4 cups freshly brewed strong coffee
½ cup granulated sugar, plus some for dipping glass rims
¾ cup amaretto or Frangelico

In a medium pot, make a syrup by bringing coffee and sugar just to a boil, then lower heat immediately. Simmer 5 minutes, stirring constantly. Remove from heat. Cool.

Add liqueur, stir, and pour into a shallow metal pan.

Place in freezer and stir with fork every 20 minutes, until coarse crystals develop and there is no unfrozen liquid. This should take several hours.

Scrape granita with fork and serve in tall glasses whose edges have been dipped first in water and then in granulated sugar. Serve immediately.

Serves 4 or more

■ ■ ■

Cool Spaghetti

Tomato-Mascarpone Soup, Basil Chiffonade

"Pasta @ Noon"

Marsala-Poached Pears, Crushed Amaretti

9 ingredients

This menu is short on prep and deliciously simple — perfect for a warm weekend afternoon.

Prepare the soup and dessert early in the day when it's still cool in your kitchen, for they both need ample time to chill.

The pasta should be prepared at noon — about an hour before you are ready to eat, because it's at its best served at room temperature.

GRAPENOTE

Balance the salty and herbal flavors with a cool refreshing white: Italian *pinot grigio* from Villa Marchesini or French Picpoul de Pinet, produced just a few miles from the Mediterranean.

TOMATO-MASCARPONE SOUP, BASIL CHIFFONADE

28-ounce can good-quality plum tomatoes in puree *
¾ cup (6 ounces) mascarpone
¼ cup packed fresh basil leaves

Place plum tomatoes with puree in medium saucepan. Bring to a boil, lower heat to medium, cover, and cook for 10 minutes. Let cool 10 minutes.

Put tomatoes in a blender with ½ cup mascarpone. You may need to do this in 2 batches. Puree until very smooth. Transfer to a bowl and let cool. Cover and chill several hours, until very cold.

Add salt and freshly ground black pepper to taste. Blend with small wire whisk. Add up to ¼ cup cold water if too thick.

Stack basil leaves on top of one another and roll tightly like a cigar. Cut into very thin strips with a sharp knife. Divide the soup evenly into chilled flat soup plates. Garnish each with 1 tablespoon mascarpone and basil chiffonade.

Serves 4 (makes approximately 3½ cups)

* Do not substitute crushed tomatoes.

"PASTA @ NOON"

¾ pound spaghetti or linguine
4 ounces (2 2-ounce cans) anchovies with capers in oil
25 to 30 oil-cured black olives

Bring a large pot of salted water to a boil. Add pasta and cook until al dente, 10 to 12 minutes. Meanwhile, chop anchovies coarsely and save all the oil. Pit olives and coarsely chop. Put anchovies, capers, oil, and olives in a large ceramic bowl.

When pasta is done, drain it thoroughly, saving

⅓ cup cooking water. Add pasta and cooking water to bowl with anchovies, capers, oil, and chopped olives.

Toss well and let cool to room temperature. Season to taste with lots of freshly ground black pepper.

Serves 4

MARSALA-POACHED PEARS, CRUSHED AMARETTI

4 large ripe Bartlett, Anjou, or Comice pears, with long stems
1 cup marsala
*¾ cup crushed amaretti cookies ***

Peel pears, leaving stems intact. Cut a thin slice from the bottoms, so pears will stand without wobbling. Put peeled pears in heavy, medium saucepan with 1 cup marsala and enough water just to cover. Bring to a boil.

Lower heat and cook pears for 30 minutes, or until soft. Remove pears with slotted spoon. Let cool, then refrigerate until cold.

Bring liquid in saucepan to a boil. Cook over medium-high heat until liquid is reduced to 1 cup. Let cool.

Before serving, roll bottom third of pears in amaretti crumbs. Place pears in each of 4 flat soup plates. Spoon marsala sauce around the pears.

Serves 4

* Use 16 to 18 small cookies, 8 to 9 large. An easy way to crush the cookies is to put them in a plastic Ziploc bag and crush with a rolling pin.

■ ■ ■

The First Cherries

Pithiviers *of Smoked Ham and Port Salut*

Mâche and Granny Smith Salad, Apple Vinaigrette

Fresh Cherry Soup

Brown Sugar Shortbread

12 ingredients

This festive lunch can be shuffled like a deck of cards, since, except for dessert, the order is arbitrary.

A pithiviers *is a grammatically and gastronomically singular double-crust puff-pastry tart, sometimes sweet and sometimes savory. Here it is filled with layers of smoked ham and creamy French Port Salut.*

The salad is a sort of three-ingredient gambol, since apples are used for crunch and contrast to soft greens, and then used again to provide body and acidity to the dressing.

Good cherries come to market in late May, which is the proper time to serve this meal. Speaking of shuffling the deck, in Monte Carlo it's a lovely tradition to close your eyes and make a wish upon the first cerises *of the year.*

GRAPENOTE

A good, flowery Beaujolais Village would be a lovely choice, as would an off-dry Riesling from the Finger Lakes (Hermann Wiemer) or a modest Kabinett-grade Riesling from Germany.

PITHIVIERS OF SMOKED HAM AND PORT SALUT

2 sheets frozen puff pastry (17¼ ounces)
*16 ounces Port Salut cheese ***
12 ounces thinly sliced smoked ham

Thaw puff pastry as directed on package. Preheat oven to 375°.

Remove rind and then cut cheese into thin slices. Lightly roll out each piece of puff pastry to form 2 9½-by-9½-inch squares.

On 1 sheet of pastry, layer ham and cheese, leaving a 1-inch border on each side: begin with a layer of ham, add a layer of cheese, and alternate, ending with ham. Sprinkle liberally with freshly ground black pepper.

Gently brush borders of pastry with cold water and cover with second sheet of puff pastry. Seal edges tightly by pressing down with fingers. Trim edges evenly with sharp knife.

Place on baking sheet and bake 35 to 40 minutes, until pastry has puffed and is golden brown. Remove from oven, let sit 10 minutes, and cut into 6 to 8 squares. Serve immediately.

Serves 6 to 8

* Use French Port Salut or substitute Danish Port Salut, also known as Esrom.

MÂCHE AND GRANNY SMITH SALAD, APPLE VINAIGRETTE

3 large Granny Smith apples
3 tablespoons good-quality olive oil
2 large bunches mâche lettuce*

Peel 1½ apples and cut into quarters. Remove seeds and cut into chunks. Place in a blender. Add 3 tablespoons cold water and 3 tablespoons olive oil. Puree until very smooth. Transfer contents to a small bowl. Add salt to taste. (This is an example of how salt magically works to balance tart and sweet flavors, but amount of salt will depend on the acidity of the apple.) You will have ¾ cup.

Wash lettuce and dry well. Cut remaining 1½ apples into very thin wedges or fine julienned strips.

Divide tufts of mâche evenly onto 6 to 8 large plates. Place apple wedges or julienned apple on top and cover each salad with 1½ to 2 tablespoons apple vinaigrette. Serve immediately, as dressing will turn brown. Pass the pepper mill.

Serves 6 to 8

---

* If you cannot find mâche, also known as lamb's lettuce, you may use baby watercress or tender leaves of green or red leaf lettuce.

FRESH CHERRY SOUP

1½ pounds fresh red cherries
½ cup Ginger Sugar (see page 11)
3 tablespoons arrowroot

Wash the cherries and pit them. Save pits. Place the cherries, sugar, and 2½ cups water in a heavy medium saucepan. Add a pinch of salt and freshly ground black pepper. Bring to a boil. Cover pot and cook over low heat for 1 hour.

At the same time, put pits into small saucepan and cover with 2 cups water. Bring to a boil and simmer 30 minutes. Pour through a strainer, reserving liquid.

In a small bowl, mix the arrowroot and ¼ cup of the strained cherry-pit liquid. After cherries have cooked for 1 hour, add mixture to cherries, stirring constantly.

Bring just to a boil, reduce heat, and cook 2 minutes. Cool, then refrigerate until very cold. Serve in chilled soup cups or in flat soup plates.

Serves 6 to 8 (makes approximately 6 cups)

BROWN SUGAR SHORTBREAD

2 cups flour, sifted
½ cup light brown sugar
1 cup unsalted butter, softened

Preheat oven to 350°.

Combine flour, sugar, and ⅛ teaspoon salt. Work the butter in gradually until well mixed, using electric mixer. Add a few drops of cold water if necessary.

Place dough on floured surface and pat out (do not roll) to ¼-inch thickness. Cut into 1½-inch rounds with a cookie cutter. Prick several times in center with tines of fork to make a design.

Place on ungreased baking sheet. Bake 20 to 22 minutes, until golden.

Makes 24 to 28 cookies

■ ■ ■

A Poem for the Table

Lemony Tuna Salad, Tuna-Tahina Dressing

Sweet Pepper Green Beans

Fruit Salad Vino Cotto

9 ingredients

I love the flavors of this simple menu; the immodest use of several prepared or "convenience" foods; the ease of its preparation.

I like its candor. And its colors. Served with a crusty baguette, it's a trip to the beach; a picnic on the grass; a poem for the table.

The crowning glory is a mélange of strawberries and grapefruit awash in "cooked wine," a syrupy reduction of white grape juice.

Refreshing and vibrant, this is a pick-me-up for the palate.

GRAPENOTE

This dressed-up tuna is rich — try a midweight Italian white like *vernaccia* or *verdicchio*.

LEMONY TUNA SALAD, TUNA-TAHINA DRESSING

5 6-ounce cans solid-pack light tuna in olive oil
3 tablespoons tahina (sesame paste)
4 large lemons

Place the contents of 1 can tuna and its oil in a blender. Add tahina. Grate the rind of 1 or 2 lemons on the medium holes of a box grater, so that you have 1 tablespoon grated zest. Add to blender with 5 tablespoons of freshly squeezed lemon juice. Add freshly ground black pepper, and puree until very smooth, thick, and creamy, adding 1 to 2 tablespoons cold water if too thick.

Drain oil from remaining cans of tuna. Turn out tuna onto each of 4 large plates and top with tuna-tahina dressing. Garnish with wedges or slices of remaining lemons.

Pass the pepper mill.

Serves 4

SWEET PEPPER GREEN BEANS

1 pound tender green beans
12-ounce jar sweet salad peppers*
¾ cup (3 ounces) pitted large oil-cured black olives

Wash green beans and trim ends. Bring a medium pot of salted water to a boil. Add green beans and cook 10 to 12 minutes (depending on the size and age of beans), until beans are tender but still bright green.

Meanwhile, drain most of the liquid from the peppers. Reserve liquid and place peppers in a large bowl. Toss with olives and freshly ground black pepper.

When beans are done, drain immediately in a colander under cold water.

Pat beans dry and toss with pepper-olive mixture. Add a few tablespoons of reserved liquid from peppers. Toss again and serve.

Serves 4 or more

*B & G has a sprightly product called sweet salad peppers, easily found in grocery stores.

FRUIT SALAD *VINO COTTO*

3 cups white grape juice
4 large white grapefruits
1 pint medium-large ripe strawberries

Put grape juice in a medium saucepan. Bring to a boil. Lower heat and cook until liquid is reduced to 1 cup. This will take approximately 30 minutes. Let cool.

Cut 2 grapefruits in half, through the "equator." Using a grapefruit knife, cut around circumference of fruit and remove gently, as you want to save shells for serving. Cut along membranes to release segments, making sure all white pith is removed. Place segments in a bowl.

Using a small sharp knife, cut rind from 2 remaining grapefruits, making sure to remove all the white pith. Cut along membranes to release segments. Add to bowl.

Wash berries, remove stems, and cut in half. Add to bowl with grapefruit. Pour reduced grape juice over fruit. Chill for at least 30 minutes.

Fill grapefruit shells with fruit salad, mounding high on top. Add as much of the fruit juices as possible. Place in a bowl and serve with a spoon.

Serves 4

■ ■ ■

An Accidental Guest

Sardines Baked in Grape Leaves, Tomato Reduction

Tubetti *with Zucchini*

Coffee Ice Cream with Toasted Almonds, Prune Syrup

9 ingredients

Knock, knock . . .

This is a sophisticated meal you can whip up when someone comes for lunch without much notice.

Most of this menu can be prepared with ingredients found in your pantry: sardines, jarred grape leaves, tomato juice, a box of pasta, chicken broth.

Its methodology is reductionist: From tomato juice to prune juice, everything gets reduced to maximize flavors.

The results are seductive. Sardines are wrapped like cigars in briny grape leaves and smothered in tomato essence; the confetti, tiny cubes of zucchini, in the tubetti *recipe are glazed with a shimmer of reduced chicken stock (replacing unnecessary fat).*

Prune juice, thickened by reduction, flows like the best chocolate sauce you've ever had.

. . . Come in.

GRAPENOTE

Having a bottle of Belvedere chardonnay in your fridge should be no accident. Open it now and replace it with another bottle.

SARDINES BAKED IN GRAPE LEAVES, TOMATO REDUCTION

2 cups tomato juice
12 grape leaves in brine
*About 14 ounces skinless, boneless sardines in pure olive oil**

Place tomato juice in medium saucepan. Bring to a boil, lower heat, and simmer until juice is reduced to 1 cup.

Preheat oven to 350°.

Remove grape leaves from brine and pat dry. Remove sardines carefully from can and reserve the oil. Place 1 sardine (or put together several pieces) on each grape leaf. Roll like a cigar, folding in side panels as you go. Wrap all the sardines so that you have 12 rolls that are approximately 4 inches long and 1 inch wide.

Place side by side in a shallow casserole or baking dish large enough to hold the sardines in one layer. Spoon 3 tablespoons sardine oil evenly over the sardines. Add a liberal grinding of black pepper. Spoon reduced tomato juice over all the grape leaves. Bake for 15 minutes. Serve while warm.

Serves 4

* You may need to use 4 3¾-ounce tins. King Oscar or Season are good-quality brands.

TUBETTI WITH ZUCCHINI

3 small to medium zucchini (about ¾ pound)
2 cups chicken broth
½ pound tubetti pasta

Wash zucchini. Trim ends. Cut zucchini in half through the diameter. Then slice lengthwise into ⅛-inch-thick slices. Meticulously cut slices into little cubes, ⅛-inch dice. You will have 2 heaping cups.

Bring a large pot of salted water to a boil.

At the same time put chicken broth in a small saucepan and cook over medium-high heat until broth is reduced to ½ cup.

When large pot of salted water is boiling, add *tubetti*. Cook for 8 minutes, add diced zucchini, and cook 4 more minutes. Drain in fine-mesh sieve.

Toss *tubetti* and zucchini with reduced broth. Add lots of freshly ground pepper. You will not need to add salt. Serve hot, warm, or at room temperature.

Serves 4

COFFEE ICE CREAM WITH TOASTED ALMONDS, PRUNE SYRUP

2 cups prune juice
1 cup (4 ounces) sliced almonds
1 pint premium-quality coffee ice cream, frozen hard*

Place prune juice in heavy, small saucepan. Bring just to a boil. Lower heat to medium and cook until prune juice is reduced to ¾ cup. This will take 15 to 20 minutes. Let cool. Syrup will be thick and look like chocolate sauce.

Meanwhile, place almonds in a medium nonstick skillet. Cook several minutes over low heat, shaking the pan occasionally, until almonds turn golden brown and produce a nutty, toasted aroma. Set aside.

To serve, remove cover from ice cream. Set container on its side on a cutting board. With a large, sharp knife, cut container into 4 1½-inch-thick disks. Place 2 tablespoons toasted almonds in center of each of 4 large plates. Top with ice-cream disk. Sprinkle with 2 more tablespoons toasted almonds and drizzle with 3 tablespoons prune syrup.

Serves 4

* Buy ice cream packed in a round container so you end up with disks.

■ ■ ■

Lunch for Picasso

Roasted Pepper "Sandwiches"

Bay Scallops with Parsley Puree

Tomatoes Provençale

Poached Oranges in Lemon Syrup, Citrus Granita

12 ingredients

Although his early hangout was the dank Three Cats Bar in a meandering Barcelona alley, later in life Picasso could be spotted wandering Cap d'Antibes in a small bathing suit.

Often as Pablo sat on the terrace overlooking La Méditerranée, a halcyon soared over his head, which not only cast a calming, tranquil veil over the artist but also upon the azure sea, especially during lunch.

Picasso ate lightly, but well, and was rarely ever blue.

Every day at three, he anticipated the voice of Françoise traversing the pebbly beach. The sunlight cut her image into cubelike forms. "Ciao, Pablo, ciao," she would say in that throaty yet kind voice. "Let me have a puff of your Gauloise."

Every day, Pablo would put his cigarette between her lips and kiss her eyelids.

She would quench her thirst with the last of the cool granita and lick the plate clean.

GRAPENOTE

A soft white from southern France would surely have pleased Monsieur. Château du Campuget from the area around Nîmes is an artistic blend of chardonnay, *clairette*, *grenache*, and *roussane*.

ROASTED PEPPER "SANDWICHES"

3 large squarish bell peppers, 2 red and 1 yellow
12 thin slices prosciutto (4 ounces)
6 thin slices fontina cheese (4 ounces)

Preheat broiler.

Cut 4 sides from each pepper to make a total of 12 panels. They will become the slices of "bread" for the sandwiches.

Place 2 slices prosciutto, folded in half, and 1 slice of cheese on top of each of 6 pepper panels. Cover with another pepper panel.

With a sharp knife, neatly trim edges of sandwiches.

Place on baking sheet. Broil 3 minutes on one side until peppers begin to blacken and blister. Carefully turn over using a spatula or tongs and broil on other side for 3 minutes.

Remove from oven. Let cool 5 minutes. Cut in half on the diagonal, like a sandwich, and serve 3 halves per person. Serve warm or at room temperature.

Serves 4

BAY SCALLOPS WITH PARSLEY PUREE

1¾ pounds bay scallops
2 or more large bunches curly parsley (3 cups packed leaves)
3 tablespoons unsalted butter, melted

Pat scallops dry and set aside.

Bring a medium pot of salted water to boil. Put parsley leaves in water and boil for 1 minute. Drain parsley. Puree in blender with 2 tablespoons cold water and 2 tablespoons melted butter. Add ½ teaspoon salt and freshly ground black pepper. Blend until creamy and thick. Transfer to a small saucepan. Keep warm.

Put remaining tablespoon melted butter in a large nonstick skillet. Add scallops and cook over high heat for 1 to 2 minutes, stirring often. Cook until scallops just become opaque.

Remove scallops with slotted spoon. Reduce any pan juices over high heat for 30 seconds and pour over scallops. Serve scallops with warm parsley puree.

Serves 4

TOMATOES PROVENÇALE

2 medium ripe tomatoes (4 ounces each)
¼ loaf semolina bread
2 tablespoons garlic oil *

Preheat oven to 400°.

Remove stems from tomatoes. Cut tomatoes in half, through the equator, so that you have 4 halves. Place tomatoes cut side up in a baking pan.

Process bread in food processor to make ¾ cup crumbs. Put crumbs in a medium nonstick skillet with garlic or herb-flavored oil. Over medium heat, toast crumbs, stirring constantly with a wooden spoon, until they become golden and crunchy. This should take about 2 minutes. Add salt and pepper to taste.

Pile crumbs on top of tomatoes to cover completely. Bake for 10 to 15 minutes, until tomatoes begin to soften but still retain their shape.

Serve hot, warm, or room temperature.

Optional garnish: Drizzle with a little additional oil.

Serves 4

* See page 8 for homemade Garlic Oil, or you may use store-bought garlic or herb-flavored oil.

POACHED ORANGES IN LEMON SYRUP, CITRUS GRANITA

1 cup sugar
6 large oranges
4 to 6 large lemons

To make granita: In a medium saucepan put 1½ cups water, ½ cup sugar, ½ cup fresh orange juice (from 2 oranges), and ⅓ cup fresh lemon juice (from 2 or 3 lemons). Bring to a boil, lower heat, and cook 1 minute, until sugar dissolves. Remove from heat and cool. Pour mixture into a 9-by-13-inch metal or glass dish and freeze for 3 hours. Every 30 minutes break up ice crystals with a fork.

To poach oranges: Cut rind from 4 oranges using a small sharp knife, making sure to remove all the white pith. Grate the rind from 2 lemons. In a pot large enough to accommodate oranges in one layer, heat 2 cups water and ½ cup sugar. Add the grated zest and the juice of 2 or 3 lemons, approximately ⅓ cup. Add peeled oranges and bring to a boil. Lower heat and cover the pot. Cook over low-medium heat for 20 minutes, or until oranges begin to soften but still retain their shape. Remove oranges with slotted spoon.

Cook liquid over high heat until slightly syrupy. Pour over oranges. Cool, then refrigerate until cold. Serve oranges with lemon syrup and granita on top. If possible, serve in a clear glass dish so you can appreciate the colors.

Serves 4

THE FOLLOWING PHOTOGRAPHS DEPICT:

Sweet Corn Soup with Scallion Butter (page 107)

Pithiviers of Smoked Ham and Port Salut (page 75); Mâche and Granny Smith Salad, Apple Vinaigrette (page 76)

Polenta "Lasagne" with Smoked Mozzarella (page 69); Blasted Green Beans with Niçoise Olives (page 70)

Bay Scallops with Parsley Puree (page 86); Tomatoes Provençale (page 87)

Seared Salmon Steak with Cornichon Vinaigrette (page 108); Horseradish Potato Salad (page 108)

Moroccan Chicken with Preserved Lemons and Green Olives (page 120); Pilaf Baked in Lavash (page 121)

Chicken Roulades with Roasted Peppers and Soppressata (page 116); Dutch Noodles with Aged Gouda (page 117)

Skirt Steak with Salsa Verde, Raw and Roasted Garlic (page 138); Sour Cream Mashed Potatoes with Skillet-Roasted Corn (page 139)

How to Eat a Mussel

Salad of Watercress, Orange, and Chorizo

Steamed Mussels **Crema di Salsa**

Country Garlic Bread

Pink Grapefruit Sherbet, Pink Grapefruit Syrup

12 ingredients

Like the great mussel eaters of Belgium and France, you must never use a fork.

Rather, take the blue-black shell of half of a mussel, using its sharp edge to dislodge the flesh of the other half, and then scoop up the sauce.

When you get tired, you may use your garlic bread as a yeasty sponge, careful not to waste a single drop of bracing crema di salsa.

The flavors of this menu undulate, then break like a wave.

A new genus of mussel has recently come to town: a rope-cultured Mediterranean, Mytilus gallop rovincialis, *from California and Washington State, is rivaling its East Coast cousin, the "blue" or "edible" mussel,* Mytilus edulis, *for affection.*

"Med" mussels are great in summer, and so is this meal. If Mediterranean mussels are not available in your area, they can be ordered directly from Taylor Shellfish Farms, at (360) 426-6178.

GRAPENOTE

Oh so delicious with a dry Spanish *rosado* from the Navarre. Look for one from Ochoa or Vega Sindoa to wet your whistle.

SALAD OF WATERCRESS, ORANGE, AND CHORIZO

2 large bunches watercress
8 medium juice oranges
4 ounces smoked chorizo sausage *

Remove stems from watercress. Wash watercress and spin dry. Divide evenly among 4 large plates.

Cut rind from 4 oranges with small sharp knife, removing all the white pith. Cut along edge of membranes to release segments. Scatter orange segments on watercress.

Cut 2 oranges in half. Squeeze juice evenly on top of orange-watercress mounds. Sprinkle lightly with salt.

Slice chorizo on the bias, about ⅛-inch thick. Heat in large nonstick skillet until fat is rendered and sausage slices are browned on both sides.

Cut remaining 2 oranges in half, and squeeze their juice into hot pan over chorizo. Cook for 30 seconds over medium-high heat.

Place chorizo slices evenly on top of watercress and oranges and pour pan juices over salads. Serve immediately.

Serves 4

* Available in many supermarkets. Stick pepperoni may be substituted.

STEAMED MUSSELS *CREMA DI SALSA*

2 pounds (about 72) fresh New Zealand or Mediterranean mussels
⅔ cup heavy cream
2 cups mild thick-and-chunky salsa

Wash mussels. Remove beards if necessary.

In a large heavy pot with a cover, put cream, salsa, and ⅓ cup water.

Bring to a boil. Add mussels. Cover pot and lower heat to medium. Cook 8 to 10 minutes, shaking pot back and forth as mussels cook.

Peek into pot after 8 minutes. If all the mussels have opened, remove immediately from heat. Otherwise, cook 1 more minute. Discard any mussels that haven't opened.

With slotted spoon, place mussels in 4 to 6 large flat soup plates. Heat liquid in pot over high heat for 1 minute, until thickened slightly.

Pour *crema di salsa* evenly over mussels and serve immediately.

Serves 4 to 6

COUNTRY GARLIC BREAD

1 pound round loaf country, peasant, sourdough, or Tuscan bread
¼ cup or more extra-virgin olive oil
4 large cloves garlic

Preheat oven to 300°.

Slice bread into 8 or more ½-inch slices. Brush very lightly with some oil. Place on baking sheets and bake in oven for 10 minutes, or until bread begins to get a bit dry and golden.

Peel garlic cloves and cut in half. Rub roasted bread, on one side only, with cut side of garlic. Put bread on platter and drizzle with more olive oil. Serve warm.

Serves 4 or more

PINK GRAPEFRUIT SHERBET, PINK GRAPEFRUIT SYRUP

2 medium pink grapefruits
1½ cups superfine sugar
3 cups buttermilk

Grate the rind of 1 grapefruit on the fine holes of a box grater so that you have 1 teaspoon of zest. Be careful not to include the white pith, as it is very bitter.

Cut grapefruit in half. Squeeze grapefruit halves so that you have 2 cups fresh grapefruit juice.

Place 1 cup grapefruit juice in a medium bowl and set 1 cup aside for later.

Reserve ¼ cup sugar for syrup. Add 1¼ cups sugar to grapefruit juice and stir until dissolved. Add 1 teaspoon grated grapefruit rind, buttermilk, and ¼ teaspoon salt. Stir well and chill 4 hours or overnight, until very cold.

Freeze mixture in an ice-cream maker according to the manufacturer's instructions.

To make pink grapefruit syrup, put remaining 1 cup grapefruit juice and ¼ cup sugar in small nonreactive saucepan. Bring to a boil, lower heat immediately, and simmer until reduced to 6 tablespoons. Let cool.

Scoop sherbet into pretty glasses and drizzle with syrup.

Serves 6 or more

■ ■ ■

Homage to Jean-Georges

Roquefort Mousse and Celery Crudités

Sea Bass Steamed in Lettuce, Rosemary Oil

Potato Silk

Almond Water Ice with Fresh Cherry Salad, Cherry Syrup

12 ingredients

Vongerichten. He's the chef's chef.

In the culinary kingdom of great talent and artistry, it's quite remarkable to soar to the top — and then stay there — with every new endeavor. Chef Jean-Georges, of restaurants JoJo, Vong (New York and London), the Lipstick Cafe, and the four-star eponymous Jean-Georges, rules! Disciples gather.

He's the original juice man. He replaced heavy sauces and stocks with vibrant vegetable juices. He's a zealot, and his exquisitely light style of cooking sparked a culinary revolution in America.

And now he's in the weeds. For his latest contribution to the ever-changing world of taste lies in the wild: little-known leaves, weeds, and flowers like Queen Anne's lace, chicory root, and pigweed, more poetically called lamb's-quarters.

His Sassafras Chicken is the first three-ingredient recipe to be published by a four-star chef in the New York Times.

I do hope he'll come for lunch. I'll make a pot of nettle tea.

GRAPENOTE

To match the delicate flavors, try a sylvaner: Look for one from Alsace (where Jean-Georges is from) or from northern Italy.

ROQUEFORT MOUSSE AND CELERY CRUDITÉS

1 bunch celery, with leaves
1 pound cottage cheese*
4 ounces Roquefort or Bleu d'Auvergne cheese, at room temperature

Remove some of the leaves from the celery and wash. Finely chop leaves so that you have 2 tablespoons. Reserve celery for later.

Place the cottage cheese in the bowl of a food processor. Cut blue cheese in small pieces and add to processor with a grinding of black pepper. Add chopped celery leaves to cheese mixture.

Process until mixture is smooth and mousselike: light and fluffy. Transfer to a ramekin large enough to hold the mixture. Cover with plastic wrap and refrigerate a minimum of 1 hour for a very fresh taste —

or a maximum of 1 day, when the flavors will have matured.

When ready to serve, wash celery and leaves. Cut half the ribs severely on the bias so that you have long, thin oval slices. Cut remaining ribs into long, thin slices with leaves attached.

Let cheese come to room temperature and serve with cold, crisp celery, little bowls of butcher-grind black pepper, and French sea salt.

Serves 4 to 6 (makes 2 cups cheese)

* Also delicious made with goat's milk cheese curds, available from Coach Farms, Pine Plains, New York, at (518) 398-5325, or other local goat cheese producers.

SEA BASS STEAMED IN LETTUCE, ROSEMARY OIL

4 8-ounce black or Chilean sea bass fillets
8 large green leaf lettuce leaves
2 teaspoons plus 6 tablespoons rosemary oil *

Remove any little bones from fish. Season fillets lightly with salt and freshly ground black pepper.

Bring a large pot of water to a boil. Add lettuce leaves and boil for 1 minute, or until just pliable. Remove immediately to a colander. Rinse under cool water, being careful not to tear the leaves. Pat dry with paper towels.

Brush ½ teaspoon rosemary oil on each piece of fish. Wrap each fillet in 2 lettuce leaves, pressing down to tightly and completely enclose fish.

Bring a large pot of water fitted on top with a flat steamer basket to a boil. Place wrapped fish in the basket in a single layer, cover, and cook over medium heat for 15 to 20 minutes.

While fish is cooking, gently heat 6 tablespoons rosemary oil in a small pot with 3 tablespoons water and a liberal pinch of salt. Keep warm.

Carefully remove fish from steamer and transfer to plates. Drizzle warm sauce over the fish. Serve immediately.

Serves 4

* You can make your own (see page 9), or you can use a good brand of prepared rosemary oil, such as Carlucci, Colavita, or Consorzio.

POTATO SILK

1½ pounds large Yukon Gold potatoes
1 cup milk or more, as needed
10 tablespoons unsalted butter or more, as needed

Scrub potatoes well. Place in a medium pot with salted water to cover by 1 inch. Bring to a boil. Lower heat and cook over medium heat for 30 to 40 minutes, or until potatoes are very soft.

Drain potatoes immediately. When cool enough to handle, peel potatoes and cut into small pieces. Push potatoes through a potato ricer into a medium pot.

Heat milk to a boil. Remove from heat.

Slowly add bits of butter to riced potatoes, whisking well after each addition.

Add milk slowly, mixing until you get a soft, creamy consistency.

Push entire mixture through a fine-mesh sieve into another medium pot. Add more milk or butter as needed to make a very fine, silky puree. Add salt and freshly ground white pepper to taste.

Serves 4 to 6

ALMOND WATER ICE WITH FRESH CHERRY SALAD, CHERRY SYRUP

²/₃ cup plus 2 teaspoons orzata *(almond syrup)* *
1¹/₂ pounds fresh red cherries
1 bunch fresh peppermint or spearmint

Three hours, or more, before serving this dessert, prepare the almond water ice: In a small metal container (a pie tin or small loaf pan) mix together ²/₃ cup *orzata* plus 1¹/₃ cups cold water. Place in freezer. Every 30 minutes, break up ice crystals with a fork. Continue for 2¹/₂ to 3 hours, or until a milky white ice is formed.

To prepare cherry syrup: Wash cherries. Remove the stems and pits from ¹/₂ pound cherries and discard. Place cherries in a small saucepan with ¹/₂ cup water plus 2 teaspoons *orzata*. Bring to a boil. Lower heat to medium and cook for 15 minutes, stirring frequently. Place cherry mixture in a fine-mesh sieve and press down hard. Mash cherries through sieve with the back of a large spoon until all the cherries have been sieved. You will have approximately ³/₄ cup syrup. Return to saucepan and reduce over high heat to 6 tablespoons. (Discard the leftover cherry "mash.")

Set aside.

To prepare dessert, remove stems and pits from remaining cherries. Cut cherries in half. Divide evenly onto 4 plates. Julienne mint so that you have 4 tablespoons. Scatter mint over halved cherries. Top with a scoop of almond ice and drizzle with cherry syrup.

Serves 4

* *Orzata* can be purchased in specialty-food stores, especially those specializing in Italian products.

■ ■ ■

Mod Cod

Roasted Red Onion and Feta Salad

Crispy Cod with Potato Flakes

Courgettes with Basil

Watermelon Granita with Chocolate "Seeds"

12 ingredients

Chefs today have taken a fancy to rolling their fillets, like hip fish sticks, in all manner of crunchy coatings: shredded wheat, kataifi *(shredded phyllo);* arare *(Japanese puffed rice), or* panko *(Japanese bread crumbs). Instant potato flakes make a more refined slipcover but also a palooka of a vegetable.*

(I'd never tried them before this recipe, but with enough butter . . .)

Chefs today also have taken to roasting their vegetables until singed, first practiced by two gentlemen in Verona centuries ago: They roasted big purple onions over charcoal until black, then sold them to be taken home, peeled, and eaten with good olive oil and salt. Substitute a thin slice of feta for the salt, and you'll have a most "mod"-est first course.

This repast tastes like virtual summer but is perfect any time of the year you can snag a watermelon.

GRAPENOTE

Madfish Bay chardonnay from Australia seems to be the right white for Mod Cod, but this mesmerizing wine is a bit steep. An under-ten-dollar but equally delicious choice is sauvignon blanc, such as the Swartland or Kronendal from South Africa.

ROASTED RED ONION AND FETA SALAD

2 very large red onions
⅓ cup extra-virgin olive oil
8-ounces feta cheese, in 1 piece

Preheat oven to 400°.

Cut each unpeeled onion into 4 wedges. Coat each wedge with ½ teaspoon olive oil. Place in heavy baking pan and roast 1 hour, turning once on each side.

Remove from oven and let cool.

Remove skin from onion wedges. Arrange 2 wedges each on 4 large plates, separating layers in a circular pattern. Sprinkle with salt.

Cut feta cheese into thin slices and place in center of plate. Drizzle each salad with approximately 1 tablespoon olive oil.

Pass the pepper mill.

Serves 4

CRISPY COD WITH POTATO FLAKES

1½ pounds thick cod, cut from the center
6 tablespoons unsalted butter
1½ to 2 cups potato flakes *

Cut fish into 8 3-ounce portions.

Season fish with salt and freshly ground white pepper. In small pot melt butter. Using a pastry brush, lightly brush fish on all sides with butter.

Place potato flakes on large plate and dredge fish in flakes, coating well on all sides. Pat flakes on firmly with your hands.

To cook fish: Pour remaining melted butter in very large nonstick skillet. Heat butter, but do not brown. When hot add fish, and cook over medium heat for 2 to 3 minutes (depending on thickness) on each side, until potato flakes are golden brown and crisp, and fish is opaque.

Serve 2 overlapping pieces on top of *Courgettes* with Basil (see the following recipe).

Optional garnish: Serve with potato puree. Bring 1¾ cups water, 2 additional tablespoons butter, and ⅛ teaspoon salt to a boil. Remove from heat. Stir in 1¼ cups potato flakes and fluff with a fork.

Serves 4

* Make sure you purchase potato flakes and not powdered mashed potatoes.

COURGETTES WITH BASIL

1 pound medium zucchini
⅓ cup packed chopped fresh basil, plus small leaves for garnishing
1 tablespoon unsalted butter

Wash zucchini, dry well, and grate on large holes of box grater.

Place in bowl. Add basil, salt, and freshly ground black pepper. Toss well.

In large nonstick skillet melt butter. Add zucchini mixture. Cook over medium heat for 10 minutes, stirring often. Do not let brown. Cook until zucchini is soft. Add salt and pepper, if necessary. Serve garnished with small basil leaves.

Serves 4

WATERMELON GRANITA WITH CHOCOLATE "SEEDS"

1 large chunk ripe red watermelon, enough for 4 cups diced flesh
¾ cup granulated sugar
½ cup miniature chocolate chips

Remove seeds from watermelon and discard. Cut melon into small dice so that you have 4 cups. Puree in a food processor until very smooth.

Add sugar and continue to process until smooth and sugar is dissolved.

Spread mixture into a shallow metal pan and place in the freezer.

When the mixture becomes slushy, break it up with a fork and return it to freezer, mixing again as it begins to harden. Repeat this process every 20 minutes (about 6 times) until mixture is frozen.

Scrape the frozen watermelon's surface with a spoon and place shavings in chilled wineglasses. Sprinkle with chocolate chips.

Serves 4

■ ■ ■

At the Niçois Table

Gougonettes *of Turbot in Chickpea Flour*

Celery Salad with French Black Olives and Truffle Oil

Polenta with Sugar and Oranges

9 ingredients

My mouth watered as I read Colman Andrews's recipe for Polenta with Oranges — "a simple but unusual dessert" — in his mesmerizing book Flavors of the Riviera. *I could taste it in my head, but it was even better than expected.*

It helped that the polenta I used came from Italy (you can find it, too); that the oranges were juicy and perfumed, and just tart enough to balance the sugar. Bright chilled orange slices atop warm yellow polenta: truly, the food of the sun.

Cuisine du Soleil. That was the name of the cooking school I attended run by master chef Roger Vergé, by day. At night, I crawled back in time to the Old Town of Nice where, by intuition, I found the best socca *imaginable — a wood-grilled, rough-hewn crepe of chickpea flour and powerful olive oil — at the ancient Nizza Socca, old enough to have welcomed Cocteau.*

Daytime again, and I was alone at the swank Hotel Negresco, eating from a menu loosely translated from dialect as "A Wink from the Niçois Table."

There was ratatouille, of course. But also little strips of lightly fried fish known as gougonettes, *and an unforgettable salad of crisp celery, black olives, and truffles.*

Back home, I thought of Old Town and decided to coat my gougonettes in chickpea flour. A wink to Colman Andrews, who is sure to tell you that life in Nice is nice.

GRAPENOTE

In the hills just above Nice and Cannes, they make a lovely white wine — just right for these dishes: Vin Blanc de Cassis.

GOUGONETTES OF TURBOT IN CHICKPEA FLOUR

1½ pounds turbot fillets, skin removed
1½ cups chickpea flour*
3 tablespoons good-quality olive oil, plus more for frying

Remove any small bones from fish. Cut fillets, using a sharp knife, into strips that are 3½ inches long by ½ inch wide.

Place chickpea flour in a large bowl. Stir in 2 teaspoons salt and lots of freshly ground black pepper.

Lightly coat strips of fish with 3 tablespoons oil, making sure all of the fish is coated, as this will help the flour to stick.

Gently toss the oiled fish strips with the chickpea flour. Make sure the flour thickly coats the fish. Pack it on well, using your hands.

Place olive oil to the depth of ⅛ inch in 1 very large or 2 smaller nonstick skillets. Heat oil, then add the fish. Cook over medium heat until a golden-brown crust is formed, about 3 minutes. Turn fish and cook the other side until crisp and golden, about 2 minutes.

Remove fish to a platter using a slotted spoon, and sprinkle lightly with salt. Serve immediately.

Serves 4

* Available in most Middle Eastern food stores and shops specializing in herbs and spices.

CELERY SALAD WITH FRENCH BLACK OLIVES AND TRUFFLE OIL

1 large leafy bunch celery
1 cup pitted large oil-cured French black olives
2 tablespoons truffle oil *

Cut bottom from celery and separate the stalks. Save the dark green outer stalks for another use; for this recipe you want primarily the inner pale celery stalks plus the leaves.

Wash celery stalks and leaves thoroughly. Roughly dice celery and leaves into ¼-inch cubes and measure so that you have 5 cups chopped celery including the leaves. Save some of the uncut darker green leaves for garnishing.

Place chopped celery in a medium bowl. Add olives, truffle oil, and a good amount of freshly ground black pepper. Stir well. Let sit at room temperature for 20 minutes before serving. Adjust with a little salt, depending on the saltiness of the olives.

Drizzle with additional truffle oil if desired and garnish with whole celery leaves.

Serves 4

* Available in specialty-food stores.

POLENTA WITH SUGAR AND ORANGES

6 small juice or blood oranges, if in season, at room temperature
1⅓ cups quick-cooking polenta, imported from Italy *
6 teaspoons granulated sugar

Cut rind from oranges using a small sharp knife. Slice oranges into ¼-inch-thick circles, removing any seeds, making sure to collect all the juice. Set orange slices and juice aside in a medium bowl.

In a medium pot, bring 4 cups water plus 1 teaspoon salt to a boil. Slowly add polenta, stirring constantly with a wooden spoon. Lower heat to medium and cook for 5 minutes, or until polenta is thick and creamy and beginning to come away from the sides of the pot. Remove from heat.

Divide polenta evenly onto the centers of 4 large plates. Sprinkle each evenly with 1 teaspoon sugar.

Arrange orange slices on top of polenta and spoon juice over oranges. Sprinkle oranges with ½ teaspoon sugar. Serve immediately.

Serves 4 (makes about 4 cups)

* Available in specialty-food stores. I've used Colavita and Tre Monti brands with great success.

Lunch on the Fourth of July

Sweet Corn Soup with Scallion Butter

Seared Salmon Steak with Cornichon Vinaigrette

Horseradish Potato Salad

Red, White, and Blueberries

12 ingredients

This menu is a regiment of flavors and colors, as impressive as any fireworks. It will make you feel like a patriot.

For added fanfare, use little red, white, and purple-blue potatoes (from Peru) in your salad!

GRAPENOTE

Have an all-American Fourth! A rich, butterscotchy chardonnay like Morro Bay from the central coast of California with the soup; then with the salmon, a light pinot noir from Talus or Pepperwood.

SWEET CORN SOUP WITH SCALLION BUTTER

6 large ears yellow sweet corn
2 large bunches scallions
5 tablespoons unsalted butter, softened

Using a sharp knife, cut corn kernels from cob; you will have about 5 cups.

Cut white parts from scallions and chop them finely so that you have ⅔ cup. Set green part aside to make scallion butter and to use as a garnish.

To make scallion butter: Place 3 tablespoons softened butter on flat surface. Finely chop enough green scallions to get 2 tablespoons. Work scallions into butter using your fingers. Place on waxed paper and roll into a small log, about 1 inch in diameter. Freeze until solid.

Meanwhile, melt 2 tablespoons butter in heavy medium pot. Do not let brown. Add ⅔ cup chopped scallions and ½ cup water. Cover and simmer for 10 minutes. Add corn kernels, 5 cups cool water, 2 tea-spoons salt, and ¼ teaspoon freshly ground white pepper. Bring to a boil, lower heat, and simmer, covered, for 10 minutes, or until corn is tender.

Puree the soup in small batches in a blender or food processor for several minutes, until very smooth. Strain the puree through a sieve, pressing hard on the solids. You will have approximately 4½ cups. Discard solids and set puree aside until ready to serve.

To serve, heat soup in pot just until boiling. Add salt and pepper to taste. Ladle soup into 4 flat soup plates. Top each with several slices of frozen butter. Chop remaining scallion greens and scatter over soup.

Serves 4 (makes about 4½ cups)

SEARED SALMON STEAK WITH CORNICHON VINAIGRETTE

6 tablespoons good-quality olive oil
½ cup French cornichons, with pickling liquid reserved
4 8-ounce salmon steaks

In small saucepan put olive oil and 4 tablespoons pickling juice from cornichons.

Finely mince enough cornichons so that you have 6 tablespoons. Add to saucepan with a grinding of black pepper. Warm gently over low heat for 30 seconds and set aside.

Season both sides of salmon steaks with salt and pepper.

Heat a large nonstick skillet until very hot. Place salmon steaks in pan and cook over high heat until salmon is browned and crisp on one side, approximately 3 minutes. Carefully turn over with spatula and cook for 2 to 3 minutes, or until salmon is cooked to desired doneness. Do not overcook.

Place salmon steaks on individual plates or on large platter. Pour vinaigrette into hot pan to warm slightly. Spoon vinaigrette over fish and garnish with additional cornichons, if desired. Serve hot.

Serves 4

HORSERADISH POTATO SALAD

1 pound small Red Bliss or mixture Red Bliss and small Peruvian purple-blue potatoes
⅓ to ½ cup light mayonnaise
2 teaspoons or more prepared white horseradish

Wash potatoes well. Put in pot with water to cover and bring to boil. Cover pot, lower heat, and cook potatoes 40 to 45 minutes, or until tender.

Drain in colander under cold water. Peel half of the red potatoes with small sharp knife, leaving half unpeeled. Peel the blue potatoes, if using. Cut potatoes in 1-inch chunks or wedges. Put in bowl and toss with mayonnaise, 2 teaspooons horseradish, and salt and freshly ground black pepper to taste. Chill. Taste before serving. You may want to add a little more horseradish.

Serves 4

RED, WHITE, AND BLUEBERRIES

4 8-ounce containers blueberry yogurt
1 pint fresh raspberries
2 cups vanilla yogurt

Drape a 4-cup coeur à la crème mold (with drainage holes) with a double layer of cheesecloth. Or you may line a large sieve with cheesecloth.

Put blueberry yogurt in a bowl and mix well, making a dark blue homogenous mixture. Place into cheesecloth-lined mold or sieve and cover with overhanging cheesecloth. Place in pan to catch liquid and refrigerate for 24 hours. Discard liquid.

Unmold thickened blueberry yogurt onto a large decorative platter. If using sieve, turn over and form into thick cake shape.

Wash raspberries, being careful not to crush. Dry well. Carefully place raspberries, one by one, on top of thickened blueberry yogurt.

Beat vanilla yogurt until creamy and serve alongside.

Serves 4 or more

■ ■ ■

Pan-Asian Primer

Tiny Clams with Wasabi and Pickled Ginger

Pan-Grilled Swordfish, Pepper-Lime Sauce

Jasmine Rice and Poppy Seeds

Pineapple Flan

12 ingredients

The introduction of Asian flavors has had extraordinary culinary impact in both America and France. Instead of clashing, many ingredients fuse elegantly within a classical framework of technique and style. My Pan-Asian menu, for example, is a synthesis of many trips to Pacific Rim countries — Australia, Japan, Taiwan — informed by years of French influences.

I was lucky to be the only woman to cook in the kitchen of Le Plaisir in New York, under the direction of revered Chef Masa Kobayashi, in the early 1980s. His prescient style inspired a generation of American chefs at the same time that great French chefs began to look east for inspiration.

This meal succinctly tells the story of West greets East.

GRAPENOTE

To start? Warm sake — you'll love the flavor match and the contrast of temperatures with the ice-cold clams. With the fish, try a full-bodied chardonnay like Raymond Amber Hill from California or Château Ste. Michelle from Washington State.

TINY CLAMS WITH WASABI AND PICKLED GINGER

36 tiny littleneck clams, well chilled
4 tablespoons wasabi powder
½ cup pickled ginger, with ginger juice

Have your fishmonger pry open clams for you, but do not open them completely. Lay them flat in a container so that you do not lose any of the clam juices.

In a small bowl, mix wasabi powder with 2 tablespoons cold water, stirring to form a thick paste.

Remove top shell of each clam and discard. With small knife, cut clam from bottom shell so it can be easily eaten.

Top each clam with 2 thin slices pickled ginger and a small dollop of wasabi. Drizzle a little pickled ginger juice over each clam.

To serve, place 9 small mounds of kosher salt on each of 4 large flat plates. Place clams — 9 per order — on each mound of salt. Serve immediately.

Serves 4

PAN-GRILLED SWORDFISH, PEPPER-LIME SAUCE

4 6½-ounce swordfish steaks
6 large limes
8 tablespoons unsalted butter, chilled and cut into small pieces

Place swordfish steaks on a platter. Cut 1 lime in half and squeeze juice over fish. Sprinkle each piece of fish with salt. Let sit 20 minutes at room temperature.

Cut rind from 3 limes using small sharp knife. Cut along edge of membranes to release lime segments. Cut remaining 2 limes in half and squeeze so that you have ⅓ cup juice. Set aside.

Heat a very large nonstick skillet until very hot. Add fish, and cook over medium-high heat until golden brown, about 2 to 3 minutes. Turn fish carefully and cook for 2 to 3 minutes, until fish is cooked but still very moist.

Remove fish to serving platter. To juices in pan add ⅓ cup lime juice, cold butter, and ½ teaspoon butcher-grind black pepper. Cook 1 minute over high heat until sauce gets creamy, stirring constantly. Add lime segments and swirl into sauce for a few seconds also over high heat. Pour over fish and serve immediately.

Serves 4

JASMINE RICE AND POPPY SEEDS

1 cup jasmine rice*
2 tablespoons unsalted butter
1 teaspoon poppy seeds

Bring 2 cups water plus ¼ teaspoon salt to a boil in a medium saucepan. Add rice and immediately lower heat. Cover and simmer 20 minutes, or until the rice has absorbed all the water.

Meanwhile, melt butter in a small nonstick skillet and add poppy seeds. Cook over low heat for 30 seconds.

When rice is ready, fluff with a fork and add warm butter–poppy seed mixture. Add salt and freshly ground black pepper to taste.

Serves 4 (makes 3 cups)

* Available in many supermarkets and specialty-food stores. You may substitute basmati rice or other fragrant rice varieties.

PINEAPPLE FLAN

1 cup granulated sugar
8 extra-large eggs
2 cups unsweetened pineapple juice

Preheat oven to 350°.

In small nonstick skillet put ½ cup sugar. Cook over medium-high heat, stirring constantly with wooden spoon so that sugar melts completely into a dark liquid. This will take a few minutes. Immediately divide among 6 6-ounce custard cups or ramekins to coat bottom of each.

Separate yolks from 4 eggs. Reserve the whites for another use. In the bowl of electric mixer place 4 egg yolks, 4 whole eggs, and ½ cup sugar. Beat for 1 minute, until eggs and sugar are well blended.

Slowly add pineapple juice, little by little, and continue to beat until juice is incorporated. Do not let the mixture become too frothy.

With a ladle, divide mixture evenly among the custard cups or ramekins.

Place cups or ramekins in a large, deep pan. Create a water bath by adding boiling water to the pan so that the water level almost reaches the tops of the molds. Carefully place in oven.

Carefully slide rack into oven and bake 40 to 45 minutes. Remove molds from water bath. Let cool and then refrigerate until very cold, ideally overnight. Unmold carefully onto large flat plates, loosening sides with small sharp knife if necessary.

Caramel will coat the top and sides of the flan.

Serves 6

■ ■ ■

Sunday "Dinner"

Yellow Pea Soup with Dill

Chicken Roulades with Roasted Peppers and Soppressata

Dutch Noodles with Aged Gouda

Gingersnap Baked Apples

12 ingredients

Sunday dinner — a powerful symbol of family life in days gone by — is nostalgically expressed by this reassuring meal, both inexpensive and unpretentious. Especially since it's served in the afternoon.

It says, "Sit down, you're one of the family," music to the ears and manna for the soul to many of us unaccustomed to this most genial of institutions.

GRAPENOTE

The strong flavors of roasted peppers, salami, and cheese take this meal into red-wine territory. Try a medium-weight Chianti like the Spalleti or a nice Rioja from Paternina Banda Azul.

YELLOW PEA SOUP WITH DILL

1 pound yellow split peas
2 smoked ham hocks (1¼ pounds)
1 bunch fresh dill

Wash peas in colander, picking out any stones. Place peas in large pot with ham hocks and cover with 8 cups cold water. Cut 1 inch off stems of dill and discard. Chop ¼ cup dill and save for later use. Set aside some dill sprigs for garnish. Put remaining dill fronds in pot. Add ½ teaspoon salt and ¼ teaspoon black peppercorns. Bring to a boil. Lower heat and simmer until peas are very soft, approximately 1½ hours.

Remove ham hocks and, using a sharp knife, remove small pieces of meat. Cut meat into ¼-inch dice. Set aside.

Puree three-quarters of the soup in food processor, including all the cooked dill fronds. Process until very smooth and combine with remaining soup. Return pot to stove. Add reserved ¼ cup chopped dill to soup with salt and freshly ground black pepper.

Heat until soup comes just to a boil. Garnish with diced ham and additional sprigs of dill.

Serves 4 or more (makes 6 cups)

CHICKEN ROULADES WITH ROASTED PEPPERS AND *SOPPRESSATA*

4 8-ounce boneless chicken breast halves, skin on
4 ounces thinly sliced soppressata *
1 6-ounce jar sweet roasted peppers

Preheat oven to 350°.

Remove "tenders" from chicken breasts and set aside. (Tenders are the small muscles running the length of the breast, approximately ½ inch in diameter, under each chicken breast half.) Place breasts on flat surface, skin side down. Flatten slightly with cleaver or mallet.

Sprinkle chicken lightly with salt and freshly ground black pepper.

Cover chicken with overlapping slices of *soppressata*. Place roasted red pepper in center of chicken. Place chicken tender on top of pepper.

Roll chicken breasts tight, jelly-roll style, to completely envelop the filling.

Place roulades in shallow baking pan. Bake for 25 minutes, then place under broiler for 30 seconds to crisp skin.

Remove from oven. Let rest 5 minutes. Cut each breast into 6 slices. Serve overlapping slices with pan juices. Serve immediately.

Serves 4

* You may use Genoa or Hungarian salami.

DUTCH NOODLES WITH AGED GOUDA

8 ounces aged Gouda cheese
8 ounces home-style egg noodles (½ inch wide)
5 tablespoons unsalted butter, cut in small pieces

Remove rind from cheese. Cut cheese into small cubes. Put in food processor and process until cheese is finely ground to the size of gravel. Set aside.

Meanwhile, bring a large pot of salted water to a boil. Add noodles and cook as directed on package, stirring often, until just soft. Do not overcook.

Reserve ¼ cup cooking water, then drain noodles in colander.

In a warmed bowl, put drained noodles, all the cheese except ¼ cup, and butter. Toss well with wooden spoon, mixing gently until butter melts. Add ¼ cup hot cooking water, ½ teaspoon butcher-grind black peppercorns, and salt to taste. Mix thoroughly.

Serve immediately, sprinkled with remaining ¼ cup cheese and additional black pepper if desired.

Serves 4 or more

GINGERSNAP BAKED APPLES

4 large Golden Delicious apples (½ pound each)
About 16 to 20 gingersnap cookies
¼ cup honey

Preheat oven to 375°.

Wash apples, but do not peel. Core apples, being careful not to cut through the bottom. You want to create a neat, ½-inch-wide cavity.

Place gingersnaps in a food processor and process until you have 1 cup coarse crumbs. Add 2 tablespoons honey and process until fairly smooth.

Pack each apple tightly with cookie mixture, mounding on top. Reserve some gingersnap-honey crumbs for garnish, if desired.

Place apples in shallow baking pan with ¼ inch water on the bottom. Cover tightly with foil and bake 40 minutes. Uncover and bake 5 minutes longer. Remove apples with a slotted spoon to a plate.

To any liquid remaining in casserole, add 2 tablespoons remaining honey and ¼ cup water. Bring to a boil and let cook over high heat for 1 minute, or until syrupy. Pour over apples. Let cool and serve. You may garnish plates with additional gingersnap-honey crumbs, if desired.

Serves 4

■ ■ ■

Med-Rim Mosaic

Warm Feta Cheese and Cherry Tomato Compote

Moroccan Chicken with Preserved Lemons and Green Olives

Pilaf Baked in Lavash

Vanilla Bean Ice Cream with Orange-Flower Water and Pistachios

12 ingredients

I've named and nurtured the concept of "Med-Rim" cuisine in America and heralded its debut in a piece in the New York Times *several years ago. Almost ten years earlier, I created menus for New York's first pan-Mediterranean restaurant, Café Greco, where* shish ta-uok *(Egypt),* moussaka *(Greece), and* za'atar *pita (Israel) could be found coexisting happily.*

This big, inclusive style of cooking encompasses ingredients and traditions of all the countries whose borders hug the Mediterranean coastline: Olive oil enriched and vibrant, this pro-"fusion" of flavors can be found mingling intelligently on one table, as many of America's best chefs have discovered.

Med-Rim means a mosaic of strong flavors: feta cheese, made of sheep's or goat's milk, is ubiq-uitous; preserved lemons are Morocco's national "pickle," adding verve to stews and tagines; *and olives of all kinds connect you with the region's ineffable, ageless earth.*

The unusual pilaf preparation that follows, authentically Persian, comes from Arlene Voski Avakian, editor of Through the Kitchen Window, *a collection of delicious essays by women exploring the intimate meaning of food and cooking. In her recipe, lavash, a soft, thin Armenian flat bread, crisps as it bakes and becomes an edible "bowl" for the rice.*

Orange-flower water and pistachios turn a simple dessert into an exotic one.

These flavors have always been my favorite. They smell like a bazaar-in-a-bottle.

GRAPENOTE

You can sip arrack from Turkey throughout this meal. When mixed with water, it turns milky white. Or slowly savor golden-hued retsina from Greece, served chilled. Corvo bianco would be a more neutral choice.

WARM FETA CHEESE AND CHERRY TOMATO COMPOTE

1 pound small cherry tomatoes
3 tablespoons olive oil, plus more for drizzling
8 ounces feta cheese, in 1 piece

Remove stems from cherry tomatoes. Cut half the tomatoes in half and leave the rest whole.

In a large nonstick skillet, heat olive oil. Add halved and whole tomatoes. Cook over high heat, stirring constantly, until tomatoes begin to soften and the tomato halves begin to blacken. Add salt and freshly ground black pepper to taste. Do not cook more than 3 minutes. Set aside. Cool to room temperature.

Slice cheese into 4 rectangular slabs approximately ¼ inch thick.

Preheat broiler.

Place cheese on baking sheet and broil until it turns golden brown and begins to bubble, 1 or 2 minutes. Remove immediately.

With a spatula, place warm cheese on top of room-temperature tomato compote and drizzle with additional olive oil.

Serves 4

MOROCCAN CHICKEN WITH PRESERVED LEMONS AND GREEN OLIVES

3½ pound chicken, cut into 8 pieces
3 whole Salt-Preserved Lemons (see page 10)
½ cup unpitted green olives, such as picholine

Remove fat and giblets from chicken. Place fat in a large nonstick skillet big enough to hold the chicken in one layer. You will need a cover for the skillet later on.

Discard liver and place giblets in a small saucepan with 1½ cups water and bring to a boil. Lower heat and continue to simmer 30 minutes while you prepare the chicken.

Melt chicken fat in skillet. Place chicken pieces skin side down in skillet and cook over medium heat for 10 to 15 minutes, or until skin becomes golden brown. Turn chicken pieces over and brown for 10 minutes on other side.

Strain broth from giblets (you will have about 1 cup) into the skillet. Turn heat up high and cook for 5 minutes. Lower heat to medium.

Meanwhile, wash preserved lemons thoroughly to remove salt. Dry lemons and cut 2 of them into small pieces, approximately ¼-inch dice, and cut remaining lemon into 4 wedges. Add to skillet with freshly ground black pepper. Cover skillet and let cook over medium-low heat for 45 to 50 minutes.

Uncover skillet, add olives, and cook uncovered over medium-high heat for 5 to 6 minutes. The chicken will be tender, browned, and the sauce will thicken.

Serve immediately.

Serves 4

PILAF BAKED IN LAVASH

1½ cups basmati rice
6 tablespoons unsalted butter
1 or 2 large lavash breads (very thin, soft Armenian flat bread)

Soak rice in refrigerator overnight in a bowl of salted water.

Preheat oven to 350°.

Drain rice and wash in bowl until water is clear. Drain again. Bring 2 cups water to a boil in a medium pot. Add rice and cook for approximately 10 minutes, stirring often. The center of rice should still be hard. Stir in a pinch of salt and freshly ground black pepper. Drain rice in colander.

Spread 1 tablespoon butter on bottom of a shallow 9-by-11-inch ovenproof casserole that is large enough to hold rice. Melt remaining butter. Place a thin layer of lavash in casserole so that the bread covers bottom and comes up the sides. Add rice and pour melted butter over top.

Cover casserole tightly and bake in oven for 45 minutes. Remove from oven. Serve rice with some of the crisped lavash bread.

Serves 6

VANILLA BEAN ICE CREAM WITH ORANGE-FLOWER WATER AND PISTACHIOS

3 cups best-quality vanilla ice cream with vanilla bean flecks
1½ to 2 tablespoons orange-flower water
6 tablespoons chopped pistachio nuts

Soften ice cream in the bowl of an electric mixer, using the paddle. Add orange-flower water. The amount you use will depend on your preference and the strength of the orange-flower water. Mix well.

Put "foil collars" around 4 small ramekins, making sure foil comes up at least 1 inch above top of ramekin. Pack ice cream in molds so that ice cream comes up to the top of the foil to make a "soufflé" shape.

Place chopped pistachios in a small nonstick skillet and cook over medium heat until you smell a faint nutty aroma. Let cool.

Top ice cream with toasted chopped pistachios and place in freezer. Remove foil collar before serving.

Serves 4

■ ■ ■

Afternoon Fiesta!

Chilled Green Bean Soup, Sour Cream Dollop

Chicken Chipotle with Red Onions

Tostones: *Fried Plantains and Fresh Lime*

Margarita Sorbet, Sugared Raspberries

12 ingredients

Traditions often outlive their usefulness, like taking a siesta after every fiesta. So scrap the nap, and instead spend your time making tostones: firm, green plantains that are sliced and fried, then smashed like hockey pucks and fried again. They are at once sweet and starchy, and like a great French fry have a crisp exterior and a creamy texture.

*Tostones are a wonderful accompaniment to my chicken chipotle, made smoky hot with dis-*tinctive chipotle peppers, which are dried and smoked jalapeños packed in vinegary adobo sauce. You buy them in cans at Latino food shops or good supermarkets.*

Like any respectable shot of tequila, tostones, too, benefit from a squeeze of lime and a lick of salt.

The fiesta begins and ends with something chilled: the first to whet the appetite, the last to cool it down.

GRAPENOTE

For this south-of-the-border menu, start with a crisp chardonnay from Chile, the Casillero del Rio; then surprise your guests with an amiable red from Baja California, Mexico — the Santo Tomas *tinto* — a combo of Barbera, cabernet, and *tempranillo*. Tecate beer is pretty good, too.

CHILLED GREEN BEAN SOUP, SOUR CREAM DOLLOP

1 pound tender fresh green beans
1 large Spanish onion
1¼ cups sour cream

Wash the green beans, and snap off the ends. Cut in half. Place in a medium pot. Peel onion, slice thin, and add to pot with 5 cups water and 1 teaspoon salt.

Bring to a boil. Lower heat and simmer 15 minutes. Drain in colander, saving all the cooking liquid. Place beans in a bowl of ice water to fix color. Drain.

Place drained beans and cooking liquid in a food processor in 2 batches and puree until very smooth. Pass mixture through coarse-mesh sieve into a clean bowl, pressing hard to release all liquid from the solids. Discard solids. Add 1 cup sour cream to soup with salt and freshly ground black pepper to taste. Refrigerate several hours, or until very cold.

Serve with 1 tablespoon sour cream on top of each serving and a sprinkling of sea salt and butcher-grind black pepper.

Serves 4 (makes approximately 4 cups)

CHICKEN CHIPOTLE WITH RED ONIONS

4 8-ounce chicken breast halves, bone in and skin on
3 medium-large red onions (6 ounces each)
5 tablespoons chipotle peppers in adobo sauce*

Place chicken breasts in a large bowl. Peel onions. Grate 1 onion on large holes of box grater. You will have approximately 6 tablespoons. Add to chicken. Thinly slice remaining onions and add to chicken.

Finely chop chipotle peppers, along with the sauce that adheres to them, and add 4 tablespoons to chicken. Save 1 tablespoon for later use. Toss chicken with ½ teaspoon salt and onion-chipotle mixture to coat. Cover and let sit 1 hour in the refrigerator.

Preheat oven to 350°.

Place chicken and marinade on baking sheet or on broiler pan, slipping onion slices under the breasts. Bake 40 minutes, or until chicken is cooked to desired doneness. Do not overcook. You want the chicken to be juicy and moist.

Remove chicken and place onions on breasts. Serve hot, with a dab of chipotle peppers on top of each.

Serves 4

---

* These are canned, smoked jalapeños and are available in many supermarkets and specialty-food stores.

TOSTONES: FRIED PLANTAINS AND FRESH LIME

2 large firm plantains
Corn oil for frying
2 limes

Peel the plantains. Cut diagonally into ½-inch pieces, approximately 12 slices per plantain.

Heat 1 inch of oil in large skillet. Fry plantains for several minutes over medium-high heat until golden around the edges.

Remove from the oil with a slotted spoon. Place between 2 sheets of waxed paper. Using the bottom of a glass, smash each to ¼-inch thickness.

Dip each in a bowl of salted water (4 cups water plus 1 tablespoon salt). Reheat oil. Shake off excess water and return them to the hot oil. Be careful because they spatter. Fry until golden brown. Drain on paper towels.

Sprinkle with salt and serve hot with limes that have been cut into wedges. Or keep in warm oven until ready to serve.

Serves 4

MARGARITA SORBET, SUGARED RASPBERRIES

2 pints (12 ounces net weight) big fresh raspberries
4 tablespoons sugar
1 pint margarita sorbet, frozen solid **

Wash berries gently and pat dry with paper towels.

In a bowl, mix raspberries with sugar and let sit at room temperature for 30 to 40 minutes (or longer), until berry juices flow and sugar is dissolved.

Remove lid from sorbet. Using a very sharp chef's knife, cut container of sorbet lengthwise, into 4 wedges, cutting through the cardboard container and through the sorbet.

To serve, divide berries and juices evenly onto 4 large chilled plates.

Top each with a wedge of sorbet.

Serves 4

* Häagen-Dazs makes this variety, and it's great.

■ ■ ■

Lunch with Chinese Flavors

Immune Soup

Chili-Cooked Garlic Spareribs with Cilantro

Rice with Water Chestnuts and Sesame Oil

Lychee Sorbet and Almond Cookie Dessert

12 ingredients

Wise Chinese saying: "He who cooks simplest, cooks best."

Immune Soup, adapted from a lovely book by Bob Flaws and Honora Wolfe entitled Prince Wen Hui's Cook *(1983), is a prime example. Scallions and sherry magically transform the most elemental of chicken broths (made with long-simmered chicken wings, water, and salt) into a multidimensional palliative with distinct Chinese taste.

Authentic flavors follow: cilantro, chili paste, sesame oil, lychees, ginger, and Stella D'Oro Chinese dessert cookies!? Hey, it's the multicultural nineties.*

GRAPENOTE

A glass of fino sherry with the starter. Lightly chilled, it's a contrast to the hot soup and guaranteed to cure most anything. Move on to a spicy red from South Africa — a *pinotage* from Cape Bay, Springbok, or Backsberg. Having a crowd? Open a magnum of Sable View and still be under ten dollars!

IMMUNE SOUP

3½ pounds chicken wings
3 scallions
1 tablespoon dry sherry

Place chicken wings in medium pot with cold water just to cover. Add ½ teaspoon salt, ¼ teaspoon white peppercorns, and 2 scallions that have been thinly sliced. Use the white and green parts.

Bring to a boil. Lower heat. Cover pot and cook over medium heat for 1½ hours.

Strain soup through a fine-mesh sieve into a clean pot. Save chicken wings. Continue to cook soup until broth is reduced to 4 cups. Remove as much visible fat as possible, using a large spoon. Add sherry and remaining scallion that has been very thinly sliced. Cook 5 minutes.

Remove as much of the meat as possible from the chicken wings. You should have 1 to 1½ cups.

To serve soup, divide cooked chicken among 4 large flat soup plates. Add 1 cup of hot soup to each bowl. Serve immediately.

Serves 4 (makes 4 cups)

CHILI-COOKED GARLIC SPARERIBS WITH CILANTRO

3 pounds pork spareribs in racks, trimmed
6 tablespoons Chinese chili paste with garlic*
2 large bunches cilantro

Place spareribs in a large bowl. Rub 5 tablespoons chili paste into flesh of ribs, making sure to cover front and back of ribs. Add a generous grinding of black pepper. Coarsely chop 1 bunch cilantro and add to bowl. Let ribs marinate for 1 hour, at room temperature, turning once or twice in bowl.

Preheat oven to 350°.

Place ribs with cilantro in a single layer on a broiler pan, meat side up. Bake for 1 hour, turning once after 40 minutes, then again after 10 minutes.

Remove pan from oven and place ribs on a cutting board. With a pastry brush, lightly brush ribs with a mixture of 1 tablespoon chili paste mixed with 1 tablespoon pan drippings. Chop remaining bunch of cilantro and sprinkle ribs with chopped leaves. Cut between ribs and serve while hot.

Serves 4

* Available in many supermarkets and Asian specialty stores. Use brands such as Thai Kitchen or Lan Chi.

RICE WITH WATER CHESTNUTS AND SESAME OIL

1½ cups short-grain white rice
8 ounces whole water chestnuts in water
3 teaspoons Oriental roasted sesame oil

Wash rice in a fine-mesh sieve. Place in a large saucepan with 2 cups water and ½ teaspoon salt. Bring to a boil, lower heat, and cover. Simmer for 20 minutes, or until all water is absorbed.

Meanwhile, drain water chestnuts in a colander. Pat dry with paper towels. Cut water chestnuts into quarters. Heat 1½ teaspoons sesame oil in a small nonstick skillet. Add water chestnuts and cook over medium heat until they turn golden and a little crisp.

When rice is done, remove cover and fluff with a fork. Add water chestnuts, remaining 1½ teaspoons sesame oil, and salt and freshly ground black pepper to taste. Serve immediately.

Serves 4

LYCHEE SORBET AND ALMOND COOKIE DESSERT

2 11-ounce cans peeled whole lychees in heavy syrup
4 Stella D'Oro Chinese dessert cookies *
4 tablespoons julienned candied ginger

Freeze unopened cans of lychees for a minimum of 8 hours. Dip unopened cans in hot water for 10 seconds to loosen filling.

Remove both ends of cans with can opener and force filling out. Cut frozen fruit into chunks and place in bowl of food processor.

Puree long enough to become smooth without getting too soft. Refreeze if you are not ready to serve dessert. Makes 3 cups sorbet.

Place a cookie in the center of each of 4 large plates. Using an ice-cream scoop, top each cookie with a large scoop of lychee sorbet.

Top each with 1 tablespoon julienned candied ginger and scatter any loose toasted sliced almonds that you can find in the cellophane cookie bag around and on top of the sorbet. Serve immediately.

Serves 4

* You can find Stella D'Oro Chinese dessert cookies in the supermarket.

■ ■ ■

Autumn Picnic

Mustard-Molasses Lamb Riblets

Cabbage "Cream" Slaw

Lemon Yellow Beans

Warm Apple Kissel, Apple Chips

12 ingredients

When there's a nip of fall in the air, here's an uncomplicated meal best eaten with family or close friends, among whom you may unabashedly lick your fingers.

Slow cooking turns inexpensive lamb riblets into a sensuous and generous dish. Its "mustard plaster" marinade mellows into a glaze of beguiling sweetness. Time-honored cabbage salad once known as cream slaw adds a gentle tang with its distinctive cream-and-vinegar dressing. Yellow beans bathed in lemon oil add dramatic color.

Kissel, a Russian dessert traditionally made from sweetened red fruit (like cranberries), is also delicious when made with Golden Delicious apples. Tart, mildly sweet, and ultimately satisfying.

GRAPENOTE

Serve with a youthful and spicy zinfandel or a flavorful beer imported from Belgium.

MUSTARD-MOLASSES LAMB RIBLETS

1 cup unsulphured molasses
1½ cups coarse Pommery mustard
3 pounds lamb riblets, cut into individual ribs by your butcher

Bring ½ cup water to a boil in a small saucepan. Combine molasses and mustard in large bowl. Whisk until smooth, slowly adding boiling water. Add riblets and freshly ground black pepper. Mix well and marinate several hours in refrigerator.

Preheat oven to 325°.

Remove riblets from marinade, and set marinade aside. Place riblets on broiler pan fitted with a rack. Cover tightly with aluminum foil and bake for 45 minutes.

Meanwhile, put reserved marinade in a small saucepan and bring to a boil. Remove from heat.

Remove foil from riblets and bake another 45 minutes, basting frequently with reserved marinade, using a pastry brush. Remove from oven and serve immediately.

Serves 4

CABBAGE "CREAM" SLAW

1 small green cabbage (about 1½ pounds)
½ cup heavy cream
3 tablespoons distilled white vinegar

Shred cabbage very thin with sharp knife. Sprinkle with 1 tablespoon kosher salt and put in colander with weight on top. Let sit 30 minutes. Rinse well under cold water. Dry thoroughly with paper towels, or use a salad spinner.

Put cabbage in a bowl and pour cream over. Mix.

Add vinegar and freshly ground black pepper. Toss well. Chill 1 hour before serving. Add salt to taste and toss again.

Serves 4 or more

LEMON YELLOW BEANS

1 pound yellow wax beans
¼ cup extra-virgin olive oil
Grated zest and juice of 1 lemon

Wash beans and trim. Bring a pot of salted water to a boil. Add beans. Lower heat and cook for 10 to 15 minutes, or until tender but not too soft. Drain well in colander.

In small bowl whisk together oil, lemon zest, and juice. Season with salt and pepper and toss immediately with warm beans. Reheat gently or serve at room temperature.

Serves 4

WARM APPLE KISSEL, APPLE CHIPS

7 Golden Delicious apples
2 tablespoons plus ½ cup granulated sugar
1 tablespoon fresh lemon juice

Peel, core, and cut 5 of the apples into ½-inch chunks. Combine 2 tablespoons sugar with 1 cup water, and bring to a boil in a very large pot. Add the apple chunks and lemon juice. Lower heat and simmer 20 minutes, until apples are very soft. Let cool slightly before serving. Or make ahead of time and warm gently before serving. Makes approximately 2¾ cups. Serve with apple chips.

To make apple chips: Preheat oven to 200°. Mix 1 cup water plus ½ cup sugar in small nonreactive bowl.

Slice 2 remaining unpeeled apples vertically into paper-thin slices, removing seeds. Place in sugar water for 15 minutes. Drain apples and arrange in single layer on baking sheets lined with parchment paper. Bake in oven for 2 hours, turning once. Apples will dry, curl a little, turn slightly brown, and become crisp. Remove from oven. Use immediately or store in container. Makes about 65 chips.

Serves 4 or more

In Honor of James Beard

Oysters with "Malted" Mignonette

Skillet Chopped Steak with Scallions and Soy

Cremini Mushrooms, Sherry-Pepper Cream

Old-Fashioned Rice Pudding

12 ingredients

Beard, the iconoclastic father of American cooking, taught a nation to respect its culinary heritage.

In April of 1992, James Beard inscribed my husband's copy of the book American Cookery: *"For Mike, who loves food and its lore!" Jim and Michael both shared this passion and worked together with Joe Baum to create one of the country's most famous restaurants, the sky-scraping Windows on the World towering 107 floors above downtown Manhattan. It was re-created by the Joseph Baum & Michael Whiteman Company in May 1996.*

What Beard identified as a renaissance of interest in food in the mid-1940s crescendoed, some fifty years later, into an explosion of culinary nationalism. Although in 1972 he opined, "We are barely beginning to sift down into a cuisine of our own," today he would surely agree that the American palate is at its zenith.

In that spirit, he helped Michael create honest food like this for the Market Bar & Dining Rooms on the ground floor of the World Trade Center, a three-star restaurant that, like Beard, exists only as a strong memory.

GRAPENOTE

Muscadet is an honorable partner for briny oysters. With the chopped steak, a cabernet from Jean Dulong (aged in oak for eighteen months — a steal from Bordeaux for $6.99!) or Dunnewood Vineyards from California's north coast.

OYSTERS WITH "MALTED" MIGNONETTE

24 or 36 bluepoint oysters
½ cup malt vinegar
2 tablespoons very finely chopped shallots

Open the oysters, or have your fish store do it, so that you have 2 or 3 dozen oysters on the half shell. Keep chilled until ready to use.

In a small bowl, mix vinegar, shallots, 2 tablespoons cold water, 1 teaspoon butcher-grind black pepper, and a pinch of salt. Stir. You will have ¾ cup mignonette sauce.

Serve 6 or 9 oysters per person. Place oysters on a bed of crushed ice or kosher salt on large plates. Place a small ramekin of mignonette sauce in center of each plate. Serve immediately with small oyster forks for easy dipping.

Serves 4

SKILLET CHOPPED STEAK WITH SCALLIONS AND SOY

3 pounds good-quality chopped ground round
½ cup finely chopped scallions, white and green parts, plus 2 whole scallions
5 tablespoons soy sauce

In a large bowl, put chopped meat, ½ cup finely chopped scallions, and 3 tablespoons soy sauce. Mix well with your hands, and add a generous grinding of black pepper.

Form into a large "cake," approximately 10 inches in diameter and 1½ inches high.

Heat a heavy iron skillet until hot and sprinkle lightly with salt. Place the "cake" in the pan and cook over high heat, turning only once, using 2 spatulas. Each side should take approximately 6 to 8 minutes. Each side should be rather charred and crisp, while still rare in the center.

When finished, turn out onto large round platter. Sprinkle with remaining 2 tablespoons soy sauce and remaining 2 scallions that have been thinly sliced on the bias.

Cut into wedges and serve hot.

Serves 4

CREMINI MUSHROOMS, SHERRY-PEPPER CREAM

8 ounces fresh cremini or shiitake mushrooms
6 tablespoons heavy cream
3 tablespoons dry fino sherry

Wipe mushrooms with a damp cloth. Cut mushrooms in half or into thirds if very large.

In a medium nonstick skillet heat heavy cream. Let cook over high heat until it starts to thicken and bubble. Add 2 tablespoons sherry and the mushrooms.

Stirring constantly, cook mushrooms over medium heat until they begin to soften, approximately 3 minutes.

Add remaining tablespoon of sherry, salt, and lots of coarse, freshly ground black pepper.

You may adjust the sauce by adding a little more cream or more sherry.

Cook 1 or 2 minutes longer, until mushrooms give up some of their liquid. Most of the sauce will be absorbed by the mushrooms. The mushrooms should be tender but not soft and still retain their shape. Serve hot.

Serves 4

OLD-FASHIONED RICE PUDDING

4 tablespoons short-grain rice*
1 quart whole milk
½ cup Vanilla Sugar (see page 11)

Wash the rice in a fine-mesh sieve. Put rice in a small bowl with ½ cup water and let soak for 30 minutes at room temperature.

In a heavy medium pot, bring the milk and sugar to a boil. Add rice and soaking water.

Lower heat and simmer mixture for 1½ hours, until most of the liquid has been absorbed. Stir frequently with a wooden spoon during cooking.

Spoon into 4 custard cups or wineglasses and let cool. Pudding will thicken as it sits.

* Sushi rice works well in this recipe.

Optional garnish: You may "sugarcoat" each serving: Spoon into heatproof cups. Chill until very cold. Preheat broiler. Sprinkle each cup with 1 teaspoon additional Vanilla Sugar. Place under broiler until sugar caramelizes, about 30 seconds. Let cool and serve.

Serves 4

More Tex Than Mex

Jalapeño and Pepperoni Tortilla Flat

Skirt Steak with Salsa Verde, Raw and Roasted Garlic

Sour Cream Mashed Potatoes with Skillet-Roasted Corn

Tequila Melon

12 ingredients

Most Americans confuse Mexican food, which is balanced and restrained, with the go-for-broke macho cooking of our own Southwest, where aggression in food is a virtue. This menu, full of outdoorsy flavors cooked on your range, makes no claim to subtlety and contains the kick of a burro.

GRAPENOTE

Intense flavors permeate this menu — so start with a robust "field blend" like Reds (from Laurel Canyon), then move to a fairly woody Rioja like Codice or Marques de Riscal.

JALAPEÑO AND PEPPERONI TORTILLA FLAT

4 8-inch flour tortillas
8 ounces jalapeño Havarti cheese
4 ounces pepperoni stick (1-inch diameter)

Preheat oven to 400°.

Place tortillas on 2 baking sheets.

Grate cheese on large holes of box grater. Distribute evenly on top of each tortilla, leaving ½-inch border.

Slice pepperoni ⅛ inch thick and place 7 or 8 slices on top of cheese, distributing evenly.

Bake for 5 minutes, until cheese begins to melt, then place under broiler for about 30 seconds or until lightly browned. Remove from oven. Let sit 2 to 3 minutes before serving. Cut into quarters with a large, sharp knife.

Serves 4

SKIRT STEAK WITH *SALSA VERDE*, RAW AND ROASTED GARLIC

2 large heads garlic (2 ounces each), plus 4 large cloves
2 pounds skirt steak
2 cups jarred medium-hot salsa verde *with tomatillos*

Preheat oven to 400°.

Wrap 2 heads garlic loosely in aluminum foil. Place in pie tin and bake for 1 hour. Remove from oven and let garlic cool.

In large bowl place skirt steak and 1½ cups *salsa verde*. Cut garlic heads in half through the diameter and squeeze out soft garlic pulp. Add to bowl. Slice remaining 4 cloves garlic paper thin, lengthwise. Add to bowl and mix ingredients thoroughly. Cover. Place in refrigerator and let marinate a minimum of 6 hours, or overnight.

Heat 2 large nonstick skillets. Cut steak into 4 portions. Place steaks in pans and cook over high heat 3 to 5 minutes on each side, until desired doneness. You want the steak to blacken and caramelize on the outside. I love it rare on the inside.

Add salt to taste and cut steaks, on the bias, into ¼-inch-thick slices. Serve each with 2 tablespoons remaining *salsa verde*.

Serves 4

SOUR CREAM MASHED POTATOES WITH SKILLET-ROASTED CORN

1¼ pounds Yukon Gold potatoes
1 large ear yellow sweet corn
½ cup sour half-and-half*

Scrub potatoes well, but do not peel. Bring a large pot of salted water to a boil. Add potatoes, cover, and cook over medium heat for 30 to 40 minutes, or until very tender.

Meanwhile, husk corn, removing all the silk. With a sharp knife, cut kernels off the cob. You will have about 1 cup. Put in a nonstick skillet. Cook for a few minutes over medium-high heat, stirring often, until corn kernels are lightly browned. Add pinch of salt and stir. Reserve.

Drain potatoes in colander, saving ⅔ cup cooking liquid. Peel potatoes under cool running water.

Put peeled potatoes in large bowl. Mash well with potato masher.

Add sour half-and-half, ½ to ⅔ cup reserved cooking liquid, and salt and freshly ground white pepper to taste. Add two-thirds of the corn and stir well. Scatter remaining corn on top and serve. If you are serving later, reheat with a little water in a heavy saucepan, then sprinkle with reserved kernels.

Serves 4

* This is low-fat sour cream available in all supermarkets.

TEQUILA MELON

1 large ripe cantaloupe (2½ pounds)
½ cup top-quality tequila, plus some for dipping glass rims
4 tablespoons sugar, plus some for dipping glass rims

Cut cantaloupe in half. Scoop out seeds. Make balls using a melon baller. Place melon balls in a medium bowl. Add the tequila, sugar, a big pinch of salt, and coarsely ground black pepper. Stir well to dissolve sugar. Cover, and refrigerate for 20 minutes.

Dip the rims of 4 wineglasses into tequila and then into a saucer filled with sugar. Sugar will cling to the rims and dry.

Carefully fill glasses with marinated melon balls. Pass the saltshaker. Depending on the sweetness of your melon, there is a delicate balance of sweet tempered with a little salt.

Serves 4

3

Night

■ ■ ■

DINNER

First Courses

Roasted Asparagus and Provolone Salad

Endive and Grapefruit Salad

White Beans and Shrimp in Pesto Broth

Bresaola *and Mango, Parmesan Shards*

A Rainbow of Roasted Tomatoes in Peppers

Fusilli Cacio e Pepe

Fennel Wafers with Poached Eggs

Scallops-in-Shiitakes

Consommé with Marrow

Frisée *and Beet Salad, Goat Cheese Dressing*

Jumbo Lump Crab, Avocado Sauce

Chilled Tomato-Orange Soup with Tarragon

Turkish Eggplant Flan

Spinach and Smoked Salmon Terrine Lutèce

Warm Duck Liver Salad

Roasted Beet Soup with Pickled Beet Greens

Asiago-Pepper Roulades

Portobello Mushroom Melt

Fennel and Orange Salad

Chicken Liver Royale with Red Onions and Bacon

Zucchini Vichyssoise

Labaneh-*Stuffed Tomatoes with Olive Oil*

Chickpea Soup with Cilantro and Red Onions

Arugula Salad with Sweet Garlic Dressing

Warm Goat Cheese with Fresh Mint Salad

Tomato Polenta

Butternut Squash Soup with Leek Cream

Baby Beets with Roquefort Cheese and
Hazelnut Oil

Prosciutto-Wrapped Shrimp Sticks

Pickled Shrimp in Rice Vinegar

Onion, Wild Mushroom, and Brie Soup

Smoked Salmon Tartare, Dill Mousse

Main Courses

Warm Salad of Pasta and Chickpeas

Globe Artichokes Stuffed with Sun-Dried
Tomato Couscous

Salmon Prunier with Tomato Julienne and Mint

"Osso Buco" of Salmon

Pavé of Cod, Herbes de Provence

Baked Halibut with Sour Cream and Parmesan

Sea Bass in Cartoccio, *Black Olive Tapenade
and Oranges*

Braised Swordfish Stuffed with Watercress

Barbecued Tuna, London-Broil Style

Pot-au-Feu: Chicken, Beef Shin, and Leeks

Chicken Fricassee with Pearl Onions and Lardons

Chicken Paillards, Adobo Style

Manchego Chicken with Prosciutto

Fesenjune: *Chicken Breasts in Walnut and
Pomegranate Sauce*

Cornish Hens with Tarragon Rice

Crisped Duck with Roasted Turnips,
Port Wine Reduction

Brine-Cured Turkey Breast with Turkey Bacon and
Roasted Pears, Roasted Pear "Gravy"

Pork Loin and "Packed Rack" with Dried Fruit and
Fennel Sausage

Pan-Roasted Breast of Veal, Marcella Hazan

Veal Chops with Lemon and Basil

Veal Roast with Caramelized Soup Greens,
Vegetable Jus

Veal Shanks with Forty Cloves of Garlic,
Pinot Noir Reduction

Lamb Chops with Goat Cheese and Lavender

Shish Kebabs with Onions and
Pomegranate Molasses

Oven-Braised Lamb Stew with Cumin and
Fresh Tomato

Roast Lamb Shoulder with Comté and Rosemary

Bombay Leg of Lamb with Yogurt and Lime

Calf's Liver, Venetian Style

Wine-Dark Short Ribs

Beef Chuck Braised for Hours, Orange Essence

Gorgonzola-Grappa Rib Steak

Bay-Smoked Chateaubriand with Truffle Oil,
Truffle-Roasted Salt

Stuffed Tenderloin with Black Olives and
Sun-Dried Tomatoes

Salt-and-Pepper Prime Rib with Horseradish Sauce
and Yorkshire Pudding

Side Dishes

Homemade Focaccia

Zucchini Flan

Fresh Spinach and Lemon Oil

Savoy Cabbage with Lardons and
Champagne Vinegar

A Twirl of Fresh Pasta, Parsley-Garlic Sauce

Fresh Artichokes with Mint

Sugar Snaps with Diced Bacon and Radishes

Warm Onion Gratin

Simple Green Beans

Boiled Potatoes with Caper Vinaigrette

Celery Root Gratin

Smoky Pink Beans and Rice

Açorda: Garlic Bread Pudding

Pepper Confit with Sherry Vinegar

Toasted Orzo with Rice

Belgian Endive and Blue Cheese Gratin

Smooth and Chunky Turnip Puree,
Caramelized Shallots

Sweet Potato–Cheddar Gratin

Ruby Cranberries with Sun-Dried Cherries:
Relish and Compote

Onions Disguised As Marrow Bones

Slow-Cooked Zucchini with Thyme

Red Pepper–Potato Cakes

Truffled White Bean Puree

Sautéed Red Swiss Chard

Watercress Sauté with Garlic Chips

"Short-Stack" Tomatoes and Onions

Whole Wheat Pita Bread

Barley with Dates

Bulgur Wheat with Caramelized Onions

Green Beans and Potatoes in Pesto

Curried Couscous with Currants

Braised Eggplant, Balsamic Syrup

Brown Rice with Sun-Dried Cherries

Polenta with Tiny Broccoli Florets

Pan-Fried Sage Potatoes

Fingerling Potatoes with Roasted Garlic and Brie Fondue

Roasted Garlic Flan

Spinach and Celery Puree

Yorkshire Pudding

Brussels Sprouts and Tangerine Beurre Noisette

Desserts

Pears in White Wine Caramel

Chocolate Dacquoise

Gelato d'Arancina, *Candied Orange Peel*

Panna Cotta *with Amber Crystals*

Pear-Poire-Pepper Sorbet

Roasted Nectarines with Amaretto Syrup and Amaretto Cream

Rhubarb Compote and Sour Cream Ice Cream, Rhubarb-Pepper Syrup

Black Grapes and Rum Raisins, Black Grape Granita

Apples Talibur *in Puff Pastry, Apple Confit*

Warm Banana Tarts

Coconut Ice Cream with Blue Curaçao

Baked Chocolate Crema

Poached Prunes with Cardamom Yogurt

Crème Brûlée

A Simple Strudel

Pumpkin-Eggnog Flan, Custard Sauce

Lemon-Curd Yogurt Tarts

Anisette Espresso Coupe

Chocolate Biscotti Terrine

Limoncello *Zabaglione*

A Kind of Spumoni

Strawberry Gratin à la Sabayon

Fig Confit with Sesame and Honey

Turkish Grapes with Wild-Thyme Honey and Yogurt

Brutti ma Buoni (Ugly but Good) Cookies

Chilled Sliced Oranges with Rosewater and Dates

Chocolate Semifreddo

Valrhona Profiteroles

Strawberries in Cassis, Crème Fraîche

Chocolate-Chocolate Tartufo

Chocolate Climax

Fresh Fruit en Papillote

Oven-Roasted Pears with Stilton, Warm Honey Syrup

■ ■ ■

Supper from the Antipasto Table

Roasted Asparagus and Provolone Salad

Warm Salad of Pasta and Chickpeas

Globe Artichokes Stuffed with Sun-Dried Tomato Couscous

Homemade Focaccia

Pears in White Wine Caramel

15 ingredients

Most sophisticated Italians would agree that the best food in Italy is found in the hundreds of family-run trattorie *scattered across the country.*

A gastronomic semaphore of the trattoria is the antipasto table, frequently wooden and worn, decked out with platters of room-temperature dishes. Trattorias make me think of robust flavors, tiny cups of strong espresso, a warm welcome.

Start preparing this convivial meal four hours before your guests arrive. This gives ample time for your dough to rise twice, letting the aromas of freshly baked bread fill your kitchen. The same amount of time is just right for marinating fresh pears, whose perfumed juices are transformed into a liquid caramel.

Buffet style or course by course, this vegetarian menu, solo verdure, *serving four can easily serve eight simply by doubling the recipe for the pasta and stuffed artichokes.*

GRAPENOTE

Fragrant Arneis, an ancient wine of Italy, is a lovely apéritif with small plates of roasted asparagus salad, or you can try a crisp Orvieto. Use the same wine to make dessert. With the meal, crack open something unintimidating, a bottle of Dolcetto d'Alba or Barbera d'Asti.

ROASTED ASPARAGUS AND PROVOLONE SALAD

1½ pounds fresh medium asparagus
1½ tablespoons extra-virgin olive oil
6 ounces provolone cheese, ⅛-inch-thick slices

Preheat oven to 500°.

Trim woody bottoms from asparagus and discard. Wash asparagus, then cut into thirds on the bias. Toss with ½ tablespoon oil to coat lightly.

Place asparagus on a shallow baking sheet in one layer. Roast in oven for 10 minutes, shaking the sheet once or twice to prevent sticking. Remove from oven and place asparagus in a bowl.

While asparagus is in the oven, cut cheese into thin julienne sticks, approximately 1½-inch long by ⅛-inch wide. Add to asparagus. Add salt and freshly ground black pepper to taste. Toss gently. Add remaining 1 tablespoon olive oil and toss again.

Serve while warm.

Serves 4

WARM SALAD OF PASTA AND CHICKPEAS

½ pound dried chickpeas
½ pound imported penne pasta
½ cup garlic oil*

Soak chickpeas overnight or use quick-soak method: Cover beans with 2 inches of water, bring to a boil, boil 2 minutes and remove from heat. Cover and let sit 1 hour. Drain well. Put chickpeas in heavy medium pot with fresh cold water to cover by 2 inches.

Bring to a boil. Lower heat and simmer for 1¾ to 2 hours, or until chickpeas are tender.

When tender, add more water if necessary, so that chickpeas are still covered by 2 inches. Add kosher salt to taste. Bring to a boil again, and add pasta. Stir frequently with wooden spoon. Cook 15 minutes, or until pasta is tender.

Drain excess water in colander, leaving pasta a little wet. Put pasta and chickpeas in warm ceramic bowl. Toss with garlic oil, 1½ teaspoons butcher-grind black pepper, and coarse salt to taste. Toss again. Serve hot or at room temperature.

Serves 4

* See page 8 for recipe, or you may use a good-quality store-bought garlic oil such as Consorzio or Colavita.

GLOBE ARTICHOKES STUFFED WITH SUN-DRIED TOMATO COUSCOUS

1 cup fine-grain couscous
½ cup sun-dried tomatoes in oil (about 12 pieces)
4 large globe artichokes

In medium nonstick skillet, toast couscous over medium heat for several minutes until lightly brown. Add 1½ cups boiling water, stir, cover pan, and cook 5 minutes, lowering heat to medium. Chop tomatoes coarsely and add to couscous along with 3 tablespoons tomato oil. Add ½ teaspoon to 1 teaspoon salt and freshly ground black pepper. Reserve. This makes 3 cups couscous.

To prepare artichokes, cut off stems and reserve. Slice 1 inch off top of each artichoke. With a scissors, trim all leaves by one-fourth. With small sharp knife, cut out inner portion and remove choke with spoon. Cook artichokes and reserved stems in large quantity of salted water over medium-high heat until tender, about 45 minutes. Remove and allow to cool.

Spread artichoke leaves apart and fill cavity of artichokes with couscous mixture, also pushing some between the leaves. If desired, mince artichoke stems and scatter on top.

Cook in a steamer basket until artichokes and couscous are hot, or preheat oven to 350°, put artichokes in baking dish, cover with foil, and heat 15 to 20 minutes. Drizzle with additional sun-dried tomato oil. Serve hot or at room temperature.

Serves 4

HOMEMADE FOCACCIA

3 cups unbleached flour
1 package (2¼ teaspoons) active dry yeast
6 tablespoons olive or rosemary oil *

To make dough, place flour, yeast, and 2 teaspoons salt in bowl of a food processor and mix for a few seconds. With the motor running, pour in 4 tablespoons oil and 1 cup warm water. Process until dough forms a ball on the blade. (If mixture is too wet to form a ball, add a bit more flour. If too dry, add a few drops water.) Continue to process for about 45 seconds to "knead" the dough.

Remove dough from processor, knead a few times by hand, and then form dough into a tight ball.

Place dough into a lightly oiled mixing bowl and turn to coat fully with oil. Cover lightly, and let rise about 2 hours, or until doubled in bulk.

Brush a large baking sheet with oil. Punch dough down and roll or pat on lightly floured surface to an approximate 8-by-12-inch rectangle about ½-inch thick and place in the prepared pan. Use your thumb to make several light dimples or indentations in the dough. Gently brush with 2 tablespoons oil and sprinkle with sea salt.

Preheat oven to 450°.

Let rise 30 minutes. Bake in the lower third of the oven for 20 to 22 minutes, until focaccia is rich golden brown and its edges are crisp.

Serves 4 or more

* Try the rosemary oil from Consorzio, or see page 9 for recipe.

PEARS IN WHITE WINE CARAMEL

2 pounds (4 to 6) ripe fragrant Comice, Bosc, or Bartlett pears
2 cups dry white wine
1 cup granulated sugar

Peel pears with a vegetable peeler. Cut them lengthwise into 8 wedges. Remove the seeds with a small knife.

Place pears in a large, shallow serving dish and pour wine over pears. Let marinate 30 minutes at room temperature.

Put sugar in a large, heavy skillet over medium heat, stirring often with a wooden spoon. Cook until the sugar melts completely into a caramel sauce, about 15 minutes. Do not overcook.

Pour the caramel over the marinated pears to cover completely.

Cover and refrigerate for at least 3 hours. Remove the pears with a slotted spoon to a platter. Place marinating liquid in a small saucepan and reduce the sauce over medium-high heat to ¾ cup. Drizzle the warm sauce over the pears and serve.

Serves 4 or more

Dinner on the Right Bank

Endive and Grapefruit Salad

Salmon Prunier with Tomato Julienne and Mint

Zucchini Flan

Chocolate Dacquoise

12 ingredients

It was at Restaurant Prunier-Madeleine in the summer of 1982 that I had the specialité du jour, *which was, happily, salmon* en papillote *cooked with fresh mint. I remember it to this day and have transformed it effortlessly into a menu worthy of fond memories. (The original Prunier was founded in 1872 in the rue Duphot in Paris, known equally for its great fish and its famous customers, such as Sarah Bernhardt and Oscar Wilde.)*

This might be your first experience cooking en papillote, *classically done in a pouch of parchment paper, but successfully achieved using aluminum foil. The foil puffs like a balloon, sealing in aromas, flavors, and precious natural juices. It is the perfect way to cook fish, eliminating the need for any fat.*

Save those calories for delightfully rich chocolate cake, a specialty of southwestern France, made surprisingly light with traditional layers of meringue.

Bake the cake several hours before dinner. The rest of the meal can be prepared in forty-five minutes.

GRAPENOTE

Open a bottle of Alsatian pinot blanc right after you finish your salad. Try a glass of French Banyuls, a ruby portlike wine made from *grenache noir,* with dessert, or a less expensive Sandeman ruby port.

ENDIVE AND GRAPEFRUIT SALAD

6 large Belgian endives
2 pink grapefruit
6 tablespoons herb-flavored oil*

Trim bottoms from the endives. Set 2 endives aside. Cut 4 endives on the bias into ¼-inch-thick slices. Put in a large bowl.

Cut rind off the grapefruit using a small sharp knife, making sure all white pith is removed. Cut along membranes to remove segments. Add grapefruit segments to the bowl with the endives. Squeeze remaining cut membranes to release all the juice and add to bowl. Add 4 tablespoons of herb-flavored oil, salt, and freshly ground white pepper. Toss gently.

Cut ½ inch from bottom of remaining 2 endives and remove all the leaves one by one. On each of 4 large plates, arrange leaves like petals of a flower.

Mound salad in center of plates. Drizzle ½ tablespoon oil and any accumulated juices around the leaves on each plate.

Serves 4

* Try store-bought basil- or rosemary-flavored oil, or make your own (see page 9).

SALMON PRUNIER WITH TOMATO JULIENNE AND MINT

4 8-ounce center-cut salmon fillets, with skin
8 large ripe plum tomatoes
2 large bunches fresh mint

Preheat oven to 400°.

Lightly season salmon fillets with salt and freshly ground black pepper. Tear off 4 18-inch pieces of aluminum foil or parchment paper. Wash mint and dry well. Pluck 4 or 5 good-looking leaves from each bunch of mint for garnish later on, then divide mint into 4 mounds. Six inches from one end of each piece of foil put a mound of mint. Top with salmon fillet.

Wash tomatoes and dry well. Cut tomatoes in half lengthwise and scoop out seeds. Cut tomato shells into julienne strips. Place tomato julienne on top of each salmon fillet.

Fold each piece of foil or parchment in half over fish to make an envelope. Seal all the edges, creating a leakproof package. Place on baking sheet and bake 18 minutes. Envelopes will puff up with steam. Transfer to plates. Serve *en papillote,* or remove fish, mint, tomatoes, and accumulated juices to a plate. Julienne reserved mint leaves and scatter on top of fish.

If serving *en papillote,* slice package open and scatter leaves inside. Serve immediately.

Serves 4

THE FOLLOWING PHOTOGRAPHS DEPICT:

Pavé of Cod, Herbes de Provence *(page 162); Savoy Cabbage with Lardons and Champagne Vinegar (page 163)*

Sea Bass in Cartoccio, *Black Olive Tapenade and Oranges (before cooking) (page 170)*

Sea Bass in Cartoccio *(page 170) with Fresh Artichokes with Mint (page 171)*

Crisped Duck with Roasted Turnips, Port Wine Reduction (page 208)

Pork Loin and "Packed Rack" with Dried Fruit and Fennel Sausage (page 218); Onions Disguised as Marrow Bones (page 219)

Veal Chops with Lemon and Basil (page 227); Red Pepper–Potato Cakes (page 228)

Lamb Chops with Goat Cheese and Lavender (page 241); Watercress Sauté with Garlic Chips (page 242); "Short-Stack" Tomatoes and Onions (page 242)

Stuffed Tenderloin with Black Olives and Sun-Dried Tomatoes (page 286); Roasted Garlic Flan (page 287); Spinach and Celery Puree (page 287)

ZUCCHINI FLAN

4 medium zucchini (1½ pounds)
4 extra-large eggs
1½ cups freshly grated Parmigiano-Reggiano cheese

Preheat oven to 400°.

Wash zucchini and pat dry. Dice zucchini into ¼-inch cubes. Bring a large pot of salted water to a boil. Add zucchini and cook over medium heat for 5 minutes. Drain in colander while you prepare the rest of the ingredients.

Separate eggs. Put egg whites and a pinch of salt into the bowl of an electric mixer. Beat until whites are stiff.

Put cooked zucchini in a large bowl. Add egg yolks, grated cheese, and freshly ground white pepper. Mix well. Fold whites into zucchini-yolk mixture.

Place in an 8- or 9-cup soufflé dish coated with vegetable spray. Bake 20 minutes, until puffed and golden on top. Serve immediately.

Serves 4 or more

CHOCOLATE DACQUOISE

4 extra-large eggs
1 cup granulated sugar
8 ounces good-quality semisweet chocolate, plus 4 tablespoons shaved chocolate

Preheat oven to 275°.

Separate eggs. Put egg whites into bowl of electric mixer. Add pinch of salt and slowly add sugar, beating well after the addition of each tablespoon. Beat until egg whites are stiff.

Melt 2 ounces chocolate in small saucepan over low heat. Add chocolate to egg whites and gently mix. Line 3 9-inch pie tins with parchment paper. Evenly divide chocolate mixture among pie tins, making a thin layer. Bake for 60 to 70 minutes, or until layers are crisp. Remove from oven and set aside.

In a heavy medium saucepan melt 6 ounces chocolate with 2 tablespoons water until smooth. Keep warm.

Put egg yolks in top of a double boiler over simmering water. Add 2 tablespoons cool water and beat several minutes with a whisk to cook yolks slightly and to increase the volume. Working quickly, add whipped yolks to melted chocolate using a flexible rubber spatula. Fold gently.

"Ice" meringue layers with this chocolate filling. Carefully remove meringue layers as you proceed. Start by placing a meringue base on a cake plate; top with ⅓ filling; another meringue layer, ⅓ filling; meringue layer, and finish with the final ⅓ filling smoothed with flexible metal spatula. Let cool.

Scatter shaved chocolate on top as a garnish. Cut into wedges with a serrated knife.

Serves 6 or more

■ ■ ■

A Dinner of Shrimp and Salmon

White Beans and Shrimp in Pesto Broth

"Osso Buco" of Salmon

Mustard Beurre Blanc

Fresh Spinach and Lemon Oil

Gelato d'Arancina, *Candied Orange Peel*

15 ingredients

Guests will surely enjoy this riff on classic osso buco made with salmon instead of veal shank. "Osso buco" means "bone with a hole," and a big sea scallop centered in a rosy steak of salmon simulates that bone. Your guests will be duly impressed with its accompanying suave beurre blanc . . . the kind of sauce three-star chefs are made of.

This is a splashy menu for all seasons, requiring only a bit of advance prep. Prepare your dessert the day before, and soak the beans overnight. Begin the meal two hours before your guests arrive by simmering the beans for the pretty first course of pink shrimp in a pesto broth and prepping the ingredients for your main course, which will require only ten minutes of cooking. This will leave you time for a well-deserved glass of wine.

GRAPENOTE

This menu, decidedly Italian in spirit, would be complemented by a *pinot grigio*, the affordable Castello d'Albola from Umbria, followed by the decidedly less affordable but magnificent Angelo Gaja chardonnay.

WHITE BEANS AND SHRIMP IN PESTO BROTH

4 ounces (about ¾ cup) dried small white beans
½ cup good-quality prepared pesto
1 pound uncooked medium shrimp, in their shells

Soak beans overnight in water to cover.

Drain beans in colander. Place beans in medium pot with water to cover by 1 inch. Add 2 tablespoons pesto. Bring to a boil. Cover pot and lower heat. Simmer beans for 1¼ to 1½ hours, or until beans are tender.

Meanwhile, remove shells and tails from shrimp. Put shrimp shells and tails in medium pot with 4 cups cold water. Bring to a boil, then lower heat to a simmer. Add ½ teaspoon salt and simmer 20 minutes. Strain shrimp broth through a fine-mesh sieve into another pot, and discard shells and tails.

Add raw shrimp and 6 tablespoons pesto to strained broth. Cook over low heat for 3 minutes, or until shrimp just become opaque. Add salt and freshly ground black pepper to taste.

Drain beans and add to soup. Heat soup gently before serving. Divide evenly into 4 large flat soup plates and serve immediately.

Serves 4 (makes about 6 cups)

"OSSO BUCO" OF SALMON

4 10-ounce, 1-inch-thick salmon steaks
4 very large sea scallops
4 slices bacon

Remove any little bones from salmon steaks, leaving small center bone in place. Cut skin from salmon using a small knife and discard.

Place 1 sea scallop in between flaps of each salmon steak, up against the small center bone. Cut off 1-inch piece from the end of one flap so that you can easily wrap flaps around sea scallop. The goal is to make a tight round shape to resemble osso buco.

Preheat oven to 400°.

Cut each slice of bacon in half lengthwise to make 2 very long strips. Wrap 2 bacon strips around edges of salmon package and secure tightly with several toothpicks.

Place salmon "osso buco" on flat shallow baking sheet. Sprinkle with salt. Bake 10 minutes, or until salmon is cooked to desired doneness. Do not overcook.

Remove toothpicks and serve immediately with Mustard Beurre Blanc. (See the following recipe.)

Serves 4

MUSTARD BEURRE BLANC

¾ cup dry white wine
7 tablespoons unsalted butter, chilled and cut into small pieces
1 tablespoon Dijon mustard *

Place wine in a small nonreactive saucepan. Cook over medium-high heat until the wine is reduced to 2 tablespoons.

Remove from stove. Whisk in 6 tablespoons cold butter, whisking constantly. Sauce will begin to thicken. Add mustard and continue whisking.

Add remaining tablespoon butter, a pinch of freshly ground white pepper, and continue whisking.

Serve immediately or let cool. This sauce can be reheated gently in small saucepan over very low heat.

Makes ¾ cup

* Use a brand such as Maille or other French-imported Dijon.

FRESH SPINACH AND LEMON OIL

2 tablespoons extra-virgin olive oil
1 large lemon
1 pound curly fresh spinach leaves

Put olive oil in a small bowl. Grate rind of lemon so that you have ½ teaspoon lemon zest. Add to oil. Squeeze lemon so that you have 2 tablespoons lemon juice. Add to oil and mix.

Wash spinach well. Remove stems. Bring ¼ cup water to a boil in a medium-large pot. Add spinach, toss, and cook until just wilted. Drain off any liquid.

Add lemon oil to spinach. Add salt and freshly ground black pepper to taste. Toss to coat. Serve immediately.

Serves 4

GELATO D'ARANCINA, CANDIED ORANGE PEEL

4 large oranges
1¼ cups Vanilla Sugar (see page 11)
1 cup heavy cream

Wash oranges. Grate rind of oranges so that you have 1 tablespoon grated orange zest making sure you don't include any white pith. Remove the rind from remaining oranges in large pieces and set aside to make candied peel. Squeeze oranges into a small bowl until you have 1 cup juice.

In a medium saucepan, put 2 cups water, grated orange zest, orange juice, and 1 cup Vanilla Sugar. Bring to a boil and boil for 2 minutes. Strain syrup through a fine-mesh sieve into a clean medium bowl. Let syrup cool to room temperature. Stir in heavy cream. Refrigerate 4 hours, or until very cold. Transfer to an ice-cream maker and freeze according to the manufacturer's instructions. Serve immediately, or pack into a container and store in freezer until ready to serve.

To make candied orange peel: Cut the white pith from the large reserved pieces of orange rind. Cut rind into julienne strips ⅛ inch wide by 2 inches long. Place in a small saucepan, cover with water, and boil 20 minutes. Repeat the process 2 more times, discarding and replacing the cooking water each time. After cooking, put drained rind and ¼ cup Vanilla Sugar in the saucepan. Cook over low heat a few minutes until the sugar melts and the skins are clear and coated with syrup. Let cool.

Serve cooled orange peel on top of gelato.

Serves 4 or more

Where France and Italy Meet

Bresaola *and Mango, Parmesan Shards*

Pavé of Cod, **Herbes de Provence**

Savoy Cabbage with Lardons and Champagne Vinegar

Panna Cotta *with Amber Crystals*

12 ingredients

Joined geographically from the Alps southward to the seaside town of Menton, France and Italy are also joined at the hip gastronomically speaking, where their culinary repertoires often coalesce. This evocative menu shuttles across the borders and is meant to stimulate more than the taste buds. It also is remarkably simple to prepare.

Bresaola, or air-dried beef, comes from Italy and is sliced paper thin like its porky cousin, prosciutto. It bridges the sweet and salty flavors of mango and Parmesan, respectively.

Pavé of cod is an idea borrowed from Paul Minchelli in Paris, where a coating of herbes de Provence *simulates the "skin" of the cod. Slowly braised cabbage, fattened with lardons and balanced by vinegar, becomes a discreet foil for the fish.*

Dessert hails from Emilia-Romagna in Italy, where trendy panna cotta, *or "cooked cream," is next of kin to French crème brûlée.*

GRAPENOTE

Something from Italy and something from France. First, a sparkling prosecco from the Veneto, followed by Domaine Tempier Bandol rosé from near Provence.

BRESAOLA AND MANGO, PARMESAN SHARDS

2 medium-large ripe mangoes
4 ounces bresaola, *very thinly sliced* *
2-ounce chunk Parmigiano-Reggiano cheese

Peel mangoes, using a very sharp knife.

Cut mangoes in half, navigating around the large pit in center. Cut each half lengthwise into ½-inch-wide slices. Reserve 2 slices for later use. Place overlapping slices in the center of 4 large plates. Distribute a liberal amount of freshly ground black pepper over mango slices.

Drape *bresaola* slices evenly over mangoes to cover completely.

Using a cheese slicer or vegetable peeler, cut Parmigiano Reggiano into paper-thin slices. Scatter around and on top of *bresaola*.

Cut remaining 2 mango slices into tiny dice. Scatter around edges of *bresaola*.

Pass the pepper mill.

Serves 4

* Air-dried beef from Italy. If unavailable, substitute prosciutto.

PAVÉ OF COD, *HERBES DE PROVENCE*

4 8-ounce thick cod fillets, skin removed
4 tablespoons unsalted butter
4 tablespoons herbes de Provence*

Make sure all little bones are removed from cod. Season fillets lightly with salt and pepper.

Melt 2 tablespoons butter in a small pan. With a pastry brush, coat tops of fillets with melted butter. Press 1 tablespoon herb mixture firmly onto top of each fillet. Make sure top of fish is completely covered.

In a 12-inch nonstick skillet, melt remaining 2 tablespoons butter. Place fish fillets, herbed side down, in skillet.

Cook over low heat for 10 minutes. The success of this dish lies in low-heat slow cooking. After 10 minutes, carefully turn fish over. Herb mixture should have formed a crust. Continue to cook over low heat for 8 minutes.

Carefully transfer fish to plates with a spatula. Serve immediately.

Serves 4

* You can buy these prepackaged and imported from France. *Herbes de Provence* is a combination of thyme, rosemary, lavender, savory, sage, and basil.

SAVOY CABBAGE WITH LARDONS AND CHAMPAGNE VINEGAR

1 large head Savoy cabbage (2½ pounds) *
4-ounce piece slab bacon
3 tablespoons champagne vinegar

Remove all dark leaves from cabbage and save for another use. Remove the core and discard. Cut cabbage in half and then across into thin shreds. Toss with 1 tablespoon kosher salt and place in a large colander. Place weight on top (a pan with an unopened can of fruit is a good idea) and let sit 1 hour. Rinse cabbage well and pat dry.

Meanwhile, cut bacon into lardons or julienned strips that are 1½ by ¼ by ¼ inch. Heat slowly in a very large casserole or pot with a cover until fat is rendered and bacon begins to get crisp.

Add cabbage and cook over low heat, with cover askew, for 1½ hours, or until cabbage is very soft, adding a few tablespoons water if needed. Stir frequently during cooking so that nothing sticks in the pan. During the last 15 minutes of cooking, add vinegar, salt, and freshly ground black pepper to taste. Cook uncovered for 15 minutes and serve hot. This can be reheated easily.

Serves 4

* Napa cabbage can be substituted successfully.

PANNA COTTA WITH AMBER CRYSTALS

1¾ cups heavy cream
3½ tablespoons plus 4 tablespoons sugar
1½ teaspoons powdered gelatin

Place cream in a medium saucepan. Add 3½ table-spoons sugar and simmer the mixture for 3 to 4 minutes, or until sugar is completely dissolved.

Place 3 tablespoons cold water in a cup. Sprinkle gelatin over water and let sit 1 minute.

Add dissolved gelatin to warm cream mixture and beat well with wire whisk. Cook over low heat for 1 minute, whisking constantly. Divide mixture evenly into 4 5-ounce ramekins or small decorative cups. Let cool to room temperature, then refrigerate for a minimum of 2 hours.

To make amber crystals: Put 4 tablespoons sugar in small nonstick skillet. Cook over medium-high heat until sugar dissolves into a smooth caramel-colored liquid. Stir with wooden spoon to prevent lumps from forming. Place a double layer of waxed paper on flat surface. Using a spoon, carefully drizzle hot caramel onto waxed paper in long thin lines. Let cool. Sugar will harden.

Remove "amber" from waxed paper. Chop very finely with a chef's knife until you have very fine crystals. You may want to chop it between layers of waxed paper so it doesn't fly around. Sprinkle on top of *panna cotta* immediately before serving.

Serves 4

Dinner for Mr. Loble

A Rainbow of Roasted Tomatoes in Peppers

Baked Halibut with Sour Cream and Parmesan

A Twirl of Fresh Pasta, Parsley-Garlic Sauce

Pear-Poire-Pepper Sorbet

12 ingredients

Several months after Recipes 1-2-3 *was published (and already in its fourth printing), a letter arrived from a Mr. David Loble of Greenwich, Connecticut.*

Inside were instructions for a three-ingredient recipe he had created thirty years before. The merger of foodstuffs, featuring halibut, was an unlikely one, but his description had me hooked. "When you get it right," he said, "you get the sweet, almost dry fish, the tart, fatty cream, and the best cheese in the world as a top note."

I tried it. I liked it. And I created a menu in his honor.

Prepare dessert early in the day, giving it ample time to chill. This elegant sorbet begins with a can of pears in the freezer — which, by the way, is a nifty technique for creating low-fat desserts in a hurry. I suggest this method once more, on page 168.

Begin the rest of the menu an hour before your company rings the bell.

GRAPENOTE

California chardonnay all the way: Joseph Phelps, Calloway, or Saintsbury. Or try all three!

A RAINBOW OF ROASTED TOMATOES IN PEPPERS

6 large square-shaped green, yellow, and orange bell peppers (2 each)
6 large ripe tomatoes, slightly smaller than peppers
6 tablespoons or more good-quality olive oil

Preheat oven to 400°.

Cut peppers in half through the core. Remove seeds. Set aside.

Bring medium pot of water to a boil. Make small X in bottom of tomatoes. Drop tomatoes in water. Let cook 1 minute.

Remove tomatoes. Place in colander and cool under cold water. Remove peel with small knife. Cut tomatoes in half through the core end.

Place tomato halves, cut side down, inside peppers. Place peppers, cut side up, in heavy shallow baking pan. Sprinkle with salt and freshly ground black pepper. Drizzle each with ½ tablespoon olive oil.

Bake for 20 minutes. Carefully turn over with spatula and bake 15 minutes longer.

Turn again and place on platter. Let cool completely. Drizzle with extra olive oil before serving, if desired.

Serves 6

BAKED HALIBUT WITH SOUR CREAM AND PARMESAN

3 thick 1-pound halibut steaks
1 cup sour cream
1 cup freshly grated Parmigiano-Reggiano cheese

Preheat oven to 375°.

Place fish in a large, shallow baking pan covered with foil. Sprinkle fish with salt and press it in with your fingers.

On each fish steak, thickly spread ⅓ cup sour cream to completely cover. Add freshly ground white pepper and sprinkle cheese evenly over sour cream.

Bake for 15 minutes, until fish is cooked through but not dry. Cheese should be golden brown. If you wish a drier crust, you may put fish under the broiler for 30 to 60 seconds.

With a sharp knife, cut each fillet along the center bone, separating from the bone to form 2 pieces of fish. You will have 6 pieces. Serve immediately.

Serves 6

A TWIRL OF FRESH PASTA, PARSLEY-GARLIC SAUCE

¼ cup garlic oil*
2 large bunches flat-leaf parsley
9 ounces fresh linguine

Freeze garlic oil by placing it in a small cup or ramekin and putting in freezer for 2 hours.

Wash parsley and dry. Pick off leaves from heavy stems, leaving a few of the thinner stems near the top of the bunch. Pack tightly into a 1-cup measure, then pack again. You will need a total of 2 packed cups parsley leaves.

Bring a medium pot of salted water to a boil. Add parsley leaves and boil for 1 minute. Drain and plunge leaves in ice water to fix color. Drain immediately and squeeze dry.

Chop leaves and stems coarsely. Place in a blender with ¼ cup cold water. Process until parsley is finely chopped. With the motor running, add frozen garlic oil by the teaspoonful. Continue to blend, adding ½ teaspoon kosher salt and an additional 3 to 4 tablespoons cold water. Blend until fairly smooth. You will have about 1 cup. Set aside.

When ready to serve pasta, bring a large pot of salted water to a boil. Add fresh pasta and cook 3 minutes, until pasta is tender but not too soft. This time will vary according to the brand of pasta used.

Drain pasta in colander. Place pasta in a large warm bowl and add parsley sauce. Add lots of freshly ground black pepper. Toss thoroughly. To serve, twirl a mound of pasta around the tines of a large 2-tine fork, so that you have 6 pasta mounds. Place a mound of pasta on each of 6 large plates.

Optional garnish: Drizzle additional room temperature garlic oil over pasta.

Serves 6

---

* Use homemade Garlic Oil (see page 8) or a store-bought brand such as Consorzio.

PEAR-POIRE-PEPPER SORBET

2 16-ounce cans pear halves in heavy syrup
3 tablespoons Poire Williams pear brandy or pear liqueur, plus more for drizzling
2 pints fresh raspberries

Freeze unopened cans of pears for a minimum of 8 hours.

Dip unopened cans in hot water for 10 seconds to loosen filling.

Remove both ends of cans with can opener and force filling out. Cut frozen fruit into chunks and place in bowl of food processor.

Puree until smooth, slowly adding pear brandy. Transfer this pear sorbet to a bowl.

Fold in ¼ teaspoon butcher-grind black pepper and refreeze. When ready to serve, remove from freezer and let soften slightly, approximately 5 minutes.

Wash berries and dry well. Place some raspberries in bottom of 6 wineglasses. Top with a scoop of sorbet. Top with more berries and another scoop of sorbet. Drizzle with pear brandy and serve immediately.

Serves 6

■ ■ ■

In the Italian Kitchen

Fusilli Cacio e Pepe

***Sea Bass** in Cartoccio, Black Olive Tapenade and Oranges*

Fresh Artichokes with Mint

Roasted Nectarines with Amaretto Syrup and Amaretto Cream

12 ingredients

"Olive oil confers on the simplest dish a delicious flavor," says Patience Gray in one of my favorite books, Honey from a Weed *(1986).*

For the simple — and ancient — pasta dish cacio e pepe, *from the Lazio region of Italy, all you need is the best-quality olive oil, wonderful Pecorino Romano, and enough black pepper to speckle the cheese.*

This menu is filled with the old and the new: The traditional method of cooking in cartoccio, similar to cooking en papillote *(see page 150), en-*velops a Sicilian-inspired combination of tapenade and orange on fish; artichoke bottoms are cooked old style, à la grecque, in a steam bath of olive oil and water, with imported dried mint, preferable, in this case, to fresh.*

A finale of roasted nectarines in a syrup of amaretto and cream — an inspiration from the River Café in London — is a wink to all things new in the Italian kitchen.

All this in under one hour.

GRAPENOTE

With the first course (*primo piatto*) try a simple Galestro from Antinori. With the *secondo piatto,* the saltiness of the tapenade combined with acidity of the oranges calls for a full-bodied, full-flavored white. By all means stay in Italy, and have either a Greco di Tufo or a Fiano di Avellino.

FUSILLI CACIO E PEPE

12 ounces dried fusilli *pasta*
4 ounces Pecorino Romano cheese
4 tablespoons extra-virgin olive oil

Bring large pot of salted water to a boil. Add the *fusilli* and cook until tender, approximately 12 to 14 minutes.

Meanwhile, grate cheese on fine holes of box grater (you will have approximately 1 cup cheese). Reserve ¼ cup for later and put ¾ cup of cheese and 2 level teaspoons freshly ground black pepper into a large bowl.

Drain the *fusilli,* reserving ½ cup cooking liquid. Add the *fusilli* to bowl of cheese and toss, adding a little of the cooking liquid to moisten pasta.

Drizzle with olive oil and serve. Sprinkle with reserved cheese.

Serves 4

SEA BASS *IN CARTOCCIO,* BLACK OLIVE TAPENADE AND ORANGES

4 8-ounce sea bass fillets
6 tablespoons tapenade *
4 juice oranges

Preheat oven to 375°.

Remove skin and any bones from fish. Using a butter knife, spread each fillet with 1½ tablespoons tapenade to cover completely. Add freshly ground black pepper.

Grate orange rind to obtain 2 teaspoons zest. Peel oranges to remove all white pith, then slice them thinly, removing any pits. Place several overlapping slices of orange on top of each fillet. Sprinkle each with grated orange zest and 1 tablespoon accumulated orange juice from cutting oranges.

Cut 4 30-inch lengths of parchment paper or foil. Fold in half lengthwise. Place a fish fillet on each piece of paper or foil and fold over, crimping edges tightly to make an airtight package. The shape should look like a half-moon. Place packets on baking sheet and bake 20 minutes.

Remove from oven. Cut open packets and serve in the paper or foil, or remove fish and juices to individual plates.

Serves 4

* See page 10 for recipe or use jarred tapenade.

FRESH ARTICHOKES WITH MINT

2 large globe artichokes
3½ tablespoons olive oil
3 teaspoons dried mint leaves*

Remove all tough outer leaves of artichokes, leaving only the tender center ones. Cut 2 inches off top of artichokes and trim tops of remaining leaves. Trim stems, leaving 1 inch.

Cut each artichoke into 8 wedges using a sharp heavy knife. Remove chokes from center. Place in large nonstick skillet with 2½ tablespoons olive oil, 2 teaspoons mint, salt, and freshly ground black pepper. Cook over medium heat for 15 minutes, turning once. Artichokes should turn golden.

Add several tablespoons of water and cover skillet. Cook 10 minutes. Remove cover and raise heat to high for 2 to 3 minutes. Season with salt and pepper. Drizzle with remaining oil. Crumble remaining dry mint between your fingers and sprinkle over hot artichokes.

Serves 4

* Use imported dried whole mint leaves if possible.

ROASTED NECTARINES WITH AMARETTO SYRUP AND AMARETTO CREAM

6 large ripe nectarines
½ cup plus 1 tablespoon amaretto
½ cup heavy cream, chilled

Preheat oven to 400°.

Wash nectarines and cut in half. Carefully remove pit by cutting around it with a small, sharp knife and scooping out with a grapefruit spoon.

Place nectarines cut side down on a baking sheet. Sprinkle with 6 tablespoons water. Roast for 10 minutes, then turn them over. Roast 10 minutes longer. Remove from oven.

Place 3 halves on each of 4 large plates, 2 halves cut side down and 1 cut side up, and let cool.

Place ½ cup amaretto in small skillet and cook over medium heat until reduced to ⅓ cup. Divide evenly over nectarines.

Whip heavy cream with 1 tablespoon amaretto until thick. Spoon over nectarines. Ideally, nectarines will be slightly warm or room temperature when served.

Serves 4

■ ■ ■

Spring Dinner for Friends

Fennel Wafers with Poached Eggs

Braised Swordfish Stuffed with Watercress

Sugar Snaps with Diced Bacon and Radishes

Rhubarb Compote and Sour Cream Ice Cream, Rhubarb-Pepper Syrup

12 ingredients

The progression of courses strikes a lovely balance of flavors, textures, and weight, with an array of colors announcing the arrival of spring.

Concentrate on the simple techniques behind each recipe, and you will have stunning results: Sheathlike slices of fennel are baked to become a crunchy sky for sunny poached eggs.

Swordfish, stuffed with verdant watercress, is inspired by a simple idea from friend and fellow author Mark Bittman. (His is done with tuna and arugula.) Marinating the fish first in olive oil and then gently braising yield particularly succulent flesh.

Sugar snaps do snap, especially when showered with diced red-and-white radishes cut meticulously to mimic tiny cubes of crisped bacon.

Silken ice cream, creamy on the palate, is punctuated by tart and sweet rhubarb harmonics. Erroneously heralded as the first postwinter fruit, rhubarb is, botanically speaking, a vegetable.

Best of all, my 1-2-3 dessert is actually three recipes in one!

GRAPENOTE

Drink pink! Try a sparkling brut rosé from France or the lovely Mirabelle from California's Schramsberg Vineyards. Next . . . a still rosé from Les Baux-de-Provence or Côtes d'Oakley rosé from Cline Cellars in California.

FENNEL WAFERS WITH POACHED EGGS

2 large fennel bulbs
1 cup freshly grated Parmesan cheese
4 extra-large eggs, at room temperature

Preheat oven to 425°.

Remove stalks from fennel bulbs and reserve the feathery fronds. Cut each fennel bulb into very thin slices, approximately ⅟₁₆ inch, cutting through the core end. You will have approximately 10 to 12 fennel "wafers" per bulb.

Place wafers flat on a foil-lined baking sheet. Sprinkle each with 2 teaspoons grated cheese to cover completely.

Bake for 15 minutes. Cheese will be golden brown, and wafers will be rather crisp. Remove wafers from baking sheet.

Arrange 5 or 6 wafers in an overlapping pattern in center of 4 large plates.

In a large nonstick skillet bring 1 inch of water and 1 teaspoon salt to a boil. Reduce heat. Break eggs one at a time and slip into water. Cook until whites are firm. Cover skillet for 30 seconds. Uncover and remove eggs with slotted spoon. Drain on paper towels.

Lift eggs carefully with slotted spoon and place on fennel wafers in center of plates. Garnish with reserved fennel fronds, finely chopped, and freshly ground black pepper. Serve immediately.

Serves 4

BRAISED SWORDFISH STUFFED WITH WATERCRESS

4 10-ounce, 1-inch-thick swordfish steaks
1 cup olive oil
2 bunches watercress

Place swordfish steaks in shallow casserole. Pour olive oil over fish to cover. Let fish marinate for 1 hour at room temperature.

Remove fish from olive oil. Make a horizontal slit through the center of the fish to create a pocket.

Wash watercress well and dry. Discard stems. Roll watercress leaves in oil and sprinkle lightly with salt. Stuff pockets with watercress, packing tightly.

Place fish in a very large nonstick sauté pan. All 4 steaks will fit into a 12-inch pan. Add 3 to 4 tablespoons of the olive oil. Cook over low heat for 2 min-

utes. Cover pan and continue cooking very slowly until fish is cooked through and tender, turning once with a spatula. This will take approximately 5 to 6 minutes on each side, depending on thickness.

Remove fish from pan, with any pan juices poured over the fish. Sprinkle fish lightly with salt. You will not need pepper, since the watercress has a peppery bite. Serve immediately.

Optional garnish: Serve with additional watercress.

Serves 4

SUGAR SNAPS WITH DICED BACON AND RADISHES

¾ pound sugar snap peas
3 ounces medium to large red radishes
3 ounces slab bacon

Wash snap peas and dry. Trim the ends of the snap peas and remove the strings running down the length of the pods. Set aside.

Wash radishes and dry. Trim ends of radishes. Meticulously cut radishes into ⅛-inch cubes. Set aside. Cut slab bacon into ⅛-inch cubes to resemble the size of the radishes. Place bacon in medium nonstick skillet. Cook over medium heat until fat is rendered and bacon is cooked, approximately 3 minutes.

Meanwhile, bring a pot of salted water to a boil. Add snap peas and diced radishes. Cook 3 to 4 minutes, until beans are tender but not soft. Drain in colander. Pat dry with paper towels.

Immediately add snap peas and radishes to pan with bacon. Stir. Heat gently and serve immediately.

Serves 4

RHUBARB COMPOTE AND SOUR CREAM ICE CREAM, RHUBARB-PEPPER SYRUP

1¼ pounds (6 to 7 stalks) fresh rhubarb
1⅜ cups sugar
1½ cups sour cream

To make compote: Wash rhubarb and remove any leaves. Coarsely chop into ½-inch pieces until you have 5 cups chopped rhubarb. Put 2 cups water and ¾ cup sugar in heavy medium saucepan. Bring to a boil, and boil sugar syrup for 5 minutes. Add 4 cups rhubarb. (Reserve remaining cup for later.) Poach gently over medium heat for 10 minutes, stirring frequently. Rhubarb will soften and result in a thick compote. Remove from heat. Cool, then refrigerate until very cold. You will have approximately 3½ cups.

To make ice cream: In small saucepan, put 6 tablespoons sugar and 6 tablespoons water. Bring to a boil, and boil 30 seconds. Remove from heat. Whisk in sour cream. Place in refrigerator until very cold.

Freeze in an ice-cream maker according to manufacturer's instructions.

To make rhubarb-pepper syrup: In small saucepan add 1 cup water and remaining ¼ cup sugar. Chop remaining 1 cup rhubarb very fine and add to syrup. Bring to a boil. Lower heat and simmer for 30 minutes. Strain through a fine-mesh sieve. Return syrup to pan. Add ¼ teaspoon butcher-grind black pepper and reduce over medium-high heat to ⅓ cup. Let cool.

To serve, divide compote among 4 to 6 flat soup plates. Top with small scoops of ice cream and drizzle with syrup.

Serves 4 to 6

A Great Fish Dinner

Scallops-in-Shiitakes

Barbecued Tuna, London-Broil Style

Warm Onion Gratin

Simple Green Beans

Black Grapes and Rum Raisins, Black Grape Granita

15 ingredients

A thoughtful progression of flavors and subtle connections among ingredients compose the inexplicable alchemy that makes menus click.

This fish dinner is purposefully "beefy" and responds to today's style of cooking fish as if it were meat. Scallops pick up a beeflike essence from shiitake mushrooms; and the inspiration for tuna London-broil style comes from chef David Burke of the Park Avenue Café in New York and Chicago. David's creativity is magical.

My dessert, on the other hand, is "black magical" — an amazing trio of black grapes, black raisins, and black rum. It also is true sleight of hand, as one dessert is concealed in another.

GRAPENOTE

Chill a light, fragrant white — a *pinot gris* from Oregon or a *viognier* from the south of France — for the scallops. Switch to a medium-weight red for the tuna, a *pinotage* from South Africa or a California *syrah* from either Zaca Mesa or EXP, which stands for "experimental" and is from H. R. Phillips Winery.

SCALLOPS-IN-SHIITAKES

20 medium 1¼-inch-diameter shiitake mushrooms
20 1-inch-diameter sea scallops (about 1 pound)
½ cup good-quality prepared pesto

Preheat oven to 450°.

Remove stems from shiitake mushrooms. Wipe mushrooms with damp cloth. Let dry.

Sprinkle inside of mushroom caps very lightly with salt and freshly ground black pepper.

Fit a scallop into each mushroom cap. Scallop should fit snugly into cap.

Top each scallop with 1 to 1½ teaspoons pesto sauce.

Carefully place mushrooms in shallow baking pan. Put several tablespoons of water in bottom of pan.

Bake 8 minutes, or until scallops turn opaque and mushrooms are hot. Serve immediately.

Serves 4

BARBECUED TUNA, LONDON-BROIL STYLE

4 10-ounce, 1-inch-thick tuna steaks
1 cup ketchup
4 tablespoons Asian sesame oil

Trim tuna of any skin and place in a shallow dish.

Mix ketchup and sesame oil in a small bowl and pour over tuna. Turn tuna several times to coat fish thoroughly with mixture.

Cover and let marinate 2 hours in the refrigerator.

Remove marinade from fish, scraping off as much as possible. Place marinade in a small saucepan with several tablespoons of water and a liberal grinding of black pepper. Heat to just below a boil, lower heat, and keep warm.

Heat 2 large nonstick skillets until hot. Sprinkle fish lightly with salt. Cook fish over high heat for 2 to 3 minutes on each side. The outside of the fish will begin to caramelize and blacken; the inside should be rare to medium rare.

Remove fish to a cutting board. With a pastry brush glaze tops of fish with warm marinade. Cut each fish steak on the bias into ½-inch-thick pieces, the way you would slice a London broil. Place on a large platter. Add water to the marinade so that you have a thin sauce. Bring to a boil. Serve fish immediately, with extra marinade poured around the fish.

Serves 4

WARM ONION GRATIN

4 medium yellow onions, peeled and each cut horizontally into 3 thick slices
3 tablespoons heavy cream
3 ounces Gruyère cheese

Preheat oven to 450°.

Fill a 9-by-11-inch shallow flameproof casserole with water. Add 1 teaspoon salt and bring to a boil. Add the onions and cook over medium heat until tender. This will take about 10 minutes. Keep the onions in their original shape, as slices will begin to separate.

Drain *all* of the cooking liquid. Pour cream over onions. Sprinkle lightly with salt and freshly ground black pepper.

Grate cheese on large holes of box grater and sprinkle over onions. Bake 8 minutes, and place under broiler for 30 seconds, until cheese is melted and golden. Serve immediately.

Serves 4

SIMPLE GREEN BEANS

¾ pound fresh string beans
3 tablespoons good-quality olive oil
1½ tablespoons red-wine vinegar

Wash string beans and trim ends.

Using a small sharp knife, cut beans in half lengthwise to make 2 long, thin halves.

Bring a medium pot of salted water to a boil. Add beans and cook 3 to 4 minutes, over high heat until beans are bright green and tender. Drain immediately.

Whisk together oil and vinegar in a small bowl. Add salt and ¼ teaspoon butcher-grind black pepper. Combine warm beans and vinaigrette and toss thoroughly to coat. Serve immediately.

Serves 4

BLACK GRAPES AND RUM RAISINS, BLACK GRAPE GRANITA

½ cup black or dark rum
1 cup black raisins
2 pounds seedless black or purple grapes

In a small saucepan, put rum, ½ cup water, and raisins. Bring to a boil. Let cook over high heat for 2 minutes. Turn off heat and let cool.

Wash grapes. Remove from stems. Place in bowl and pour rum raisins over top. Mix well.

To make granita: Transfer ⅓ grape-raisin mixture to a food processor, and process until very smooth. Place mixture in metal pie tin and put in freezer. Break up crystals with a fork every 20 minutes. It will take up to 2 hours to freeze.

Meanwhile, refrigerate remaining marinated grape-raisin mixture until very cold.

To serve, place marinated grapes and raisins in 4 or more large wineglasses. Top with granita. Serve immediately.

Serves 4 or more

■ ■ ■

An Imagined Dinner for Julia

Consommé with Marrow

Pot-au-Feu: Chicken, Beef Shin, and Leeks

Boiled Potatoes with Caper Vinaigrette

Apples Talibur *in Puff Pastry, Apple Confit*

9 ingredients

Allow me this small indulgence of preparing a menu for Julia Child — if only on paper — just in case I don't actually get the chance to cook for her in my lifetime!

As it is perfection she's often after, simplicity pleases her . . . like that cold artichoke vinaigrette we both ordered several years ago in a friend's restaurant. We laughed at its plainness. "Isn't this lovely?" she said in that remarkably lyrical and omniscient way of hers: "These are almost extinct, you know."

Short of preparing an artichoke, I thought something French might be appropriate. Three courses and a side dish, four recipes but only nine ingredients, everything stripped to its essential, well . . . essence.

And what's a talibur? *you might ask. It's a big apple, peeled, cored, and filled with vanilla sugar and baked in puff pastry, also known, as Julia will tell you, as a* pomme en cage.

Of course we'll begin with her favorite cocktail, a three-ingredient Upside-Down Martini. For each drink: Fill a cocktail shaker with 6 ice cubes. Add 2½ ounces dry vermouth and a generous splash of gin. Stir briskly and strain into a chilled martini glass. Twist a long strip of lemon zest over drink and drop into glass.

GRAPENOTE

Begin with an Upside-Down Martini (see above). Call your favorite wineshop, say Julia Child is coming for dinner, and see what they suggest. For something affordable, try a 1993 or 1994 Côtes de Beaune from a good producer.

CONSOMMÉ WITH MARROW

8 cups broth from Pot-au-Feu: Chicken, Beef Shin, and Leeks (see the following recipe)
Marrow bones from Pot-au-Feu: Chicken, Beef Shin, and Leeks

Put 8 cups of broth through a fine-mesh sieve that has been lined with a double-layer of cheesecloth. Strain into a clean medium pot. Cook broth for 20 minutes over medium heat, until reduced to 6½ cups. Add salt to taste.

Remove marrow from bones using a long, flexible, thin-bladed knife and slice into ¼-inch-thick slices. Put 2 slices marrow into bottom of each of 6 flat soup plates. Ladle hot consommé over marrow and serve.

Serves 6

POT-AU-FEU: CHICKEN, BEEF SHIN, AND LEEKS

2½-pound organic chicken, legs trussed
5 pounds beef shin, cut by butcher into ¾-inch-thick slices
3 large leeks

Place chicken and beef shin in an 8- to 10-quart casserole or soup pot with a cover.

Wash leeks, removing any grit between leaves. Trim 2 inches off green tops of leeks and discard. Trim roots. Cut leeks into 3 sections and add to pot. Add 3½ quarts cold water to pot, making sure chicken is just covered. Add ½ teaspoon whole black peppercorns.

Bring to a boil. This will take approximately 15 minutes. Cover pot.

Lower heat to a simmer. Cook for 4½ hours over low heat. Check occasionally to make sure chicken is covered with liquid. Remove from heat.

After 4½ hours, uncover and with a ladle remove 8 cups broth and marrow bones. Reserve to make Consommé with Marrow (see the preceding recipe).

When ready to serve, gently heat pot-au-feu. With slotted spoon, transfer chicken, beef shin, and leeks to a very large platter. Spoon some of the broth over everything. Allow guests to help themselves. Serve immediately with small bowls of kosher salt.

Serves 6 or more

BOILED POTATOES WITH CAPER VINAIGRETTE

2½ pounds large potatoes, Yukon Gold, Red Bliss, or other waxy potato
⅓ cup drained capers, plus 2 tablespoons caper juice
⅓ cup extra-virgin olive oil

Scrub potatoes well, but do not peel. Bring a large pot of salted water to a boil. Add potatoes, lower heat, and cook for 30 to 40 minutes, or until potatoes are very tender when tested with the point of a small sharp knife.

Meanwhile, place capers and caper juice in a blender. While blending, slowly add olive oil until thick and emulsified. Continue to blend and slowly add ¼ cup cold water. Set aside. You will have approximately ⅞ cup caper vinaigrette.

Drain potatoes in colander.

Peel potatoes with a small knife and cut into quarters. Place warm potatoes on platter and spoon caper vinaigrette over the potatoes and serve.

Optional garnish: Sprinkle with extra capers.

Serves 6 or more

APPLES *TALIBUR* IN PUFF PASTRY, APPLE CONFIT

5 large Granny Smith apples (2 pounds)
¾ cup plus 2 teaspoons Vanilla Sugar (see page 11)
1 sheet puff pastry (8¾ ounces), chilled

Preheat oven to 400°.

Wash apples. Trim bottoms so that they sit without wobbling.

Peel and core 4 apples, leaving ¼ inch of flesh in the bottom of the apples.

Fill each cavity with 1 tablespoon Vanilla Sugar.

Cut puff pastry into 4 squares that are 4½ by 4½ inches. With a rolling pin, roll each piece of pastry to enlarge 1 inch on each side, so that each puff pastry square is 5½ by 5½ inches. You want the pastry to be thin.

Place an apple in center of a pastry square and fold one side of the pastry at a time over the top of the apple. You may gently stretch the pastry to cover. Make sure the entire apple is wrapped. Repeat with remaining 3 apples.

Place apples on shallow baking sheet and sprinkle each with ½ teaspoon Vanilla Sugar. Bake 20 minutes. Pastry will be golden, and sugar will be caramelized. Remove from oven. Let sit 20 minutes before serving. Delicious slightly warm, room temperature, or cold.

Serve with apple confit: Peel and core remaining apple. Meticulously cut into ¼-inch dice. In a small saucepan, bring 1 cup water plus remaining ½ cup Vanilla Sugar to a boil. Boil 2 minutes. Add diced apples. Lower heat to very low and simmer uncovered for 30 minutes. Let cool. Apple cubes will retain their shape. Makes 1 cup.

Serves 4

THE FOLLOWING PHOTOGRAPHS DEPICT:

Red, White, and Blueberries (page 109)

Chocolate Biscotti Terrine (page 229)

Gelato d'Arancina, *Candied Orange Peel (page 159);* Brutti ma Buoni *(Ugly but Good) Cookies (page 257)*

Roasted Nectarines with Amaretto Syrup and Amaretto Cream (page 172)

Rhubarb Compote and Sour Cream Ice Cream, Rhubarb-Pepper Syrup (page 176)

Warm Banana Tart (page 189)

Lemon-Curd Yogurt Tart (page 220)

Chocolate Dacquoise *(page 154)*

Hungry Guests

Frisée *and Beet Salad, Goat Cheese Dressing*

Chicken Fricassee with Pearl Onions and Lardons

Celery Root Gratin

Warm Banana Tarts

12 ingredients

COUNTDOWN 3-2-1:

• *One and a half hours before dinner, prep the main course. Make the chicken stock and begin to simmer the fricassee.*

• *One hour before dinner, prep the ingredients for the Celery Root Gratin, then bake thirty minutes before it is to be served.*

• *Assemble salad components and dessert a half hour before guests arrive. Do not bake the tarts.*

• *Place the tarts in the oven just as you serve the main course.*

• *Excuse yourself after twenty-five minutes (everyone will be having second helpings of the gratin) and remove the tarts from the oven.*

• *Make coffee. Serve tarts, still warm.*

This menu is meant for four hungry guests but will graciously serve six. Just make two more tarts, and you're set.

GRAPENOTE

You will need two bottles of an affordable but real French red Burgundy, like Marsannay Rouge. With dessert, a little snifter of Armagnac.

FRISÉE AND BEET SALAD, GOAT CHEESE DRESSING

6 ounces fresh plain or herb-flavored goat cheese
2 bunches frisée lettuce, or 1 large head chicory
1 large bunch fresh beets, about 1¾ pounds

Crumble cheese coarsely and place in a blender. Begin to blend and slowly add ¼ to ½ cup cold water until smooth, creamy, and thick. Place in a small bowl and add freshly ground black pepper and a pinch of salt if needed. Cover and refrigerate while you prepare salad. You will have ¾ cup dressing.

Wash lettuce and dry very thoroughly, using a salad spinner if possible. Tear lettuce into small pieces and mound in center of 4 to 6 large plates.

Peel beets using a sharp knife. Cut carefully into ¹⁄₁₆-inch-thick slices. Then cut the slices into very thin threadlike julienned strips.

Spoon dressing over top of greens, covering lightly but thoroughly. Scatter julienned beets on top of salad. Serve immediately and pass the pepper mill.

Serves 4 to 6

CHICKEN FRICASSEE WITH PEARL ONIONS AND LARDONS

*4-pound chicken ***

4-ounce piece of slab bacon

½ pound tiny pearl onions, peeled

Cut breast in quarters and remaining chicken into 6 pieces, removing wing tips.

Remove giblets from chicken and any extraneous pockets of fat.

In a small nonstick skillet, place chicken fat, chicken liver, and 3 chopped pearl onions. Cook over low heat for 10 minutes and set aside.

In a small saucepan put remaining giblets, wing tips, and 1½ cups cold water. Add ¼ teaspoon salt and 10 black peppercorns. Bring to a boil. Lower heat and simmer 30 minutes. Strain through a fine-mesh sieve and set aside.

Meanwhile cut bacon into ¼-inch-thick slices, then cut across into ½-inch-wide pieces. These are lardons.

Place lardons in a very large skillet, large enough to accommodate the chicken pieces in one layer. Cook lardons over medium heat until they begin to crisp and the fat is rendered, about 5 minutes. Add chicken pieces, skin side down, and cook until golden brown and crispy, about 20 minutes.

Turn chicken pieces over and add onions. Cook over high heat until onions begin to caramelize, about 5 minutes.

Add reserved chicken stock and cook over high heat for 10 minutes.

Reduce heat to low and cover pan. Cook 1 hour or longer, until chicken is tender. Turn chicken twice during cooking.

Meanwhile, place reserved cooked liver and any juices in blender. Puree until very smooth. You will use this to thicken sauce.

When chicken is tender, remove from pan, with onions and lardons, to a platter.

Add pureed liver to pan and whisk into juices. Cook over high heat for 1 minute until sauce is thickened. Add salt and freshly ground black pepper to taste. Pour sauce over chicken and serve immediately.

Serves 4 to 6

* Use a free-range chicken if possible.

CELERY ROOT GRATIN

2 pounds celery root (1 large or 2 medium)
2 cups half-and-half
1 cup freshly grated Parmigiano-Reggiano cheese

Preheat oven to 350°.

Peel celery root with small, sharp knife. Cut into thin slices, approximately ¼ inch thick.

Place sliced celery root into a heavy medium pot with a cover.

Add half-and-half, ½ teaspoon salt, and ⅛ teaspoon freshly ground white pepper. Bring to a boil. Cover pot and cook over low heat for 15 minutes.

Transfer half of celery root with half of cream to a shallow casserole, approximately 9 by 11 inches.

Sprinkle with half of cheese and a grinding of black pepper. Add remaining celery root and cream. Top with remaining cheese.

Bake for 20 to 25 minutes. Place under broiler for 1 to 2 minutes until cheese is golden brown. Serve hot. (Any liquid that accumulates on the bottom of the casserole will be reabsorbed almost immediately after it is removed from the oven.)

Serves 4 to 6

WARM BANANA TARTS

1 sheet frozen puff pastry (8¾ ounces)
½ cup good-quality apricot jam
3 small, firm, ripe bananas

Preheat oven to 375°.

Thaw pastry according to package directions. While pastry is cold, roll out with rolling pin to stretch dough approximately ¼ inch longer and ¼ inch wider.

Cut dough into quarters so that you have 4 squares. Place a piece of pastry in each of 4 4½-inch fluted removable-bottom tart pans.

Press down with your fingers to secure dough in pan. Press pastry up sides of tart pans and remove excess dough by moving rolling pin on tops of pans. Or you may trim with a knife. Prick bottom of pastry several times with a fork.

Melt jam and 2 tablespoons water in a small saucepan over low heat. Slice bananas into very thin pieces, then arrange in tart pans in an overlapping pattern, in 2 layers.

Using pastry brush, cover tops of tarts lightly, but thoroughly, with melted jam, being careful not to let jam drip over the edges or it will be difficult to remove pastry from tart pans. Bake tarts 25 minutes. Remove from oven.

Lightly brush tops of tarts with more melted jam. Let cool in pans. Remove tarts from pans before serving.

Makes 4 tarts

■ ■ ■

Café Caribe

Jumbo Lump Crab, Avocado Sauce

Chicken Paillards, Adobo Style

Smoky Pink Beans and Rice

Coconut Ice Cream with Blue Curaçao

12 ingredients

On the little island of Tropicali at the Café Caribe is a beautiful woman who is chef.

People come from far and wide to appreciate Miss Marley's good looks but also her good cooking.

As the lowering sun casts shadows upon the coral sands, natives doff their shoes, then wrap themselves tightly in colorful sheets embroidered with golden threads.

Like clockwork this procession reggaes along the beach to the little restaurant-on-stilts.

Miss Marley, a bronzed Rapunzel, lets down her hair, which actually doubles as the dinner bell. Long strands of tiny shells flap in the wind beckoning everyone to sit down to their first course: a salad of the-sea-and-the-tree.

But for dinner you have a choice. You can have chicken and rice, or chicken or rice. It's up to you, and it's always delicious.

And every night, as the iridescent moon glitters like a disco ball, Miss Marley serves dessert: coconut ice cream in a blue lagoon.

GRAPENOTE

Have a fanciful tropical rum drink or a crisp, next-to-no-wood chardonnay: Jepson or St. Andrews from California or de Wetshof from South Africa.

JUMBO LUMP CRAB, AVOCADO SAUCE

4 small ripe avocados
1 pound jumbo lump crabmeat
4 large limes

Cut avocados in half lengthwise. Remove the pits. Cut a small slice from bottom of 4 halves, so the avocados won't wobble. Save bottom slices for garnishing.

Pick through crabmeat to remove any cartilage. Fill these 4 avocado halves with crabmeat to cover. Cover with dampened paper towels while you prepare sauce, or refrigerate, covered, until later.

To make sauce: Scoop out avocado flesh from remaining halves. Add to food processor, along with ¼ cup fresh lime juice (you will need to squeeze 2 or 3 limes), approximately ¾ cup cold water, and salt and freshly ground black pepper to taste. Process until very smooth and thick.

To serve, mound avocado sauce on top of each crab-stuffed avocado half. Stick small piece of reserved avocado shell on top. Spoon additional sauce on plates and garnish with lime slices cut from remaining lime.

Serves 4

CHICKEN PAILLARDS, ADOBO STYLE

4 whole skinless boneless chicken breasts (about 1¾ pounds)
4 large cloves garlic, pushed through garlic press
2½ teaspoons ground cumin

Cut chicken breasts in half to make 8 halves. Place breasts between waxed paper and pound lightly with mallet to flatten.

Place flattened breasts in large dish with garlic, 2 teaspoons cumin, 1 teaspoon kosher salt, ¼ teaspoon each freshly ground white pepper and black pepper. Cover and marinate in the refrigerator for 2 hours.

Heat 2 large nonstick skillets and cook breasts quickly over medium-high heat for 2 to 3 minutes on each side.

Serve immediately, dusted with remaining ground cumin.

Serves 4

SMOKY PINK BEANS AND RICE

½ pound kidney or small pink beans
4 slices hickory-smoked bacon, cut into ¼-inch dice
½ cup extra-long-grain rice

Sort beans and soak overnight or use quick-soak method: Cover beans with 2 inches of water, bring to a boil, boil 2 minutes and remove from heat. Cover and let sit for 1 hour.

Drain beans in colander. Add to heavy medium pot with 4 cups or enough water to cover and ¼ teaspoon whole black peppercorns. Let cook, with cover askew, over medium heat for 1 hour.

Heat bacon slowly in medium nonstick skillet until fat is reduced and bacon is cooked but not crisp.

Add to beans along with bacon fat. Add rice, stir well, and cover.

Continue to cook another 30 minutes, or until beans are tender and rice is cooked. Drain in fine-mesh sieve. If any liquid remains, reduce it over high heat to ¼ cup and add to beans. Season with salt and freshly ground black pepper to taste.

Serves 4

COCONUT ICE CREAM WITH BLUE CURAÇAO

2 cups whole milk
1½ cups sweetened coconut milk *
6 tablespoons blue curaçao, chilled

In a heavy medium pot bring the milk to a boil. Whisk in the coconut milk and a pinch of salt. Turn off the heat.

Pass the mixture through a fine-mesh sieve into a medium bowl. Let cool. Cover and refrigerate several hours, until the mixture is very cold.

Transfer mixture to an ice-cream maker and pre-

pare according to the manufacturer's instructions.

When ready to serve, scoop ice cream into chilled martini glasses. Spoon 1½ tablespoons blue curaçao carefully into each glass, around, not over, the ice cream. Serve immediately.

Serves 4 or more

* Use a brand such as Coco Lopez.

An Ode to Spain

Chilled Tomato-Orange Soup with Tarragon
Manchego Chicken with Prosciutto
Açorda: *Garlic Bread Pudding*
Pepper Confit with Sherry Vinegar
Baked Chocolate Crema
15 ingredients

As food consultants my husband and I travel the world — eating, drinking, and creating restaurants. One memorable excursion was two weeks of "research" (which means eating gloriously) in Catalonia to plan all the restaurants at Hotel Arts Barcelona.

Aside from Barcelona's obvious yet unforgettable attractions — the Ramblas, the architecture of Gaudi, and the palpable national pride — one remembers the food, the wine, the relaxed sophistication of dining out.

Each dish of my Catalan-inspired menu was kindled by a singular flavor, an ingredient, a preparation, an experience:

- SOUP. *Clean, vivid gazpacho-like tomato-orange flavors accented with tarragon.*

- MAIN COURSE. *Simple griddled chicken layered with nutty Manchego, a full-flavored sheep's-milk cheese from La Mancha, and mountain-cured Jabugo ham; since Jabugo is unavailable here, you'll use prosciutto.*

- SIDE DISHES. *The classic, garlic-laden açorda — a savory bread pudding — alongside a vivid confit of peppers in sherry vinegar.*

- DESSERT. *A chocolate version of the classic* crema catalana.

GRAPENOTE

Have a small glass of chilled Lustau Papirusa fino sherry with the soup. Balance the salty component of the chicken with a soft and fruity malvasia from the Toro region of Spain or a white from the adjacent area, Rueda.

CHILLED TOMATO-ORANGE SOUP WITH TARRAGON

28-ounce can best-quality whole tomatoes in puree*
1 cup freshly squeezed orange juice
1 tablespoon fresh tarragon leaves, plus extra for garnishing

In bowl of food processor, put tomatoes, tomato puree, and orange juice. Process until very smooth.

Add 1 tablespoon tarragon leaves and freshly ground black pepper. Process again until very smooth. You will not need to add salt.

Transfer contents to a container and chill several hours until very cold.

Serve in a chilled flat soup plate with a few leaves of tarragon as garnish.

Serves 4 to 6 (makes 4 cups)

* Redpack brand is a good choice.

MANCHEGO CHICKEN WITH PROSCIUTTO

12 pieces thin-sliced chicken breast cutlets (2 pounds)
12 thin slices prosciutto (about 3 ounces)
6 ounces Manchego cheese

Lightly season chicken cutlets with salt and freshly ground white pepper, and place on flat surface. Place 1 slice prosciutto on each of 6 cutlets.

Remove rind from cheese and cut into thin slices. Place several slices of cheese on top of prosciutto to cover evenly. Top with another chicken breast to make a "sandwich," pressing down to form a tight package.

Spray a large nonstick skillet with vegetable spray. Heat, and when hot, add the chicken. Sauté 3 minutes over medium heat on one side, until golden. Turn over, sauté on the other side for 2 minutes, then cover and let cook 2 or 3 minutes, until chicken is cooked through and cheese is melted. To serve, drape remaining slice of prosciutto over each breast. Sprinkle with freshly ground black pepper.

Serves 6

AÇORDA: GARLIC BREAD PUDDING

1 pound good-quality round loaf peasant, Tuscan, or sourdough bread
3 tablespoons finely chopped fresh garlic (10 to 12 small cloves)
½ cup plus 3 tablespoons extra-virgin olive oil

Preheat oven to 300°.

Cut bread into 1-inch-thick slices. Place in shallow baking pan and bake 20 minutes, until bread is dry and feels "stale." Let cool.

Preheat oven to 350°.

Crumble bread into irregular 1-inch pieces and put in large bowl with chopped garlic, ½ teaspoon salt, and freshly ground black pepper.

Slowly pour in 2 cups boiling water and stir in ½ cup olive oil. Mix well until all the bread is moistened, adding up to ½ cup more water if needed.

Transfer to a shallow casserole, 9 by 13 inches, and pack down with spatula. Drizzle 3 tablespoons oil on top. Bake 30 minutes, or until you have a crisp golden crust on top.

Serves 6 to 8

PEPPER CONFIT WITH SHERRY VINEGAR

4 large red and yellow bell peppers (about 1½ pounds)
¼ cup extra-virgin olive oil
2 tablespoons or more Spanish sherry vinegar

Wash peppers and dry. Cut each pepper into 8 large wedges. Remove core and any seeds.

Place peppers, olive oil, 2 tablespoons vinegar, and 10 whole black peppercorns in a heavy medium pot with a cover.

Bring to a boil. Cover pot and reduce heat to low. Simmer for 45 minutes without lifting cover, as the steam helps soften the peppers. Shake pot back and forth several times during cooking.

Transfer peppers and juices to a platter. Add salt if desired or sprinkle with a little more sherry vinegar. Delicious served hot, warm, room temperature, or chilled.

Serves 6

BAKED CHOCOLATE *CREMA*

2 cups heavy cream
6 ounces good-quality milk chocolate
4 extra-large egg yolks

Preheat oven to 325°.

Heat cream in a small heavy saucepan. Chop chocolate into small pieces and place in cream. Heat over low heat for several minutes until chocolate is completely melted and mixture is smooth. Stir constantly with wooden spoon or small whisk.

In the bowl of an electric mixer, beat egg yolks until slightly thickened and a paler yellow color. Pour the hot chocolate cream over yolks, a little at a time, beating constantly.

Pour mixture into 6 5-ounce molds or ramekins. Place in large baking pan and pour boiling water into pan almost to the tops of the molds.

Bake 25 minutes. Mixture will still be loose but will firm up when chilled.

Refrigerate several hours. Remove from refrigerator 30 minutes before serving.

Serves 6

A Middle Eastern Affair

Turkish Eggplant Flan

Fesenjune: *Chicken Breasts in Walnut and Pomegranate Sauce*

Toasted Orzo with Rice

Poached Prunes with Cardamom Yogurt

12 ingredients

Kitchen diplomacy.

With ancient dishes hailing from Turkey, Persia, Syria, and other sandy lands, this menu transcends politics. Without borders, these recipes from the land of figs and olives get along quite nicely.

Eggplant flan tastes like smoky baba ghanouj suspended in a feta soufflé and is lovely direct from the oven or cooled to room temperature.

Fesenjune tastes like no chicken you've ever had before. This unfamiliar Persian dish will bewitch and bewilder your palate. An amazing compilation of sweet, sour, salty, and bitter flavors seduces slowly, but completely. I am grateful to Lynn Fredericks, a food and wine writer, whose Iranian friend shared this dish with her, then she with me. Lynn says, "It's even better the second day . . . and the third. But beware: The sauce looks like chocolate."

GRAPENOTE

A challenge to be sure, but your best bets would be Penfolds Semchard from Australia, or go in another direction with Jade Mountain La Provencale, a spirited red wine made with *mourvèdre* and *syrah* grapes from California.

TURKISH EGGPLANT FLAN

2 large eggplants (1¼ pounds each)
5 extra-large eggs
10 ounces feta cheese*

Preheat oven to 450°.

Over open gas fire, or on baking sheet under the broiler, place eggplants and blacken skin for several minutes on each side. Turn carefully using tongs. You will begin to detect a smoky fragrance.

Line a pan with foil and bake eggplants on baking sheet for 50 minutes. Remove from oven. Let cool.

Reduce oven heat to 350°.

Cut eggplants in half lengthwise and remove all the flesh using a spoon. Discard skin. Place flesh in colander and let drain 10 minutes.

In bowl of electric mixer, beat eggs until light. Add eggplant and blend thoroughly. Add 8 ounces crumbled feta cheese, ¼ teaspoon salt, and lots of freshly ground black pepper. Beat well to incorporate cheese.

Put mixture in an 8-cup soufflé dish. Create a water bath by placing the filled soufflé dish in a deep baking pan that will accommodate the dish. Fill baking pan with boiling water almost up to the top of soufflé dish. Bake 45 minutes. Remove from oven, then preheat broiler. Carefully lift soufflé dish from water bath. Slice remaining 2 ounces cheese paper thin and place on top of flan. Put under broiler for 30 seconds, until cheese begins to melt. Serve flan immediately, or let cool to room temperature.

Serves 6

* You may also use a flavored feta cheese.

FESENJUNE: CHICKEN BREASTS IN WALNUT AND POMEGRANATE SAUCE

⅔ pound walnut pieces
3 split (6 pieces) chicken breasts (4½ pounds), bone in and skin on
7 tablespoons or more pomegranate molasses *

Put walnuts in bowl of a food processor and finely grind almost to a paste. In a large nonstick skillet, brown walnuts slowly over medium heat, stirring constantly with a wooden spoon. Adjust heat so they do not burn but turn dark very slowly.

After approximately 15 minutes, walnuts will be a deep chocolate color; remove from heat and place in a large, heavy pot, big enough to accommodate chicken in a single layer. A 12-inch, 8¾-quart Le Creuset casserole works beautifully.

Wipe the large nonstick skillet clean with a paper towel. Add chicken breasts skin side down and brown on both sides over medium heat until chicken is almost cooked through, about 10 minutes on each side. Season well with salt and freshly ground black pepper. Meanwhile add 3½ cups water to casserole with nuts.

When chicken is browned, remove along with pan juices that have accumulated and add to casserole. Bring to a boil, immediately lower heat, and simmer slowly until thickened, about 15 minutes. Remove chicken with slotted spoon and continue cooking until sauce is thick; the time required will vary.

Once sauce is thick, add pomegranate molasses, salt, and freshly ground pepper. Cook over medium-high heat and reduce sauce for 5 minutes longer. You will need to adjust seasonings to your liking. What you're looking for is a balance of salty, bitter, sour, and sweet. Play with the amounts of salt and pomegranate molasses. Return chicken to casserole and heat for a few minutes until hot.

Serves 6

* Use Cortas brand from Lebanon, available in many Middle Eastern food stores.

TOASTED ORZO WITH RICE

3 tablespoons unsalted butter
1 cup orzo
1 cup extra-long-grain rice

In a heavy medium saucepan with cover, melt 2½ tablespoons butter.

Add orzo and cook over medium heat, stirring often, until orzo turns a dark golden brown and butter is bubbly. Do not let butter brown. This will take 2 to 3 minutes.

Add rice and cook 1 minute, stirring constantly. Add 2 cups boiling water, ¼ teaspoon salt, and cover. Lower heat, and simmer 15 minutes. Do not uncover.

Turn off heat and let sit 20 minutes. The steam will continue to cook the orzo and rice.

After 20 minutes, remove cover. Fluff with a fork and add remaining ½ tablespoon butter, salt, and freshly ground black pepper. Serve immediately.

Serves 6

POACHED PRUNES WITH CARDAMOM YOGURT

1 pound large prunes with pits
4 cups vanilla yogurt
1½ teaspoons ground cardamom

Place prunes in medium pot with water just to cover. Bring to a boil. Lower heat, cover, and simmer for 15 minutes. Let cool in liquid. Refrigerate 1 to 2 days, until prune liquid has thickened. Or remove prunes with a slotted spoon and cook juices over high heat until reduced by a third. Add prunes to reduced liquid and refrigerate until very cold.

Drain yogurt in sieve or strainer lined with cheesecloth or a coffee filter. Place over a bowl to catch whey. Let sit 1 hour. You will have about 3 cups. Discard liquid residue.

Mix thickened yogurt with 1 teaspoon cardamom, stirring well.

To serve, place ¼ cup cardamom yogurt in bottom of large wineglass. Carefully place 6 to 8 drained prunes on top with 1 to 2 tablespoons prune liquid. Top with additional ¼ cup cardamom yogurt. You may sprinkle a little extra cardamom on top. Serve immediately.

Serves 6

■ ■ ■

Homage to Lutetia

Spinach and Smoked Salmon Terrine Lutèce

Cornish Hens with Tarragon Rice

Belgian Endive and Blue Cheese Gratin

Crème Brûlée

12 ingredients

Lutetia, as some may know, was the long-ago name for the city of Paris. Lutèce, as many more may know, is one of New York's revered restaurants, whose legendary chef André Soltner, and now Eberhard Muller, have kept classic French cuisine alive and well, but never stuck in the mud of time.

Make this menu, and you'll feel like a four-star chef. Spinach and salmon terrine, a recipe adapted from Soltner, is beautiful with its many layers of bright pinks and greens.

Cornish Hens with Tarragon Rice gets a flavor bonus from homemade stock and cooked giblets added for depth.

Its incomparable side dish of Belgian endive swaddled in blue cheese sauce is surprisingly low in calories and may be eaten with great élan.

Save room for the entremets, the sweet course. There's very little to tell you about crème brûlée that you don't already know. It's to die for, and this recipe is vintage.

GRAPENOTE

Begin with a sparkling Vouvray from the Loire. Switch to Bourgueil or Chinon, light but luscious reds, from the same region.

SPINACH AND SMOKED SALMON TERRINE LUTÈCE

1 pound fresh spinach
2 sticks (½ pound) unsalted butter, at room temperature
1 pound thinly sliced smoked salmon

Wash spinach well and remove stems. Save a few leaves as a garnish. Set aside. Bring large pot of salted water to a boil. Add remaining leaves to boiling water and cook 30 seconds. Place in colander, then plunge leaves in bowl of ice water. Squeeze spinach to remove excess water. Place spinach in food processor. Cut butter into small pieces and add, except for 1 tablespoon. Add freshly ground black pepper and process until you have a paste.

Use 1 tablespoon of butter to coat bottom of a 1½-quart terrine, loaf pan, or bowl with tall sides.

Line with plastic wrap. Put down layer of smoked salmon, ¼-inch layer of spinach mixture, layer of smoked salmon, and alternate, ending with layer of smoked salmon. You will have 3 layers of spinach.

Refrigerate 3 hours. Unmold (if necessary, dip bottom of mold quickly into hot water). Cut terrine into ½-inch-thick slices. Serve 1 or 2 slices with fresh spinach leaves as a garnish.

Serves 8

CORNISH HENS WITH TARRAGON RICE

4 medium-large Cornish hens (1¾ pounds each)
2 cups extra-long-grain rice
2 large bunches fresh tarragon

Remove giblets from Cornish hens. Discard livers.

Bring 5½ cups water to a boil in a medium pot. Add giblets, ½ teaspoon whole black peppercorns, and 1 teaspoon salt and cook over medium heat for 45 minutes with a cover askew.

Remove giblets with slotted spoon and place on a cutting board. Chop giblets into small pieces.

Preheat oven to 350°.

Bring broth back to a boil and cook over high heat until reduced to 4½ cups. Add rice and cover. Lower heat to simmer, and cook 20 minutes, until water is absorbed, but rice is still moist. Chop 1 bunch tarragon leaves so that you have 6 tablespoons, saving some whole leaves for garnish. Add chopped tarragon to rice along with chopped giblets, and stir well.

Stuff Cornish hens fully with rice mixture, packing well. Truss hens with kitchen string. Rub salt and freshly ground black pepper into skin of hens.

Scatter remaining bunch of tarragon on bottom of heavy shallow roasting pan. Place hens on top. Roast for 40 minutes, basting once during cooking with juices from bottom of pan.

Place under broiler for 1 minute, or until hens are a rich, golden brown. Remove from oven and let rest 5 minutes. Cut hens in half. Serve hens with rice, crisped tarragon, and pan juices. Sprinkle with reserved tarragon leaves that have been coarsely chopped.

Serves 8

BELGIAN ENDIVE AND BLUE CHEESE GRATIN

8 large Belgian endives (2½ pounds)
8 ounces Danish blue cheese
¾ cup heavy cream

Preheat oven to 350°.

Wash endives and trim bottoms with sharp knife. Drop into a medium-large pot of salted boiling water, bring to a boil again, lower heat, and simmer 10 minutes.

Drain, cool, and squeeze gently to remove as much moisture as possible.

Place endives in heavy shallow casserole large enough to hold them in one layer. Sprinkle with freshly ground black pepper. Crumble cheese on top of endives and pour cream over the top.

Bake in top third of oven for 30 minutes, and then put under broiler for 1 minute, until endives are lightly browned. Let cool for 5 minutes, then serve with cream sauce spooned over top of endives.

Serves 8

CRÈME BRÛLÉE

3 cups heavy cream
6 extra-large egg yolks
9 tablespoons plus ⅓ cup granulated sugar or Vanilla Sugar (page 11)

Preheat oven to 300°.

Put cream in heavy medium saucepan and cook over low heat to just below a boil. Lower heat immediately and simmer 1 minute.

Put egg yolks and 9 tablespoons sugar in bowl of electric mixer. Whip on medium speed until thick and pale yellow, about 5 minutes.

Gradually add hot cream to yolks, whipping at low speed until just blended. Ladle custard into 8 6-ounce ramekins or crème brûlée dishes. Set in large baking pan.

Add boiling water to pan to reach almost to the top of the ramekins or crème brûlée dishes.

Bake 40 minutes or until set. Remove carefully from water bath and cool for 45 minutes. Cover with waxed paper and refrigerate at least 2 hours, until custard is very cold.

When ready to serve, preheat broiler. Sprinkle each with 2 teaspoons sugar. Place under broiler to caramelize sugar. Watch carefully, as sugar burns quickly. Let cool a few minutes until sugar hardens, then serve.

Serves 8

One Duck, Two Courses

Warm Duck Liver Salad

Crisped Duck with Roasted Turnips, Port Wine Reduction

A Simple Strudel

9 ingredients

We've had many a great duck in our day: At Ferdinand's in Cambridge, Massachusetts, crisp duckling came with fresh cherry sauce; Paul Steindler's Duck Joint in New York City boasted a juicy rendition done up with green peppercorns; our favorite duck à l'orange hailed from Laserre in Paris; slow-roasted duck bedded on braised red cabbage came from the wonderful Hungarian restaurant Emke on Manhattan's Upper East Side.

The list goes on, but what all these birds had in common was their crisp, crackling exteriors and succulent, gamy flesh.

My method for cooking duck guarantees a crisp skin every time. And if you're lucky, you'll find two livers in your giblet pouch, as I occasionally do.

In Central Europe, where there's duck, there's strudel. This version relies on the inherent sweetness of dried apples, cooked and enrobed in many layers of buttery, crisp phyllo.

Prepare dessert just before you cook the duck, as the strudel is best when served within three hours of baking. All this effort results in a munificent dinner for 4, including seconds on dessert.

GRAPENOTE

My husband often starts a meal like this with a snifter of Calvados. You might want to save yours for dessert. Conventional wisdom tells us to drink what we've cooked with, but in this case a lovely Cornas or a lush-style zinfandel is in order, and not a bottle of port.

WARM DUCK LIVER SALAD

1 small head leaf lettuce
Duck skin, fat, giblets, and liver from Crisped Duck with Roasted Turnips, Port Wine Reduction
(see following recipe)
¼ cup white balsamic vinegar

Wash leaf lettuce well. Pat dry with paper towels. Tear dark outer leaves with your hands and place approximately 1 cup leaves in center of 4 large plates.

Crumble enough of the reserved cooked duck skin to make 4 tablespoons. Set aside.

Heat 3 tablespoons reserved duck fat in large non-stick skillet. Add liver and very thinly sliced giblets. Cook over medium heat for a few minutes until liver is cooked but still pink in the center.

Remove duck liver and giblets with slotted spoon.

Slice liver into 4 pieces, on the bias, and put in center of lettuce with giblets surrounding it.

Add vinegar to the pan and cook over high heat for 1 minute until syrupy. Add salt and a generous grinding of black pepper.

Pour over greens. Sprinkle with crumbled duck skin. Serve immediately while duck is resting.

Serves 4

CRISPED DUCK WITH ROASTED TURNIPS, PORT WINE REDUCTION

5-pound fresh duck
16 small white turnips (2 pounds), peeled and cut in half
2 cups tawny port

Preheat oven to 350°.

Remove giblets and wing tips from the duck. Set liver aside to make Warm Duck Liver Salad (see preceding recipe), wrapping it well and putting it in the refrigerator.

Put giblets and wing tips in a medium saucepan with cold water to cover. Add ¼ teaspoon whole black peppercorns and ½ teaspoon salt. Bring to a boil. Lower heat and cook for 1 hour. Strain through a coarse-mesh sieve into a clean pot. Discard wing tips and save giblets for making the Warm Duck Liver Salad. Cook stock over medium heat and reduce until you have ½ cup. Set aside.

Remove lobes of fat from duck and discard. Wash duck well and dry. Prick duck skin all over with a fork. Rub salt and freshly ground black pepper into skin. Truss duck with string.

Place duck on a rack fit in a broiler pan. Roast for 1¼ hours. Remove duck from rack. Pour off fat and save 3 tablespoons for Warm Duck Liver Salad. Place duck directly in broiler pan. Place turnips around

duck and return it to oven. After 25 minutes, turn turnips over. Cook an additional 20 minutes. Raise oven temperature to 500°. Cook duck 15 minutes longer. Total cooking time for duck will be 2¼ hours.

While duck is cooking, make the port wine reduction. In a medium saucepan, put ½ cup reduced duck stock and add 1 cup port. Bring to a boil and cook over medium heat until reduced to ½ cup, about 15 minutes. In a small saucepan, cook 1 cup port until it is reduced to 3 tablespoons. Add duck stock–port reduction and cook a few minutes, until sauce is syrupy. You will have approximately ½ cup. Season to taste with salt and freshly ground black pepper.

Remove duck and turnips from oven. Remove duck wings and enough skin to obtain 4 tablespoons of skin. Make salad (preceding page) and let duck rest. Remove string and cut duck into quarters or as desired.

Serve with turnips and port wine reduction.

Serves 4

A SIMPLE STRUDEL

4 cups (10 ounces) dried apple slices
5 tablespoons unsalted butter
7 sheets phyllo dough

Preheat oven to 375°.

Place dried apples in a medium pot. Add 2 cups cold water. Bring to a boil. Lower heat, cover pot, and cook over medium heat for 20 minutes.

Uncover pot. Heat over high heat for 1 to 2 minutes, until all the water is evaporated. Break up pieces gently with a wooden spoon. Add 1 tablespoon cold butter. You will have about 2¾ cups apple compote. Set aside to cool.

Melt remaining 4 tablespoons butter in a small saucepan.

Lay sheets of phyllo dough on a flat surface. Using a pastry brush, brush butter lightly on each sheet of phyllo and restack them as you go.

Place apple compote in a strip 3 inches from and parallel to one of the short sides of the phyllo, then roll up tightly, jelly-roll style. Place on a baking sheet.

Brush top generously with remaining butter and bake for 25 minutes. Let cool before serving, but do not refrigerate. Best served within 3 hours of baking.

Serves 6 or more

My 15-Ingredient Thanksgiving Feast

Brine-Cured Turkey Breast with Turkey Bacon and Roasted Pears, Roasted Pear "Gravy"

Smooth and Chunky Turnip Puree, Caramelized Shallots

Sweet Potato–Cheddar Gratin

Ruby Cranberries with Sun-Dried Cherries: Relish and Compote

Pumpkin-Eggnog Flan, Custard Sauce

"Those who cook holiday dinners at home can give thanks for the revival of that most sensible culinary trend, 'simplicity,'" proclaimed USA Today *(November 21, 1996), which asked me to create a Thanksgiving meal using only 15 ingredients.*

The menu, extremely bounteous and beautiful, relies on some interesting techniques to maximize flavors. Immersing a turkey breast in salt water creates moist, smoothly textured flesh. A mantle of turkey bacon adds a subtle smoky flavor and makes the bird "self-basting." Roasted pear gravy looks like the traditional stuff, but with no flour.

The same three ingredients, cranberries, brown sugar, and sun-dried cherries, yield two surprisingly different results: a cooked compote and an uncooked sprightly relish.

Pumpkin-eggnog flan, cooked in a water bath, has pumpkin pie flavor without the crust.

Soak the turkey for six hours before preparing the meal, and the sweet potatoes, cranberries, and dessert can be prepared the day before with great success.

Instead of a first course, I serve sherry and walnuts.

There is much to be thankful for.

GRAPENOTE

Here are *three* choices covering a spectrum of tastes: California chardonnay (Acacia) with a touch of oak and an apple-pear bouquet. It's the right white for turkey. Oregon pinot noir (Benton Lane), a softer red with mild tannins, has a cherry-berry quality. It also picks up the sweetness of the sweet potatoes. For a bigger red, try a merlot (Rodney Strong) displaying herbal and smoky notes that pick up on the bacon and cheddar flavors.

BRINE-CURED TURKEY BREAST WITH TURKEY BACON AND ROASTED PEARS, ROASTED PEAR "GRAVY"

6½- to 7-pound all-natural turkey breast
12 ounces thinly-sliced turkey bacon
8 assorted large firm pears (about 3 pounds), such as Bartlett, Comice, or Anjou

Soak breast in large bowl or pot of cold water to cover with 1 pound kosher salt. Place in refrigerator for 6 hours. Remove breast, rinse under cold water, and pat dry.

Preheat oven to 350°.

Season breast with 1 teaspoon coarse-grind black pepper. Remove pop-up if there is one. Lay strips of turkey bacon in tightly overlapping pattern to cover entire breast. Secure with toothpicks, if needed. Wrap breast tightly with double layer of cheesecloth: First wrap around the breast, then wrap front to back, making sure top, bottom, and sides are covered.

Place breast in large, heavy flat roasting pan. Cover breast tightly with foil. Roast for 1¼ hours. Wash pears. Cut them in half lengthwise and remove seeds and stems. (You may want to leave a few stems on for decorative purposes.) After 1¼ hours, place pears, cut side down, around the turkey. Roast another 45 minutes. Remove foil and turn pears over. Roast another 30 minutes, or until meat thermometer registers 160°. (Total cooking time is approximately 2½ hours.)

Remove pan from oven. Transfer turkey and pears to large platter. Let turkey rest 15 minutes while you prepare the gravy.

To pan juices add 2 cups boiling water and scrape up all drippings and brown bits. Pour through fine-mesh sieve. Reserve.

Cut half of pears into chunks and place in blender. Process until very smooth, slowly adding reserved liquid. Transfer gravy to small pot and keep warm, adding salt and freshly ground black pepper to taste.

Carefully remove cheesecloth. Present turkey to guests and then carve. Remove bacon, and slice breast. Serve turkey slices with some turkey bacon, roasted pear half, and hot roasted pear gravy.

Serves 8

SMOOTH AND CHUNKY TURNIP PUREE, CARAMELIZED SHALLOTS

3 pounds medium white turnips
¾ pound medium shallots
4 tablespoons salted butter

Peel turnips. Place in large pot with salted water to cover. Bring to a boil. Lower heat and continue cooking 30 to 35 minutes, or until turnips are soft.

Meanwhile, peel shallots. If very large, cut shallots in half. Heat butter in a large nonstick skillet and add shallots. Cook over low heat for 25 to 30 minutes, until shallots are soft, brown, and caramelized. Do not let shallots get too brown. Reserve, keeping shallots warm.

Drain turnips in colander. Cut into large chunks and process in food processor until fairly smooth, with some chunky pieces remaining. Transfer turnips to bowl and fold in half of caramelized shallots and liquid from pan. Season to taste with salt and freshly ground black pepper. Top with remaining shallots.

Serve hot or reheat gently in a large covered saucepan.

Serves 8 or more

SWEET POTATO–CHEDDAR GRATIN

3 pounds sweet potatoes
¾ pound sharp white cheddar cheese
1 cup sour cream

Preheat oven to 350°.

Boil the unpeeled sweet potatoes in salted water for 15 to 20 minutes, until you can pierce them easily with a fork, but do not let them get too soft. Drain in colander under cold water, and peel. Cut into ⅓-inch-thick slices and pat dry with paper towels.

Grate cheddar cheese on large holes of box grater. Set aside. Line the bottom of a 9-inch removable-bottom springform pan with a round of waxed paper or aluminum foil. Sprinkle ½ cup cheese on bottom.

Add a layer of sweet potato slices (overlapping slightly) until bottom is covered. Spread ⅓ cup sour cream over potatoes. Sprinkle with salt and freshly ground white pepper, and cover with a third of the remaining grated cheese. Repeat process twice, ending with a layer of cheese. Press down with spatula.

Place pan on baking sheet. Bake 40 minutes, until golden brown. Press down with spatula once during baking. Let rest 10 minutes before serving. Much of the liquid will be reabsorbed. Loosen edges of gratin with knife. Remove from pan and cut into wedges.

This is even better when reheated the next day.

Serves 8 to 12

RUBY CRANBERRIES WITH SUN-DRIED CHERRIES: RELISH AND COMPOTE

RELISH

12 ounces (about 3 cups) cranberries
4 ounces (about ¾ cup) sun-dried cherries
¾ cup packed dark brown sugar

Put cranberries and sun-dried cherries in small bowl. Mix gently. Add half of mixture to food processor container. Process until mixture is coarsely, but evenly, chopped. Transfer to bowl. Repeat with remaining mixture. Add brown sugar to cranberry-cherry mixture with pinch of salt and grinding of black pepper. Mix very well so that all sugar is incorporated and dissolved. Cover and let sit in refrigerator 24 hours before serving.

Makes 2½ cups

COMPOTE

⅔ cup packed dark brown sugar
12 ounces (about 3 cups) cranberries
4 ounces (about ¾ cup) sun-dried cherries

In a heavy medium saucepan put 1 cup water, brown sugar, pinch of salt, and 12 whole black peppercorns or a liberal grinding of black pepper. Bring to a boil; add cranberries and sun-dried cherries. Return to a boil, reduce heat, and cook over medium heat for 10 minutes, or until cranberries have popped and sauce has thickened. Cool at room temperature, cover, and refrigerate until cold.

Makes 2¼ cups

PUMPKIN-EGGNOG FLAN, CUSTARD SAUCE

2 level cups pumpkin pie filling
4 cups eggnog *
4 extra-large eggs

Preheat oven to 350°.

In bowl of electric mixer, put pumpkin pie filling and 3 cups eggnog. Mix well. Add eggs and blend very well.

Pour mixture evenly into 8 6-ounce custard cups. Place cups in a deep baking pan. Pour boiling water in pan until it reaches halfway up sides of the cups. Bake 40 minutes, until firm. Remove from water bath and refrigerate until very cold.

Serve with eggnog custard sauce: Put 1 cup remaining eggnog in small heavy saucepan. Reduce by half very slowly, 20 to 25 minutes, over low heat, whisking often. Chill custard sauce well and spoon 1 tablespoon on top of each flan, smoothing down with a small, flexible spatula or a butter knife.

Serves 8

* Use a commercial, ready-prepared dairy product.

■ ■ ■

Midwinter Magic

Roasted Beet Soup with Pickled Beet Greens

Pork Loin and "Packed Rack" with Dried Fruit and Fennel Sausage

Onions Disguised As Marrow Bones

Lemon-Curd Yogurt Tarts

12 ingredients

Even if you don't possess a fireplace, this menu is designed to cure any midwinter blues.

Make the soup a day ahead to let the flavors marry and allow the beet greens sufficient time to pickle.

However ambitious the main course sounds, it takes only three simple ingredients to yield two surprisingly showy results: a succulent pork roast stuffed with a mosaic of fruit and a "packed rack"
of sweet fennel sausage studded with fruit jewels atop a cradle of juicy ribs.

Giant slow-roasted onions pop their centers and wind up looking like marrow bones set into a jam of divinely sweet caramelized onions.

For dessert, an iconoclastic trilogy offers welcome notes of acidity (yogurt), sweetness (lemon curd), and comfort (graham crackers) all in one!

GRAPENOTE

Gamay all the way. Two different styles: a soft, fruity version from Preston Vineyards with the soup and, with the pork, a richer cru Beaujolais — Brouilly or Juliénas.

ROASTED BEET SOUP WITH PICKLED BEET GREENS

1 large bunch (4 large) beets, with leafy greens
½ cup red-wine vinegar
1 cup buttermilk

Cut beet greens from beets, then separate leaves from stalks. Wash leaves well and chop coarsely. Place in a medium pot. Add 1½ cups water, ¼ cup vinegar, 1 teaspoon kosher salt, and 12 black peppercorns. Bring to a boil. Cook over high heat for 3 to 4 minutes. Let cool in cooking liquid. Cover and refrigerate several hours or overnight.

Preheat oven to 400°.

Coarsely chop beet stalks and put in a medium pot with 1½ cups water. Bring to a boil, lower heat, and cover. Cook for 15 minutes. Set aside in cooking liquid.

Scrub beets. Place unpeeled beets in a shallow baking dish. Add ¼ inch of water and bake 1½ hours, turning once or twice. Beets will be tender and easily pierced with a knife. Remove from oven, let cool a bit, then peel.

Cut in wedges and put in food processor. Add cooked beet stalks with 1½ cups of their cooking liquid. Puree until very smooth. Add ¼ cup vinegar, salt and freshly ground black pepper to taste, and 1 cup buttermilk. Process again.

Serve hot or chill well. Add water to thin, if necessary. Adjust seasonings. Add salt, pepper, or vinegar to taste. Garnish with pickled greens.

Serves 4 to 6 (makes 4 cups)

PORK LOIN AND "PACKED RACK" WITH DRIED FRUIT AND FENNEL SAUSAGE

4½-pound center-cut rack of pork
6 ounces dried mixed fruit
¾ pound sweet fennel sausage

Have your butcher remove loin from rack and reserve bones in one piece. Have the bones trimmed neatly.

Preheat oven to 375°.

Separate pork loin from rack. Insert the handle of a large wooden spoon or a knife-sharpening steel into the center of the pork loin, making a 1-inch-diameter tunnel through the length of the loin.

Cut all the fruit into ¼-inch dice. You will have approximately 1½ cups dried fruit. Stuff ½ cup fruit into tunnel of the pork loin using the end of the spoon to pack it in. Sprinkle loin with salt and freshly ground black pepper. Place in a large baking pan and roast for about 1 hour. Meat thermometer should register 140° for moist meat.

Meanwhile, mix sausage meat and remaining diced fruit. Place rack of ribs flesh side down on a flat surface. Pack sausage mixture on top, to cover completely. After 30 minutes of roasting the pork loin, place rack of ribs in baking pan next to pork. Continue to roast for 30 to 40 minutes.

Remove roast and packed rack to cutting board. Place pan on top of stove, adding some water to pan juices to help scrape up browned bits. Bring to a boil, stirring constantly. Keep warm. Slice pork into ½-inch-thick slices and cut rack into individual ribs. Serve immediately with pan juices.

Serves 6 or more

ONIONS DISGUISED AS MARROW BONES

3 large onions (6 ounces each), plus 2½ pounds medium onions
4½ tablespoons extra-virgin olive oil
4 tablespoons balsamic vinegar

Preheat oven to 375°.

Cut large onions in half through the "equator" to make 2 halves. Do not peel. Drizzle 1 teaspoon olive oil over each of 6 cut onion halves.

Place cut side down in shallow baking pan. Bake for 1 hour, turning onions twice during baking. You want the cut side of the onions to blacken and the onions to be soft.

Meanwhile, peel remaining onions and slice very thin. Heat remaining 2½ tablespoons oil in a large heavy pot or skillet and add onions. Cook over medium-high heat for 25 minutes, stirring frequently. Onions will be browned.

Add vinegar, ¼ cup water, ¼ teaspoon salt, and freshly ground black pepper. Lower heat, cook 30 minutes longer, over medium-high heat, adding a little water as you periodically scrape up brown bits in the bottom of the pan. You want the onions to look like marmalade, thick, soft, and very dark.

Remove onions from oven after 1 hour. Using small spoon, remove centers of onions and set aside. Fill each onion with approximately ⅓ cup onion marmalade, placing onion center on top of filling. Serve immediately or reheat in 375° oven, covered, for 10 minutes.

Serves 6

LEMON-CURD YOGURT TARTS

2 cups plain yogurt
½ cup plus 4 teaspoons prepared lemon-curd*
10 whole graham crackers

Preheat oven to 350°.

Line a sieve with cheesecloth or with a coffee filter and put in yogurt. Place over a bowl to catch liquid. Let yogurt sit for 2 hours at room temperature until thickened. You will have about 1 cup. In a small bowl, mix thickened yogurt and ½ cup lemon curd. Refrigerate for 30 minutes or longer until ready to use.

Meanwhile, break up graham crackers and place in bowl of a food processor. Process until they become fine crumbs. You will have about 1⅓ cups graham cracker crumbs.

To make the crust of each tart, put ⅓ cup crumbs in a small bowl and add 1 tablespoon water, mixing with a fork. Crumbs should just become moistened.

Pack crumbs into each of 4 4½-inch removable-bottom fluted tart pans. Make sure the bottom is well covered by a layer of crumbs, pushing crumbs up the sides. Crumbs, however, will not reach the top of the pans.

Bake for 15 to 20 minutes until all moisture is evaporated and crusts are medium brown in color. Remove from oven and let cool. (Crusts can be made in advance.)

Fill tart crusts with lemon curd–yogurt mixture. Swirl 1 teaspoon lemon curd on top of each. Refrigerate tarts. Serve within 2 hours of filling.

Makes 4 tarts

---

* Use a jar of good-quality prepared lemon curd, such as Crabtree & Evelyn or Wilkin & Sons.

A Traipse Through Italy

Asiago-Pepper Roulades

Pan-Roasted Breast of Veal, Marcella Hazan

Slow-Cooked Zucchini with Thyme

Anisette Espresso Coupe

12 ingredients

In 1980, my best friend, Arthur Schwartz (food critic, author, radio talk-show host), and I went to Italy.

From lunching with the Hazans (Victor and Marcella) in a trattoria in Firenze, to a feast prepared by the nuns of Oasi della Pace near Milan, to an entire afternoon of bagna cauda *course by course (ending with a raw egg broken into the dregs of garlicky anchovy oil and a very long nap), to dinner at the home of famous couturier Biki, who was Puccini's granddaughter, . . . we had culinary adventures to last a lifetime. The trip was arranged by our friend and fellow foodie, Francesco de'Rogati.*

This menu honors them all.

Asiago comes from the Veneto region of Italy, where Marcella once lived, and is cow milk cheese, mild and milky tasting.

Marcella's veal recipe, which I have adapted only slightly, produces an impressively succulent roast.

The slow-cooking method in the zucchini recipe turns its flesh translucent.

Dessert is a "coup."

GRAPENOTE

Enjoy a full-flavored Italian white — like Gini's Soave Classico Superiore or the single-vineyard Soave from Anselmi.

ASIAGO-PEPPER ROULADES

6 large bell peppers, assorted colors
6 ounces Asiago cheese *
12 flat anchovies in oil (2-ounce can)

Preheat broiler.

Put peppers on baking sheet and broil several minutes on each side until skins are very black and blistered. Immediately seal peppers in paper bag to steam for 10 minutes. (You can also use a bowl covered with a lid or a plate if you don't have a paper bag.) Remove peppers and carefully remove all charred skin. Cut peppers in half, remove core and all seeds.

Preheat oven to 400°.

Cut cheese into 12 ½-ounce "fingers" or "sticks" approximately 2 inches long and ½ inch wide. Roll 1 piece of cheese and 1 flat anchovy in each soft pepper half to cover completely.

Place pepper roulades in baking pan. With pastry brush, brush roulades lightly with anchovy oil. Bake 10 minutes. Serve immediately.

Serves 4 or 6

* You may also use Valgrande or Manchego cheese from Spain.

PAN-ROASTED BREAST OF VEAL, MARCELLA HAZAN

3 tablespoons garlic oil*
4½ pounds breast of veal with rib bones
1 cup or more dry white wine

Heat oil over medium heat in a deep pan, with a lid, large enough to hold the meat lying in a flat position.

When oil is hot, put in breast, skin side down. Brown the meat over medium heat for 3 to 5 minutes on one side, turn over, and brown well on the other side.

Turn again. Add salt, freshly ground black pepper, and 1 cup wine. Turn up heat to medium-high and cook 5 minutes.

Lower heat to a simmer, cover pan, and cook slowly for 2½ hours. Turn several times during cook-ing. Add more wine if veal becomes dry or begins to stick.

When veal is tender, place on a cutting board. Remove bones and slice meat thinly.

Skim fat from top of pan juices. Discard. Heat re-maining juices over high heat, adding salt and pep-per to taste, for 1 to 2 minutes. Pour over meat and serve immediately.

Serves 4 to 6

* See page 8 for recipe or use Colavita or Consorzio brand.

SLOW-COOKED ZUCCHINI WITH THYME

6 small zucchini (1½ pounds)
4 tablespoons good-quality olive oil
1 large bunch fresh thyme

Wash zucchini well and pat dry with paper towels. Cut into ¼-inch-thick rounds.

Put 2 tablespoons oil in each of 2 large nonstick skillets.

Place zucchini in pans in one layer.

Cook slowly over low heat on one side for 10 minutes, until zucchini are golden. Carefully turn over and cook 10 minutes on other side, until golden.

To each pan add ¼ cup boiling water and salt. Simmer slowly 5 to 10 minutes, or until all water has evaporated and zucchini are soft but still hold their shape.

Remove zucchini to a platter. Add 3 tablespoons washed and dried thyme leaves to one of the pans along with remaining oil from the other pan. "Fry" thyme leaves for 1 minute, until they begin to get crisp. Scatter over zucchini, along with fresh, uncooked sprigs of thyme.

Add freshly ground black pepper and serve immediately.

Serves 4 to 6

ANISETTE ESPRESSO COUPE

2 pints good-quality vanilla ice cream
6 tablespoons anisette or sambuca
2 or 3 tablespoons instant-espresso granules

Soften ice cream and place in bowl of electric mixer. Add anisette or sambuca and blend quickly.

Place mixture in chilled wineglasses and sprinkle each with ½ tablespoon espresso.

Place in freezer until ready to serve.

Let sit at room temperature for 5 minutes before serving.

Serve bottle of anisette or sambuca alongside dessert for guests to add more if desired.

Serves 4 to 6

■ ■ ■

Cucina Casalinga

Portobello Mushroom Melt

Veal Chops with Lemon and Basil

Red Pepper–Potato Cakes

Chocolate Biscotti Terrine

12 ingredients

As the pace of life quickens, Italians, who by nurture consume a rigid progression of courses at every meal, are opting for fewer courses and food that is lighter and healthier.

As in America, cooks in Italy are recasting old-fashioned recipes for contemporary tastes and lifestyles. I have "lightened" some authentic trattoria recipes and created a few new ones, while preserving the spirit and flavor of the true cucina casalinga *. . . which translates as good "home cooking."*

GRAPENOTE

Start with earnest whites like Terre di Tufo and Mastroberardino's Lachryma Christi; then open a nebbiolo from Italy's northern Piedmont — a Gattinara or an Inferno from a great vintage (1990 or 1995).

PORTOBELLO MUSHROOM MELT

16 plum tomatoes *
8 medium portobello mushroom caps, 2½-inch-diameter
8 ounces smoked mozzarella cheese, thinly sliced

To make roasted tomatoes: Preheat oven to 250°. Wash tomatoes. Cut tomatoes in half, lengthwise. Place tomatoes cut side up in a single layer on a baking sheet. Bake 2½ to 3 hours, turning twice with a metal spatula. The tomatoes will retain their shape. Let cool. These can be made early in the day.

Preheat oven to 400°.

Wipe mushrooms with cloth to remove any dirt. Lightly sprinkle inside of each mushroom cap with salt and freshly ground black pepper. Place 4 roasted tomato halves, slightly overlapping, in each of 4 mushroom caps. Cover tomatoes with cheese slices. In remaining mushroom caps, place cheese slices and top each with 4 roasted tomatoes. Place filled mushrooms on baking sheets and bake 10 minutes, until cheese is melted and mushrooms are hot. Serve hot.

Serves 4

* Also known as roma tomatoes.

VEAL CHOPS WITH LEMON AND BASIL

4 large 1-inch-thick veal rib chops
2 large bunches fresh basil
2 large lemons

Have butcher trim the veal chops and give you trimmed fat; you will need 2 to 3 ounces. For a more elegant presentation you may have butcher "French" the veal bone, removing meat on the bone up to the eye of the chop.

Wash 1 bunch basil and dry thoroughly. Trim stems and discard. Place ½ bunch basil on a platter, then place chops on top. Cover with remaining basil. Wrap platter and refrigerate several hours or overnight.

When ready to cook, preheat oven to 425°.

Remove basil from chops and place basil leaves in bowl of food processor. Wash and dry remaining bunch of basil and remove all but 1 inch of the stems. Place half of it in food processor. Cut reserved veal fat into small pieces and place in processor. Grate the rind of 1 or 2 lemons until you have 2 teaspoons grated zest. Cut 1 lemon in half and squeeze so that you get 2 tablespoons juice. Add zest and juice to the food processor. Process until a fairly smooth paste is formed. Add salt and freshly ground black pepper to taste.

Season chops lightly with salt and pepper. Pack basil-lemon paste evenly on top of each chop to cover completely. Place chops on baking sheet. Bake for 25 minutes, or until desired doneness. Garnish with remaining fresh basil and thin slices cut from remaining lemon. Serve immediately.

Serves 4

RED PEPPER–POTATO CAKES

1½ pounds Red Bliss potatoes
3 tablespoons or more chili oil*
½ cup jarred roasted peppers, plus 3 tablespoons pepper liquid

Scrub potatoes well. Place in pot with salted water to cover. Bring to a boil. Lower heat and cook potatoes for 40 minutes, or until soft.

Drain potatoes in colander, saving ¼ cup cooking liquid. Peel potatoes and place in large bowl. Using potato masher, mash potatoes until smooth and creamy, but still leaving small chunks, while slowly adding cooking liquid and chili oil.

Cut roasted peppers into ¼-inch dice and add to mashed potatoes along with 1½ teaspoons butcher-grind black pepper and 1½ teaspoons salt, or to taste.

Reheat in a large covered saucepan over low heat before serving. Pack potatoes into a 3-by-1¼-inch ring to form a "cake," then remove ring. Repeat to make 4 "cakes." Or use a ½-cup measure and pat potatoes into cake form. Turn out and serve immediately. Drizzle with extra chili oil, if desired.

Serves 4

* See page 9 for recipe, or you may use a store-bought brand — such as Consorzio or Land of Canaan.

CHOCOLATE BISCOTTI TERRINE

6 anisette toasts*
½ pound best-quality semisweet chocolate
⅔ cup heavy cream

Line a small 6-by-3¼-by-2¼-inch-high loaf pan with plastic wrap so that it hangs 3 inches over edges of pan.

Chop chocolate into small pieces. Place chocolate and heavy cream in medium saucepan. Cook for several minutes over medium heat, stirring constantly until chocolate melts and the mixture is thick and smooth. Slowly pour a small amount of the chocolate mixture into the loaf pan to completely cover the bottom.

Place 3 anisette toasts, rounded side up, on the chocolate layer. Adjust the center toast so that its tip touches one short end of the pan, and the tips of the outer two touch the other end of the pan. (This will help to give the terrine a pretty "checkerboard" look when it is sliced.)

Cover this first layer of anisette toasts with more of the chocolate mixture and put the remaining 3 anisette toasts on top, this time placing them in the reverse position of the bottom 3. Slowly pour the remaining chocolate mixture over the top so that the anisette toasts are completely covered. Be sure to allow the mixture to seep into all of the crevices of the terrine.

Cover with overhanging plastic wrap and refrigerate several hours until firm. Cut into thin slices, serving 2 or 3 slices per person.

Optional garnish: Whip extra heavy cream and serve with terrine, or melt a little additional chocolate to decorate plate.

Serves 4

* Use Stella D'Oro anisette toast cookies, available in most supermarkets.

Unexpected Pleasures

Fennel and Orange Salad

Veal Roast with Caramelized Soup Greens, Vegetable Jus

Limoncello *Zabaglione*

9 ingredients

Soup greens in a fancy veal dish? Limoncello in dessert? This is the serendipity that brings pleasure to the table.

Some might argue that soup greens aren't (or isn't) one ingredient, and technically speaking they may be correct. However, soup greens are a singular package of foodstuffs (carrots, celery, parsley, leeks, dill) sold in every supermarket in America for a single price and as such have evolved as a single entity in the nation's pantry.

And aren't we lucky, for packaged soup greens save money and time, and provide, in this rather remarkable recipe for veal, both a vegetable and a sauce!

Limoncello, that trendy libation from sunny Sorrento and Capri, adds a sweetly tart layer of flavor to an otherwise monotonic Italian dessert. Limoncello is now readily available in this country and is great to sip straight from the freezer.

GRAPENOTE

For the salad, experiment with a heavier-style sauvignon blanc from Chile — one from Montes or Casa Lapostelle. Rediscover light Italian reds — Valpolicella or Bardolino — for the veal.

FENNEL AND ORANGE SALAD

2 large bulbs fennel, with lots of feathery fronds
4 large navel oranges
6 tablespoons extra-virgin olive oil

Wash fennel. Remove stalks, leaving only the bulb. Remove any dark brown spots. Cut in half through the root, then with a sharp knife, slice very thin, and place in a large bowl. Reserve feathery fronds; discard stalks.

Grate the rind of 2 oranges so that you have 1 tablespoon zest. Set aside. Cut the 2 oranges in half and squeeze halves to get ½ cup juice. In a blender put orange juice and olive oil. Add salt and freshly ground black pepper. Puree until creamy.

Cut rind from 2 remaining oranges, using a small sharp knife and discard rinds. Cut between membranes into segments. Add segments to fennel and toss. Add dressing and mix gently.

Chop fennel fronds so that you have 6 tablespoons. Scatter on top of salad, along with reserved zest.

Serves 6

VEAL ROAST WITH CARAMELIZED SOUP GREENS, VEGETABLE JUS

2 14-ounce packages fresh soup greens *
3½-pound boneless veal shoulder roast
4 tablespoons olive oil

To make stock: From soup greens packages, remove 2 carrots, 1 onion, 3 celery ribs, parsley, and dill. Peel carrots and peel onion. Cut celery, carrots, and onion into 1-inch pieces. Put all ingredients in small pot with 3 cups water and ¼ teaspoon black peppercorns. Bring to a boil, lower heat, and simmer 45 minutes.

Preheat oven to 350°.

Peel remaining carrots and parsnips and cut into 2-inch pieces. Trim unpeeled turnips and cut into quarters. Cut leeks into 1-inch pieces and wash well. Peel remaining onions and cut into quarters. Trim ends of celery and cut into 2-inch lengths.

Season veal with salt and freshly ground black pepper. Brown veal in large, heavy, shallow casserole (large enough to hold veal and vegetables), in 3 table-spoons olive oil. Quickly brown on all sides until golden and remove from pan. This should take about 5 minutes.

Add prepared uncooked cut vegetables and 1 tablespoon oil. Brown vegetables well over high heat and add ¼ cup vegetable stock. Add salt and pepper to taste. Meanwhile, strain remaining stock through a sieve, pressing down on vegetables with a spoon to extract all the juices. Set aside. Discard vegetables.

Put veal back in center of pan, surrounded by the browned vegetables, and put in the oven. Roast for 1 hour, or until desired doneness. This is particularly delicious medium-rare.

Remove from oven. Transfer veal to a cutting board. Transfer the vegetables, with a slotted spoon, to a serving platter, keeping warm. Let veal rest for 10 minutes before slicing.

Quickly, make vegetable jus. Add strained stock to roasting pan with veal drippings and vegetable drip-pings, scraping up any browned bits. Cook over high heat for a few minutes until somewhat syrupy. Add salt and freshly ground black pepper to taste.

Carve veal. Serve with warm vegetables and vege-table jus.

Serves 6

* Prepacked combination of celery, carrots, turnips, parsnips, parsley, dill, onions, and leeks.

LIMONCELLO ZABAGLIONE

9 extra-large egg yolks
½ cup superfine sugar
6 tablespoons limoncello *liqueur* *

In top of a double boiler, put egg yolks and sugar. Over simmering water, beat eggs and sugar with a wire whisk or an electric mixer until very thick and swelling in volume. This should take approximately 10 minutes. Make sure the water does not touch the bottom of the bowl. The idea is to beat in air while slowly "cooking" the yolks.

Slowly add liqueur and continue cooking while whisking until mixture is a puddinglike consistency. Let cool a few minutes, whisk again, and spoon into 6 small wineglasses. Serve warm or chilled.

Serves 6

* Use Limoni or other brand.

■ ■ ■

For My Husband's Birthday

Chicken Liver Royale with Red Onions and Bacon

Veal Shanks with Forty Cloves of Garlic, Pinot Noir Reduction

Truffled White Bean Puree

Sautéed Red Swiss Chard

A Kind of Spumoni

15 ingredients

Defenestration led to the pragmatic decision that my husband and I would never, ever cook together again. At least not side by side. Rather, Michael and I now cook systematically one after the other, each making a course (or courses), jumping over each other as in a game of hopscotch.

"Defenestration," in case you are wondering, means the act of throwing things out a window. In this case a kitchen window, leaving a crowd of guests speculating why there was a shiny copper pot — no two! — in our small backyard.

We still invite company over, but what we like best is to entertain just one couple at a time, explaining why this menu is "dinner for four."

I love my husband. He's my boss, my mentor, my landlord, my Bacchus.

And that's why I cook for him, by myself, on his birthday.

GRAPENOTE

My husband, Michael, suggests an expensive Zind-Humbrecht Gewürztraminer from Alsace. Then he wants a bottle or two of Domaine Bonserine from the Côte-Rôtie.

CHICKEN LIVER ROYALE WITH RED ONIONS AND BACON

8 slices bacon
2 cups very finely diced red onions
1 pound chicken livers

Cut 4 slices bacon into 1-inch pieces. Place in a medium nonstick skillet. Cook very slowly, over low heat, for 20 minutes, so that fat is rendered. Do not brown.

Remove bacon with slotted spoon and reserve for later use.

Add 1½ cups diced onions to fat in pan. Sauté over low heat for 10 minutes. Pat livers dry and season with salt and freshly ground black pepper. Add to pan and cook quickly over medium heat, about 3 minutes, until livers are cooked but still a little pink in the center. Transfer mixture to food processor and process until very smooth, adding salt and pepper to taste. Line 4 ½-cup ramekins or timbales with plastic wrap. Pack in liver mixture, cover, and refrigerate for several hours, until cold and firm.

To serve, cut remaining 4 slices bacon into 1-inch pieces. Cook over medium heat to render fat, about 10 minutes. Add remaining ½ cup finely diced red onions and cook over medium heat until soft, about 5 minutes. Add cooked bacon that has been set aside. Cook over high heat with ¼ cup water for 1 minute, until hot.

Put warm bacon-onion mixture in center of each of 4 large plates. Unmold chilled liver and place on top. Serve immediately. (My husband suggests you serve this with wafer-thin slices of toasted baguette.)

Serves 4

VEAL SHANKS WITH FORTY CLOVES OF GARLIC, PINOT NOIR REDUCTION

4 large 2½-inch-thick pieces veal shanks (¾ pound each)
10 large cloves garlic
2 cups pinot noir

Preheat broiler.

Place shanks in shallow broiler pan and broil on each side for 2 minutes, or until meat is browned. Place in heavy pot, large enough to accommodate shanks in one layer.

Peel garlic cloves, saving papery skin. Add 38 peeled cloves to pot with shanks. In small heavy saucepan, put garlic peels, 2 cloves garlic pushed through garlic press, 2 cups water, ¼ teaspoon salt, and ¼ teaspoon whole black peppercorns. Bring to a boil. Simmer 10 minutes and strain. You will have approximately 1¾ cups garlic stock.

To pot with shanks, add ½ cup wine and ½ cup garlic stock. Bring to a boil.

Cover, lower heat to simmer, and cook 2 to 2½ hours, or until veal is very soft.

Turn shanks after 30 minutes, adding ½ cup wine and a little garlic stock. Turn shanks every 30 minutes, keeping meat moist. There should be approximately ½-inch liquid at all times. Add water, if necessary.

Meanwhile, in small saucepan, cook 1 cup wine and 1 cup garlic stock until reduced to 1 cup. Set aside.

When veal is fork-tender, remove from pot with slotted spoon, also removing any whole garlic cloves. Turn heat to high and mash broken cloves into the sauce. Add enough reserved wine reduction to achieve a balanced sauce. Add salt and pepper to taste. Pour thickened sauce over veal shanks and whole garlic. Serve immediately.

Serves 4

TRUFFLED WHITE BEAN PUREE

½ pound small white beans
¼ cup heavy cream
1½ tablespoons truffle oil

Sort beans, removing any stones. Rinse beans in a colander. Place beans in a medium pot with water to cover by 1 inch. Bring to a boil and let boil for 2 minutes. Remove from heat. Cover pot and let sit 1 hour.

Drain beans in colander. Place beans in a clean medium pot with cold water to cover by 2 inches. Add 12 whole black peppercorns. Bring to a boil. Reduce heat to low, cover pot, and simmer for 1 hour and 20 minutes or until beans are tender.

Drain beans, saving 2 tablespoons of the cooking liquid. Place beans in the bowl of a food processor.

Process until very smooth, adding 2 tablespoons cooking liquid. With motor running, slowly add cream and 1 tablespoon of the truffle oil.

Transfer mixture to a medium saucepan. Add ½ teaspoon kosher salt or more to taste.

Cook over low heat until puree is hot, adding a little water if mixture is too thick. Stir in remaining ½ tablespoon truffle oil. Can be reheated.

Serves 4 or more

SAUTÉED RED SWISS CHARD

1½ pounds red Swiss chard
2 tablespoons or more olive oil
2 lemons

Wash Swiss chard and remove large stems. Bring a large pot of salted water to a boil and blanch chard for 1 minute. Drain immediately in colander under cold water.

Squeeze out water with your hands and coarsely chop the chard. Heat oil in a large nonstick skillet. Add chard to pan. Cook over medium heat until chard softens, about 5 minutes.

Add the juice of 1 lemon and salt and freshly ground black pepper to taste. Continue to cook until soft and tender.

Serve with extra olive oil, if desired, and wedges cut from remaining lemon.

Serve immediately.

Serves 4

A KIND OF SPUMONI

1 cup diced candied fruit
½ cup white rum
1 quart best-quality vanilla ice cream

In a small pot, put candied fruit and rum. Bring to a boil. Lower heat and simmer 5 minutes. Remove from heat. Let marinate 2 hours at room temperature.

Soften ice cream. Drain fruit in small sieve. Pat dry. Reserve liquid.

Fold ½ cup fruit into ice cream and stir to evenly incorporate fruit. Add 1 teaspoon reserved liquid and stir.

Line a 4-cup loaf pan or decorative mold with plastic wrap. Spoon in ice cream mixture, packing down well.

Freeze for several hours, until very hard.

Serve thick slices with remaining soaked diced fruit and reserved liquid spooned over the top.

Serves 4 or more

On Easter

Zucchini Vichyssoise

Lamb Chops with Goat Cheese and Lavender

Watercress Sauté with Garlic Chips

"Short-Stack" Tomatoes and Onions

Strawberry Gratin à la Sabayon

15 ingredients

This celebration dinner, meant for Easter or any other vernal Sunday, brings great rewards for modest amounts of effort.

Easter corresponds to spring, and spring, in turn, means renewal: a time for young lamb, watercress, the first zucchini, fresh lavender, and early strawberries. You'll find them all in this menu, as resplendent as an Easter parade.

GRAPENOTE

A still Vouvray would be a lovely match for the soup. For the main course choose a red from the Languedoc, like Domaine Clavel's Les Garrigues, a blend of *syrah* and *grenache noir*, or a flowery Beaujolais like Chiroubles.

ZUCCHINI VICHYSSOISE

¾ cup heavy cream
½ cup finely chopped shallots plus 1 whole shallot, optional
¾ pound fresh zucchini (2 medium-large)

In a medium pot, put cream, 1½ cups water, 1 teaspoon salt, and freshly ground white pepper.

Add chopped shallots and zucchini that have been washed and thinly sliced.

Heat mixture to just below a boil. Lower heat immediately and simmer for 15 minutes, until zucchini are soft.

Place contents in a blender in 2 batches and process until mixture is very, very smooth and a beautiful light green color.

Transfer to a bowl or container and cool. Cover soup and refrigerate several hours, until very cold.

Before serving, add salt and freshly ground white pepper to taste. Thin with a little cool water if soup is too thick. *Optional:* Peel remaining shallot and slice thin. Scatter several slices on soup.

Serves 4 (makes approximately 4 cups)

LAMB CHOPS WITH GOAT CHEESE AND LAVENDER

8 thick rib lamb chops
6 ounces fresh goat cheese
*3 tablespoons chopped fresh lavender leaves**

Have the butcher "French" the chops, cutting all meat from the bones up to the "eye" of the chops; the long exposed bone makes an elegant presentation.

Preheat oven to 375°.

In a small bowl, mix goat cheese with 2 tablespoons chopped lavender leaves. Set aside.

Season chops with salt and freshly ground black pepper. Heat a large nonstick skillet until hot and sear chops on each side until browned, leaving meat very rare inside. Transfer chops to a shallow baking pan.

Pack approximately 1½ tablespoons of the cheese mixture on one side of each chop to cover meat completely.

Place chops in the oven for 8 to 10 minutes, or until desired doneness. You may also brown the cheese under the broiler for 30 seconds before serving. Scatter remaining lavender over chops and serve immediately.

Serves 4

* You may substitute fresh rosemary leaves.

WATERCRESS SAUTÉ WITH GARLIC CHIPS

3 large bunches watercress
4 large cloves garlic
3 tablespoons good-quality olive oil

Wash watercress and dry thoroughly. Cut away most of the stems and discard.

Peel garlic cloves and cut lengthwise into very thin slices.

Heat olive oil in a large nonstick skillet until very hot. Add sliced garlic cloves and remove pan immediately from the heat. The garlic will crisp and brown, but this will prevent blackening.

Add watercress to pan with oil and garlic. Cook over high heat for 1 minute, until watercress just begins to wilt. Stir constantly with wooden spoon. Sprinkle with salt and serve immediately.

Serves 4

"SHORT-STACK" TOMATOES AND ONIONS

4 medium-large ripe tomatoes (1½ pounds)
2 large red onions
4 tablespoons extra-virgin olive oil

Preheat oven to 300°.

Using a sharp knife, cut a ¼-inch slice off the top and bottom of each tomato. Slice each tomato into 3 thick slices. Reassemble each to look like a whole tomato.

Peel red onions and slice into 8 ¼-inch-thick slices and 4 thinner slices. Layer thicker red onions in between tomato slices, ending on top with a thin slice of onion.

Drizzle 1 tablespoon oil over each and sprinkle with salt and freshly ground black pepper. Place a short skewer in center of each stack to help hold "short stacks" together.

Place in shallow baking pan and bake 1¼ hours. Baste with pan juices twice during baking, making sure tomatoes hold their shape. Remove from oven and let rest 15 minutes.

The bottom will be soft, so transfer carefully with a spatula to plate. Spoon pan juices over tomatoes and serve. Also delicious at room temperature or reheated in a 375° oven.

Serves 4

STRAWBERRY GRATIN À LA SABAYON

2 pints ripe medium-large strawberries
½ cup plus 2 tablespoons granulated sugar
4 extra-large egg yolks

Reserve 4 berries with stems for garnish. Cut stems off remaining berries. Wash well in colander, but do not pat dry.

In heavy medium saucepan with cover, place wet berries and ½ cup sugar. Cover pan and cook over medium heat for 8 to 10 minutes, or until berries are just beginning to get tender. Turn off heat. With slotted spoon, divide strawberries equally into 4 gratin dishes or small flat soup plates. Cook syrup in saucepan over medium heat until reduced to ½ cup. Pour 1 tablespoon syrup over each dish of berries. Let berries cool. Set aside 4 remaining tablespoons syrup. You may prepare up to this point several hours before serving.

About 10 minutes before serving, beat egg yolks with electric mixer or whisk in top of double boiler with 2 tablespoons sugar and 2 tablespoons strawberry syrup. Whisk over medium heat for 8 minutes, or until egg yolks are thickened and fluffy.

Divide sabayon equally over berries. Drizzle a little of the remaining syrup over top. Make fan shapes from 4 remaining berries by cutting thin slices lengthwise, stopping short of the stem so the berries remain intact, and pressing down to shingle. Garnish each gratin with a strawberry fan.

Serves 4

The "Seven Species" Dinner

Labaneh-*Stuffed Tomatoes with Olive Oil*
Whole Wheat Pita Bread
Shish Kebabs with Onions and Pomegranate Molasses
Barley with Dates
Fig Confit with Sesame and Honey
15 ingredients

. . . a land of wheat and barley, of vines, figs, and pomegranates, a land of olive oil and of honey; a land where you may eat food without stint, where you will lack nothing.
DEUTERONOMY, 8:7–10

Dinner in the Mediterranean Basin was once loosely based on foods mentioned in the Bible: wheat, barley, olives, figs, pomegranates, wine, and honey (probably made from dates), specifically known as the seven species.

This eating regime, the genesis of what currently is called the Mediterranean Diet, has health benefits that are well documented. Our first course looks like a famous Turkish dessert in which dried apricots "sandwich" a filling of thickened yogurt. Instead, I substitute slow-roasted tomatoes for the fruit and anoint them with fragrant *olive oil.*

Shish kebabs get a Med-Rim treatment of marination in grated onion, which tenderizes and softens the lamb, and a flavor jolt from pomegranate *molasses, a syrupy reduction of pomegranates, sugar, and lemon juice.*

Unhulled barley (the earliest known cereal to be cultivated) provides a nutritious oasis for sweet bits of dates, while whole wheat, ground to a flour, is used in fresh-baked pita.

Figs and wine complete the story that began at the beginning of time.

GRAPENOTE

Wine, or "vines," is one of the "seven species" mentioned in the Bible, so try something geographically correct: Begin with Gamla sauvignon blanc, then move on to Carmel Winery's Reserve cabernet sauvignon from Rishon Le Zion, one of the region's oldest wineries.

LABANEH-STUFFED TOMATOES WITH OLIVE OIL

3 cups plain low-fat yogurt
12 large plum tomatoes
4 tablespoons extra-virgin olive oil

Line a strainer or sieve with 2 layers of cheesecloth or a coffee filter. Place yogurt in strainer or sieve with a bowl underneath to catch liquid. Let sit 8 hours in the refrigerator, until yogurt becomes very thick. You will have approximately 1½ cups.

Preheat oven to 250°.

Cut tomatoes in half lengthwise. Place tomatoes cut side up on a baking sheet in a single layer. Drizzle tomatoes with 1 tablespoon olive oil. Sprinkle with salt and freshly ground black pepper.

Bake for 4 hours, turning tomatoes after each hour. Remove from oven and let cool.

Make "sandwiches" using 2 tomato halves per sandwich. Fill each with 1½ to 2 level tablespoons thickened yogurt (*labaneh*). Serve 2 or 3 per person. Drizzle with remaining olive oil. Sprinkle with additional salt and pepper.

Serves 4 to 6

WHOLE WHEAT PITA BREAD

1 tablespoon dried yeast
5 cups whole-wheat flour
2 tablespoons honey

In a small bowl, dissolve the yeast and honey in ½ cup lukewarm water. Let sit 10 minutes in a warm place.

Put 4 cups flour into a large mixing bowl. Add the yeast mixture and 2 cups warm water. Beat vigorously for 2 minutes. Add 2 teaspoons salt and ½ cup additional flour.

Turn out onto a lightly floured board and knead the dough for 10 minutes, until smooth and elastic, or use a mixer fitted with a dough hook. Add more flour, if necessary, to make a stiff dough, up to ½ cup.

Place dough in a large bowl. Cover with a dry cloth and set in a warm place. Allow dough to double in volume, approximately 2 hours.

Punch down dough and knead for 2 minutes. Divide dough into 10 balls, each the size of a baseball.

Place balls on a sheet pan and cover with a dry cloth. Let rise 30 minutes.

Preheat oven to 475°.

On a lightly floured board, roll balls out into circles that are 5 inches in diameter and ¼ inch thick. Place on ungreased baking sheets and let rest 10 minutes.

Bake for 8 minutes, or until bottoms are very lightly browned.

Breads will puff like balloons and then deflate when cool. Serve immediately, or allow to cool and put in plastic bags to be refrigerated or frozen.

Makes 10 pita breads

SHISH KEBABS WITH ONIONS AND POMEGRANATE MOLASSES

2 pounds boneless leg of lamb, cut into 1½-inch pieces (20 to 24 pieces)
4 medium onions
4 tablespoons pomegranate molasses*

Place lamb pieces in a large bowl. Peel 2 onions and cut them in half. Grate them on large holes of box grater so that you have approximately ½ cup grated onions. Mix lamb with grated onions. Add freshly ground black pepper and 2 tablespoons pomegranate molasses. Mix well and cover. Refrigerate overnight or a minimum of 8 hours.

When ready to serve, preheat broiler. Peel remaining 2 onions and cut in half through the core. Separate onion layers and cut them into 1-inch pieces. On each of 4 10- or 12-inch skewers put a piece of onion, then lamb, onion, and so on, until you have filled the skewers. Each skewer should have 5 or 6 pieces of lamb.

Sprinkle skewers with salt and pepper. Place on broiler pan and broil 3 minutes on each side, or until medium-rare.

Drizzle each shish kebab with ½ tablespoon pomegranate molasses. Serve immediately.

Serves 4

* Available at Middle Eastern food stores.

BARLEY WITH DATES

1 cup (6 ounces) unhulled barley
3 ounces whole dried dates
2½ tablespoons unsalted butter

In medium pot bring 6 cups water to a boil. Add barley and 1 teaspoon salt. Lower heat and cover pot. Cook over low heat for 40 to 50 minutes, until barley is tender.

Remove pits from dates. Dice dates into ¼-inch pieces. You will have approximately ½ cup.

In small nonstick skillet, melt 2 tablespoons butter. Add dates and cook over low heat for 2 minutes.

When it is tender, drain barley in colander. Place drained barley in a medium bowl. Add cooked dates and additional ½ tablespoon butter. Toss gently. Add salt and freshly ground black pepper. Mix again and serve immediately.

Serves 4

FIG CONFIT WITH SESAME AND HONEY

1 pound large dried figs *
½ cup orange-blossom honey
2 tablespoons sesame seeds, lightly toasted

In a medium pot, place figs. In a small bowl, mix honey with 2 cups cool water until dissolved and pour over figs.

Sprinkle 1 tablespoon sesame seeds over figs.

Bring to a boil. Lower heat and cover. Cook over very low heat for 45 minutes. Figs will plump substantially. Remove figs with slotted spoon. Place in a medium bowl.

Cook liquid in pot over high heat until reduced and syrupy, about ¾ cup. Pour over figs and let cool at room temperature.

Sprinkle with remaining tablespoon sesame seeds before serving.

Serves 4

* I recommend the variety called Calimyrna.

■ ■ ■

Israel's Mediterranean Cuisine

Chickpea Soup with Cilantro

Oven-Braised Lamb Stew with Cumin and Fresh Tomato

Bulgur Wheat with Caramelized Onions

Turkish Grapes with Wild-Thyme Honey and Yogurt

12 ingredients

Israel is affectionately known as the world's small-est melting pot. Equally diverse and exotic, Israel's emerging palate is influenced heavily by Arabic (known in Israel as Oriental) flavors, punctuated with superlative local ingredients: verdant olive oil from ancient trees in the Galilee and the hills of Jerusalem, lusty tomatoes, fragrant herbs and spices. Its Mediterranean cuisine is perhaps the greatest story never told.

This menu evokes the collision of cultures that is Israel. The hot soup is reminiscent of everyone's favorite cold snack: hummus. Chunks of lamb stew are perfectly braised and perfumed with vapors of cumin and tomato. Cracked wheat, the base of the "uncooked" salad known as tabbouleh, here gets cooked and strewn with softly burnished onions.

It should come as no surprise that dessert is a plate of "milk and honey."

B'tayavon *(good appetite).*

GRAPENOTE

A superb match for the lamb would be Yarden (Galil) merlot that has a small percentage of cabernet sauvignon for character.

CHICKPEA SOUP WITH CILANTRO

1 cup (6 ounces net weight) dried chickpeas
1 medium-large red onion
1 large bunch cilantro

Pick out stones or bad beans from chickpeas. Soak overnight in cold water to cover. Drain chickpeas. Place in large, heavy pot with a cover. Add 5 cups cool water and ½ teaspoon whole white peppercorns.

Peel onion and dice into ¼-inch pieces. You should have 1 heaping cup chopped onion. Add to pot with chickpeas and water.

Wash cilantro and dry thoroughly. Cut off stems. Chop stems coarsely and add to pot. Save cilantro leaves for garnishing later. Refrigerate until ready to use.

Bring pot of chickpeas to a boil. Cover pot, lower heat, and let simmer for 1 hour.

Uncover pot. Add 1 teaspoon salt and cook over medium heat for 30 minutes. Chickpeas should be very soft. If not, continue to cook another 20 to 30 minutes.

Reserve 20 chickpeas for a garnish. Process remaining soup in food processor, in 1 or 2 batches, until very smooth and creamy. Transfer contents back to pot and reheat gently before serving. Add salt and freshly ground black pepper to taste, if desired.

Garnish hot soup with reserved chickpeas and coarsely chopped cilantro leaves. *Optional garnish:* Top with very finely minced red onion.

Serve immediately.

Serves 4 (makes 4½ to 5 cups)

OVEN-BRAISED LAMB STEW WITH CUMIN AND FRESH TOMATO

¼ cup good-quality ground cumin
2 pounds ripe red tomatoes
3 pounds lamb stew meat, cut into large 2½-inch pieces, with bones

Preheat oven to 350°.

In a small bowl put cumin, 2 teaspoons salt, and ¼ teaspoon freshly ground white pepper. Using your fingers, rub spice mixture into each piece of lamb, covering lightly but completely. Set aside on platter.

Cut all but 1 tomato in half and scoop out seeds. Cut into ½-inch pieces and place in bottom of a large flameproof casserole with a cover.

Place lamb pieces on top of tomatoes in one layer. Cover casserole and place in oven.

Bake for 1¾ hours to 2 hours, or until lamb is fork-tender. Check several times during baking, adding a little water at a time, so tomatoes don't stick.

Remove from oven. Transfer lamb to a large platter with a slotted spoon. Place casserole containing tomato liquid on stove. Add remaining tomato, seeded and chopped into ¼-inch dice, ½ cup water if needed, and a little of the remaining spice mixture, if any, or additional cumin, salt, and pepper. Cook over high heat for 1 minute. Spoon sauce over lamb and serve immediately.

Serves 4 or more

BULGUR WHEAT WITH CARAMELIZED ONIONS

3 large yellow onions
3 tablespoons olive oil
1½ cups (8 ounces) coarse bulgur wheat

Peel onions. Cut 2 onions into ¼-inch dice. Reserve remaining onion for later.

In a large nonstick skillet, heat 2 tablespoons olive oil. Add diced onions and cook over medium-high heat for 20 minutes, or until they are dark brown, soft, and caramelized.

Transfer onions to large, heavy saucepan with cover. Add bulgur wheat, 3 cups water, and 1 teaspoon salt. Bring to a boil. Cover and lower heat. Simmer 20 minutes, or until all water is absorbed. Stir several times during cooking to make sure bulgur doesn't stick.

Meanwhile, cut remaining onion in half and then into very thin slices. Heat remaining 1 tablespoon oil in a small nonstick skillet and add onion slices. Cook over medium-high heat until they become almost blackened.

When bulgur is tender, remove from heat. Add salt and pepper to taste.

Serve immediately with blackened onions on top, or reheat before serving.

Serves 6

TURKISH GRAPES WITH WILD-THYME HONEY AND YOGURT

2 cups plain yogurt
1½ pounds seedless grapes, green, red, or a combination
½ cup wild-thyme or wildflower honey

To drain yogurt: Line a fine-mesh sieve with 2 layers of cheesecloth or a coffee filter. Place yogurt in sieve with a bowl underneath to catch any liquid. Let drain 45 minutes, at room temperature, until thickened. You will have 1⅓ to 1½ cups yogurt. Place in bowl in refrigerator until ready to use.

Wash grapes and remove from stems. Place grapes in heavy medium pot with a cover. Add honey and stir well to coat. Cook grapes over low heat, covered, until tender but not too soft. They should retain their shape. This will take approximately 10 to 12 minutes.

Remove grapes with slotted spoon to a bowl to cool slightly.

Cook honey in pot over high heat until very thick and syrupy, about 6 tablespoons. Keep warm.

To serve, spread yogurt evenly on 4 flat dessert plates, making a slight well or indentation in center. Mound grapes evenly in center of yogurt. Drizzle grapes and yogurt with warm honey syrup. Serve immediately.

Serves 4

Food and Friends

Arugula Salad with Sweet Garlic Dressing
Roast Lamb Shoulder with Comté and Rosemary
Green Beans and Potatoes in Pesto
Brutti ma Buoni *(Ugly but Good)* **Cookies**

12 ingredients

This unassuming meal for six begins with a simple salad and ends with a plate of cookies. Its rustic flavors can be found as easily in a Tuscan farmhouse or in the south of France, where, for instance, I first encountered l'aiado, *a stuffed and rolled shoulder of lamb, at the restaurant La Mère Besson.*

A tangle of bitter arugula softens under a heady but faintly sweet dressing made of roasted garlic and good olive oil. Succulent lamb shoulder is filled with Comté, a marvelous French cheese similar to Swiss Gruyère, and fresh rosemary; the lamb bones lend flavor and viscosity to homemade stock. Beans, potatoes, and pesto, or pistou *as it is known in the south of France, offer an authentic and homey triad of tastes.*

Equally rustic are cookies, compliments of my friend and fellow chef Lidia Bastianich, who calls them "ugly but good." Although deceptively simple, this meal is special enough to share with good friends.

GRAPENOTE

For this marriage of Italian and French flavors, begin with Vernaccia di San Gimignano from Tuscany, then drink a French country red such as Minervois or a Côtes de Ventoux.

ARUGULA SALAD WITH SWEET GARLIC DRESSING

2 very large heads garlic
½ cup good-quality olive oil
3 bunches impeccably fresh arugula, chilled

Preheat oven to 400°.

Wrap garlic loosely in aluminum foil to form a sealed packet. Place in baking pan or pie tin and bake 1 hour. Remove from oven. Open packet and let garlic cool.

Cut garlic heads in half horizontally through the center. Squeeze out pulp and place in bowl of food processor. You should have approximately 4 tablespoons garlic pulp. Add 6 tablespoons cold water and process.

With motor running, slowly add olive oil. Sauce will thicken. Transfer dressing to small bowl and add salt and freshly ground black pepper to taste. This makes approximately 1 cup dressing.

Wash arugula and dry thoroughly. Place arugula in bowl and toss gently with dressing.

Serve on chilled salad plates.

Serves 6

ROAST LAMB SHOULDER WITH COMTÉ AND ROSEMARY X

6-pound lamb shoulder, boned (reserve bones)
2 tablespoons fresh rosemary leaves, plus 1 large bunch fresh rosemary on branches
8 ounces Comté or Swiss Gruyere cheese

Preheat oven to 375°.

To make broth: Put bones in medium pot with 2 cups water, 1 large sprig rosemary, ¼ teaspoon whole black peppercorns, and ¼ teaspoon salt. Bring to boil and lower heat. Simmer 30 minutes over low heat, removing any scum that forms on top. Put through fine sieve. Reduce broth over high heat until you have 1 cup. Reserve the bones that have some meat on them; I like to broil them to serve along with the sliced lamb.

After lamb is boned, you will have approximately 4 pounds meat. Place lamb, boned side up, on work surface. Unroll lamb. Sprinkle with salt and freshly ground black pepper. Rub into surface of meat.

Grate cheese on large holes of box grater. Scatter evenly on lamb. Coarsely chop 2 tablespoons rosemary leaves and scatter on top of cheese.

Roll lamb, jelly-roll style. Tie with kitchen string at 2-inch intervals. Scatter rosemary branches in shallow roasting pan. Place lamb on top of rosemary.

Roast lamb until meat thermometer registers 140° for medium-rare. This should take approximately 1 hour, but check after 50 minutes with thermometer. Transfer with rosemary branches to platter and let rest 10 minutes.

Add reserved broth to pan juices and heat 2 minutes over high heat.

Slice lamb, removing string, and serve with pan juices and broiled bones, if you wish.

Serves 6 to 8

GREEN BEANS AND POTATOES IN PESTO

1 pound tender green beans
1 pound medium red potatoes
6 tablespoons good-quality prepared pesto

Trim ends of beans with a small sharp knife. Bring medium pot of salted water to a boil. Peel potatoes and cut into 1-inch chunks.

Add potatoes to boiling water. Continue to cook over high heat until potatoes are soft, approximately 15 minutes.

Add trimmed beans to pot and cook until beans are tender and bright green, approximately 4 minutes.

Drain potatoes and beans in colander. Shake off excess water. Place in bowl and toss with pesto.

Add salt and freshly ground black pepper to taste. Toss and serve. Delicious hot or at room temperature.

Serves 6

BRUTTI MA BUONI (UGLY BUT GOOD) COOKIES

1 cup (5 ounces) shelled hazelnuts, with skins, coarsely chopped
4 extra-large egg whites
1 cup confectioners' sugar, sifted

Preheat oven to 275°. Line a baking pan with parchment paper.

Place chopped hazelnuts in medium nonstick skillet. Cook over medium heat for about 2 minutes until nuts are lightly browned and toasted. Set aside.

In bowl of electric mixer beat egg whites with a pinch of salt until stiff.

In large heavy saucepan put toasted nuts, confectioners' sugar, and beaten egg whites.

Place over moderate heat and cook for 20 minutes,

stirring constantly with wooden spoon. The mixture will become a light, golden color and will come away from sides and bottom of pan.

Remove from heat. Using a tablespoon, drop batter onto a baking sheet. Bake 35 to 40 minutes until dark golden brown. Remove from oven. Let cookies cool until crisp. Remove with spatula.

Makes 20 cookies

■ ■ ■

A Dinner of Aromatics

Warm Goat Cheese with Fresh Mint Salad

Bombay Leg of Lamb with Yogurt and Lime

Curried Couscous with Currants

Chilled Sliced Oranges with Rosewater and Dates

12 ingredients

Mint, curry, currants, rosewater, lime . . .

This menu is a romp through a souk (an open-air marketplace found in North Africa and in the Middle East). While it is not specifically from anywhere, its spirit derives from parts of the world where redolence arouses the most dormant of palates.

Sweet or spicy, fragrant or pungent, aromas evoke history, buried emotions, forgotten memo- *ries, and a strong sense of place. Smell is 70 percent of taste, which explains the appeal of this olfactory meal.*

This is a great party menu, as all the recipes can be easily doubled or tripled. Marinate the lamb for six to eight hours; the rest of the menu takes a total of seventeen minutes to cook and approximately fifteen minutes to prep!

GRAPENOTE

The first course calls for a full-bodied chardonnay — try Pedroncelli's Frank Johnson Vineyard. The "aromatics" in the rest of the meal call for lots of ripe fruit: a California *mourvèdre* — L'Enfant Terrible from Edmunds St. John or Primitivo di Mandurlo from Italy.

WARM GOAT CHEESE WITH FRESH MINT SALAD

12 ounces fresh goat cheese, well chilled
1 cup packed fresh mint leaves
6 tablespoons extra-virgin olive oil

Divide cheese into 4 3-ounce portions. Pack each into a 2¾-inch ring so that cheese is ¾ inch thick. Or form cheese by hand into "cakes" that are 2¾ inches in diameter and ¾ inch thick. Pat ¼ teaspoon butcher-grind black peppercorns firmly on top of each cake.

Coarsely chop fresh mint. In small bowl, mix mint leaves well with 4 tablespoons olive oil and ½ teaspoon kosher salt. Divide mint salad among 4 large oven-proof plates, placing in the center.

Preheat broiler. Place cheese on salad in center of plate. Drizzle ½ tablespoon oil over each cheese "cake."

Put under broiler for 1 minute, until warmed and lightly browned. (Some of the mint leaves will get crispy, and that is good!) Serve warm.

Serves 4

BOMBAY LEG OF LAMB WITH YOGURT AND LIME

2-pound boned leg of lamb, butterflied
1 cup plain low-fat yogurt
2 large limes

In large nonreactive bowl, put lamb and yogurt. Grate zest of 1 lime and squeeze the juice of 2 limes (you will have approximately ¼ cup). Add to bowl along with freshly ground black pepper and ½ teaspoon kosher salt. Mix well so that lamb is thoroughly coated in yogurt marinade.

Cover and refrigerate 6 to 8 hours. Turn once or twice during the marinating period.

Preheat the broiler. Remove lamb from marinade.

Place lamb in heavy baking pan. Place marinade in small pot.

Broil lamb on each side for 6 to 8 minutes. Lamb should reach 150° on meat thermometer for rare; 160° for medium-rare. Meanwhile, warm marinade over low heat. Remove lamb from oven. Let rest 5 minutes. Slice thinly and serve with warm marinade.

Serves 4 to 6

CURRIED COUSCOUS WITH CURRANTS

2 teaspoons good-quality curry powder
4 tablespoons currants
1½ cups couscous

In a heavy medium pot with cover, bring 2¼ cups water, 1½ teaspoons curry, currants, and ½ teaspoon salt to a boil. Slowly add couscous, stirring constantly. Cook over low heat for 1 minute. Turn off heat and cover pot.

Let sit 5 minutes. Remove cover and add ½ teaspoon remaining curry. Fluff with fork. Serve immediately.

Serves 6

CHILLED SLICED ORANGES WITH ROSEWATER AND DATES

5 large navel oranges
2 teaspoons rosewater
12 good-quality large dried dates

Squeeze the juice of 1 orange; you will have approximately ⅓ cup orange juice. Put in a small bowl with rosewater and stir.

With a small, sharp knife remove rind and all white pith from remaining oranges. Cut oranges into ¼-inch-thick slices.

Arrange orange slices on 4 individual plates or on a platter. Remove pits from dates. Cut 6 dates into wedges. Finely dice remaining dates.

Put date wedges around oranges and scatter diced dates on top. Pour orange juice–rosewater mixture over top. Chill well, or serve at room temperature.

Serves 4

Dinner for a Doge

Tomato Polenta

Calf's Liver, Venetian Style

Braised Eggplant, Balsamic Syrup

Chocolate Semifreddo

12 ingredients

The flavors of tomato and butter are strangely comforting, so I especially love the simplicity and memories triggered by Tomato Polenta — something I whip up for myself on wistful days. Which is pretty much the way I feel when I dream about Venice . . . that pervasive longing for the Piazza San Marco and a vague yearning for liver!

Those cooks in La Serenissima certainly do liver right. They call it fegato alla veneziana, *and it comes in small pieces, quickly cooked and smothered with golden onions. One bite, and you'll feel like you're a doge in a palazzo overlooking the Grand Canal.*

My version of semifreddo, *a classic dessert from the Veneto, may be unorthodox, but nonetheless produces the requisite "half-frozen" mousse texture and concentrated flavor. Prepare early in the day or several hours before the meal, making sure to remove it from the freezer thirty minutes before serving.*

Eggplant can be made earlier and reheated, leaving you free to cook the polenta at the last minute.

GRAPENOTE

The whites from the Veneto region don't have quite enough acidity for this meal, so go north into the Alto Adige for a sauvignon blanc or a fuller-flavored wine made from the *riballo gialla* grape. With the liver, try a stunning red from the Veneto called Camul, or return to the Alto Adige for a bright Italian merlot.

TOMATO POLENTA

1½ cups tomato juice
4 tablespoons unsalted butter, chilled
1 cup yellow cornmeal

In a small saucepan, bring ½ cup tomato juice to a boil. Lower heat and let simmer until tomato juice is reduced to ¼ cup. Whisk in 1 tablespoon butter, off the heat, until creamy. Set aside.

In a heavy medium pot, bring 2½ cups water and 1 cup tomato juice to a boil.

Lower heat to medium. Slowly add cornmeal, letting it slip through your fingers. Stir constantly with a wooden spoon, making sure that no lumps form.

Stir until thick, but still runny and creamy, about 8 to 10 minutes. Cut 3 tablespoons butter into small pieces. Add bit by bit, stirring constantly. Season to taste with salt and freshly ground black pepper. Spoon immediately into 4 flat soup plates and drizzle warm reduced tomato juice over the top. Serve immediately.

Serves 4

CALF'S LIVER, VENETIAN STYLE

1¼ pounds (3 medium) yellow onions
3 tablespoons extra-virgin olive oil
1¼ pounds best-quality calf's liver, thinly sliced

Peel onions. Cut in half through the root end. Place cut side down on a flat surface and slice very thin.

Heat 2 tablespoons olive oil in large nonstick pan with a cover. Add onions and cook over high heat for 5 minutes, stirring onions to coat them with olive oil. Cover pan, reduce heat to very low, and cook for 45 minutes, lifting cover to stir occasionally. After 45 minutes, remove cover and cook an additional 15 minutes, until onions are very soft and golden in color. Season with salt and freshly ground black pepper.

Sprinkle liver lightly with freshly ground black pep-per. Heat remaining tablespoon of oil in another large nonstick skillet. Cut liver into 1½-inch-wide strips. Add to hot oil and cook on each side over high heat for a few minutes, until outside begins to caramelize. Remove from pan. Sprinkle with salt and drizzle with pan juices.

Serve immediately topped with hot caramelized onions.

Serves 4

BRAISED EGGPLANT, BALSAMIC SYRUP ✗

1 large firm eggplant (1½ pounds)
3 tablespoons olive oil
½ cup balsamic vinegar

Trim ends of eggplant. Wash eggplant and dry, but do not peel. Cut into ½-inch-thick slices, then cut slices into ½-inch cubes. Place eggplant cubes, tossed with 1 teaspoon salt, in a colander. Put weight on top of eggplant and let sit 1 hour.

Rinse the eggplant and dry the pieces well with paper towels. In a large nonstick skillet heat oil until hot. Add eggplant and cook over medium heat until eggplant begins to brown and soften. Stir frequently. After 15 minutes, add ¼ cup balsamic vinegar, 2 table-spoons water, and salt and freshly ground black pepper to taste. Continue to cook for 5 to 10 minutes, or until eggplant is tender when tasted.

In a small saucepan heat remaining ¼ cup vinegar and reduce over medium heat to 2 tablespoons. Serve eggplant hot (this can be reheated easily) with a little of the balsamic "syrup" drizzled on top.

Serves 4

CHOCOLATE *SEMIFREDDO* X

6 ounces good-quality semisweet chocolate
1 cup vanilla yogurt
2 extra-large eggs, separated

Melt 4 ounces chocolate in top of a double boiler. Make sure water is at a constant moderate heat so that chocolate melts evenly.

Whisk in yogurt and stir just to combine. Add egg yolks and continue to whisk mixture over moderate heat for 5 to 6 minutes, or until mixture has thickened. The chocolate mixture should thickly cover the back of a wooden spoon. Remove from the heat and let cool. Transfer mixture to a large bowl.

In the bowl of an electric mixer beat egg whites with a pinch of salt until whites are stiff. Fold egg whites into chocolate mixture. Do not overmix, but make sure whites are thoroughly incorporated.

Line 4 dessert cups or molds with plastic wrap. Spoon in mixture and place in freezer for 2 hours. Remove from freezer 30 minutes before serving. Unmold onto large plates. In a small skillet melt 2 ounces remaining chocolate with 1 tablespoon water over low heat. Drizzle chocolate syrup over *semifreddo* and serve.

Serves 4

∎ ∎ ∎

A Wonderful Autumn Dinner

Butternut Squash Soup with Leek Cream

Wine-Dark Short Ribs ✗

Brown Rice with Sun-Dried Cherries

Valrhona Profiteroles

12 ingredients

Quite advertently, the colors of this menu are shades of orange and brown. Its flavor profile also says autumn.

Butternut squash, when roasted and caramelized, produces a luxuriously flavored soup. Leeks not only flavor the broth, but are transformed into a flourish of sweet leek cream. It makes sense to prepare a large batch of this soup, which serves eight but can be stored for a day or two.

The unexpected union of hoisin sauce and zinfandel wine adds sweetness, salt, and spice to meaty short ribs. Sun-dried cherries add another burst of sweetness to nutty brown rice. Together they are a mouthwatering match.

Everyone loves profiteroles, but not everyone has the time, or patience, to make pâte à choux. Instead, make small "buns" from store-bought puff pastry. Fill them with ice cream and freeze. When ready to serve, spoon gobs of melted chocolate over the top, letting the dark brown sauce slowly enrobe each and every one.

This is just the kind of food you want to eat when you start to wonder where your overcoat is.

GRAPENOTE

The sweet roasted flavors of the soup call for a big and oaky chardonnay: Sanford, Chalone, or Gallo's single vineyard Laguna Ranch. Serve the ribs with the same zin you use to prepare them: Good choices would be Deux Amis, Seghesio, or Marietta Cellars.

BUTTERNUT SQUASH SOUP WITH LEEK CREAM

1 large or 2 medium butternut squash (3 pounds)
1 large bunch leeks (1½ pounds)
1½ cups heavy cream

Preheat oven to 400°.

Cut squash in half lengthwise. Scoop out seeds and discard. Also discard any stringy fibers.

Cut in half again, across the width of squash. Place squash pieces, cut side down, in shallow baking pan. Pour in ⅓ cup water. Bake for 1 hour, or until squash is very soft and flesh is caramelized.

Meanwhile, wash leeks very well. Cut off all but 1 inch of green parts of leeks and set greens aside. Slice white part of leeks into thin rounds.

Place sliced leeks in large, heavy pot with 3½ cups water, 1 cup cream, and 1 teaspoon salt. Bring to a boil. Cover and simmer 30 minutes.

When squash is cooked, remove from oven. When cool enough to handle, scoop out flesh and add to pot with leeks and cream. Cook over medium heat for 15 minutes.

Transfer soup to a food processor in several batches and process until very smooth. Return to pot. Add salt and freshly ground white pepper to taste.

To make leek cream: Put remaining ½ cup cream in small saucepan. Finely dice 1 cup leek greens. Add to cream and simmer 15 minutes. Transfer to blender and puree until thick and very smooth. Add salt to taste.

When ready to serve, reheat soup. Garnish with a tablespoon of leek cream, and additional finely minced leek greens, if desired.

Serves 8 (makes 8 cups)

WINE-DARK SHORT RIBS

4 pounds short ribs, cut between the bones, then into 3-inch lengths (12 pieces)
½ cup plus 2 tablespoons hoisin sauce
2 cups zinfandel (red)

Place ribs, ½ cup hoisin, and 1 cup zinfandel in large, nonreactive bowl. Cover and let marinate overnight in the refrigerator.

Remove short ribs from marinade and set aside.

Bring marinade to a boil with 3 cups water in a heavy pot large enough to hold short ribs in one layer. Add ribs and ½ teaspoon whole black peppercorns. Cover and cook slowly over low heat for 2½ hours, turning several times during cooking.

Meanwhile, place remaining 1 cup zinfandel and 2 tablespoons hoisin sauce in small, nonreactive saucepan. Reduce slowly over low heat until you have ½ cup. Reserve.

Remove short ribs with slotted spoon. Turn heat to high and cook liquid in pot until thick and syrupy. Whisk in enough of reserved wine-hoisin reduction until you have a well-balanced sauce. Add salt to taste. Pour sauce over short ribs. Serve immediately.

Serves 4

BROWN RICE WITH SUN-DRIED CHERRIES

2 cups beef broth
1 cup brown rice
½ cup (2 ounces) sun-dried cherries

In a heavy medium saucepan with cover bring broth and rice to a boil. Add freshly ground black pepper and ¼ teaspoon salt.

Lower heat, cover, and cook 10 minutes. Add sun-dried cherries, stir, and cover. Continue to cook 20 minutes, or until water is absorbed and rice is tender but not too soft.

Fluff with a fork and adjust seasonings, adding salt and pepper, if desired.

Serves 4

VALRHONA PROFITEROLES

1 sheet frozen puff pastry (8¾ ounces)
2 pints good-quality vanilla ice cream
4 ounces semisweet Valrhona chocolate

Preheat oven to 400°.

Thaw pastry according to package instructions. While pastry is still cold, cut out 12 circles using a 2-inch cookie cutter. Save remaining dough for another use, or you may cut out extra circles and bake, using the nicest ones for this dessert. Place on ungreased baking sheet.

Bake 15 minutes, or until pastry circles have puffed and are golden brown. Remove from baking sheet. Let cool.

Cut profiteroles in half, horizontally. Top each of 12 bottoms with a small scoop of ice cream, placing "hats" on top. You may freeze until ready to serve, covered with waxed paper.

To make sauce: Chop chocolate into small pieces. Place in small, heavy saucepan with ¼ cup cold water. Simmer over low heat and whisk until chocolate is melted and sauce is smooth. Keep warm. You will have approximately ⅔ cup sauce.

Place 3 profiteroles in center of each of 4 large plates. Pour sauce evenly over tops of each profiterole. Serve immediately.

Serves 4

La Bonne Table ☆

Baby Beets with Roquefort Cheese and Hazelnut Oil

Beef Chuck Braised for Hours, Orange Essence

Polenta with Tiny Broccoli Florets

Strawberries in Cassis, Crème Fraîche

12 ingredients

All good food was his delight — none was too plebeian, none too haute cuisine.
LUDWIG BEMELMANS,
La Bonne Table, 1964

This menu honors Ludwig Bemelmans, prolific writer (best known for Madeleine), *gastronome, artist, and wit, whose delightful book* La Bonne Table *presents his lifetime love affair with the art of dining.*

Bemelmans, through his writings and drawings (he collected famous menus to use as sketch pads), had the rare ability to transport readers to his world of pleasure — the grand hotels and great restaurants of Europe — recounting his memorable meals and riotous experiences behind the scenes of a world I've come to know well.

A good idea: While your chuck roast is braising for hours, sit in a big, comfy chair and read his book. Like this dinner, it is a joy.

GRAPENOTE

The natural sweetness of the beets (even with the piquant note of Roquefort) calls for a soft fruity white like *viognier* or a Riesling-style hybrid like the Müller-Thurgau from Oregon's Sokol Blosser. With the main course, Bemelmans would have loved a great red Burgundy like Gevrey-Chambertin.

BABY BEETS WITH ROQUEFORT CHEESE AND HAZELNUT OIL

2 pounds baby beets or the smallest beets you can find
5 ounces Roquefort cheese, in one piece
6 tablespoons hazelnut oil

Remove leaves from beets, leaving 1 inch of the stem. Save for another use. Cut off any roots

Scrub beets well.

Bring a large pot of salted water to a boil. Add beets and cook over medium heat for 20 minutes, or until beets are tender when tested with the tip of a sharp knife.

Drain beets in a colander. When cool enough to handle, peel with a sharp knife. Cut beets in half if very small or into 3 or 4 thick slices if larger.

Divide warm beets among 6 large plates. Slice cheese very thin and scatter evenly on tops of beets. Drizzle each plate with 1 tablespoon oil. Sprinkle lightly with salt and freshly ground black pepper.

Let cool to room temperature before serving.

Serves 6

BEEF CHUCK BRAISED FOR HOURS, ORANGE ESSENCE

3 pounds beef chuck, cut into 2-inch pieces
6 medium juice oranges
2 pounds tender young carrots

Place beef chuck in a large bowl. Grate the rind of as many oranges as you need to get 2 tablespoons grated orange zest. Mix with chuck.

Cut oranges in half and squeeze enough oranges so that you have 2 cups orange juice. Pour over chuck. Add a liberal grinding of black pepper. Cover and let marinate in the refrigerator for a minimum of 3 hours, turning once.

Preheat oven to 325°.

Peel carrots and halve lengthwise. Cut across into 1-inch pieces. Place carrots in a deep, shallow flame-proof casserole large enough to hold in one layer. With slotted spoon, place meat on top of carrots. Reserve marinade.

Cover casserole and cook for 3 hours. Every half hour, check casserole, adding a little of the marinade to prevent sticking. After 2 hours, stir beef and carrots together, adding ½ teaspoon salt. Continue to cook until beef is very tender. Uncover casserole during last 15 minutes of cooking.

Using slotted spoon, remove meat and carrots to a platter. Place casserole on top of stove and add remaining marinade. Cook over high heat, adding salt and freshly ground black pepper if needed, until sauce is thickened and syrupy, and pour over meat. Serve immediately.

Serves 6

POLENTA WITH TINY BROCCOLI FLORETS

1 large head broccoli
1½ cups stone-ground yellow cornmeal
3 tablespoons unsalted butter

Cut broccoli head into tiny florets and save stems for another use. You will have approximately 3 cups florets. In a medium pot, bring 4 cups water to a boil. Add broccoli florets and cook 5 minutes, until tender but still bright green. Drain in colander under cold running water. Set aside.

In a large pot, bring 6 cups water plus 1½ teaspoons salt to a boil.

Pour in the cornmeal by the handful, very slowly in a thin stream. Stir constantly with a wire whisk to prevent any lumps.

Cook over low heat, stirring constantly. After 20 minutes add 2 tablespoons butter, cut into small pieces, and continue to cook.

Add drained florets to pot with cornmeal. Stir well with wooden spoon to equally distribute broccoli. Add salt and freshly ground black pepper to taste.

Preheat broiler.

Pour polenta into 9-by-11-inch casserole buttered with 1 teaspoon butter. Dot with remaining 2 teaspoons butter.* Put under broiler for 1 minute and serve immediately.

Serves 6 or more

---

* You may make the dish several hours in advance up to this point. Reheat, uncovered, in 325° oven for 10 to 12 minutes. If done ahead of time, the polenta will become firm and can be cut with a knife. If made according to directions in main recipe, the polenta will be soft and creamy. Both are delicious.

STRAWBERRIES IN CASSIS, CRÈME FRAÎCHE

3 pints large fresh strawberries
9 tablespoons crème de cassis
1 cup crème fraîche*

Reserve three whole berries with stems for garnish. Remove green stems from remaining strawberries. Place berries in colander. Wash well. Let drain but do not pat dry.

Cut berries in half lengthwise. Put in bowl. Pour cassis over berries and mix. Add a grinding of black pepper and let marinate 1 hour at room temperature.

Divide berries and cassis equally among 6 wineglasses. Top each with about 2½ tablespoons crème fraîche. Cut remaining strawberries in half, lengthwise through the stem. Garnish each portion with a strawberry half.

Serves 6

* Available in dairy or cheese section in many specialty-food stores.

Father's Day Dinner

Prosciutto-Wrapped Shrimp Sticks

Gorgonzola-Grappa Rib Steak

Pan-Fried Sage Potatoes ✗

***Chocolate-Chocolate* Tartufo** ✗

12 ingredients

People pay us to think about food. And when I say "us," I mean the Joseph Baum & Michael Whiteman Company. We're a four-person restaurant "brain trust" with over 120 years of combined operating and consulting experience. We create lofty icons such as Manhattan's Windows on the World and the Rainbow Room.

So we nibble, the president (my husband, Michael Whiteman) and I. The two of us have noshed, snacked, and gobbled our way around the world, gathering ideas for recipes and identifying those factors that shape the lives of great watering holes and joyful restaurants.

Example: We're speeding down the Alps into Italy, and it's too close to dinnertime but too far to Lake Como. *So we pull into this one-street town whose entire nightlife consists of a creaky* panini *bar with an Astroturf café, and Michael asks for some beer and food. Out comes the ultimate griddled sandwich: crisped bread with a molten filling of Gorgonzola cheese spiked with grappa.*

"Wouldn't this be great on a steak?" I say.

He says, "File this one, Rozee, along with that prosciutto and shrimp thingamajig we had in Rome last year."

And that's how menus are born.

This one is dedicated to my dad; to Michael (Jeremy's dad); and to all the dads in the world who deserve a well-crafted meal to accompany a well-crafted brew.

GRAPENOTE

An icy pale ale would do nicely with the sizzling shrimp sticks. The main course requires the heft of an Australian *shiraz*. After dessert, why not a shot from a single-barrel bourbon? Pass cigars.

PROSCIUTTO-WRAPPED SHRIMP STICKS

48 uncooked medium shrimp (1½ pounds), in their shells
¾ pound thinly sliced prosciutto
3 tablespoons olive oil

You will need 8 6-inch bamboo skewers.

Preheat broiler. Peel shrimp, removing tails. Uncurl shrimp and wrap a small slice of prosciutto neatly and snugly around each to cover completely. If prosciutto slice is too long, cut in half before wrapping.

Skewer 6 shrimp so that they are parallel to one another and closely packed. Fill 8 skewers.

Place skewers on shallow baking sheet. Using pastry brush, brush oil on each side to coat prosciutto.

Place under broiler and broil 20 seconds. Turn shrimp over and broil 20 to 30 seconds. Do not overcook.

Serve immediately, 2 skewers per person. Drizzle with extra olive oil, if desired.

Pass the pepper mill.

Serves 4

GORGONZOLA-GRAPPA RIB STEAK ✕

4 thick 14- to 16-ounce rib steaks, bone in
¾ pound Italian Gorgonzola cheese
3 tablespoons or more grappa

Preheat oven to 450°.

Season steaks with salt and freshly ground black pepper.

Using 2 large nonstick skillets, sear steaks on each side over very high heat, for 3 minutes.

Place steaks on baking sheet and finish cooking in hot oven until desired doneness, approximately 5 minutes for rare.

Cut rind off cheese with a sharp knife and cut cheese into small cubes. Place in heavy medium saucepan with 3 tablespoons grappa. Heat slowly to melt cheese, stirring constantly. Continue to cook for several minutes, or until sauce is thick. If it's too thick, you may add a little more grappa or water.

Plate the steaks and pour cheese sauce over steaks. Serve immediately.

Serves 4

PAN-FRIED SAGE POTATOES

4 large red potatoes (1½ pounds)
3 tablespoons olive oil, plus ¼ cup for frying sage leaves
2 large bunches fresh sage

Wash potatoes and scrub well.

For contrast, peel 2 potatoes, leaving 2 unpeeled. Cut potatoes into quarters (to form long wedges), then cut each wedge thinly, into ⅛-inch-thick triangular pieces.

In a very large nonstick skillet, heat 3 tablespoons oil. Add potatoes. Cook over high heat for 5 minutes, stirring often. Turn potatoes over, and cook on other side for 5 minutes. Potatoes will begin to crisp and turn golden brown.

Cover pan, lower heat, and cook 5 minutes longer. Julienne half the sage so that you have ¼ cup. Un-cover pan and add julienned sage. Stir well, add salt and freshly ground black pepper to taste, and cook another 5 minutes. Total cooking time will be 20 minutes.

Meanwhile, in small nonstick pan heat ¼ cup oil over high heat. When oil is very hot, add 8 to 12 whole sage leaves. Sage will crisp in 30 seconds. Remove sage from oil.

Transfer cooked potatoes to a platter. Garnish with fried sage leaves.

Serves 4

CHOCOLATE-CHOCOLATE *TARTUFO*

1½ pints best-quality chocolate ice cream
2½ cups miniature chocolate chips
¾ cup heavy cream, chilled

Put ice cream in large bowl. Let soften enough to form into 4 large balls, using a large ice-cream scoop.

Place ice-cream balls on waxed paper in a pie tin and immediately place in freezer. Freeze until very hard. Remove ice-cream balls.

Place 2 cups miniature chocolate chips on flat surface. Working quickly, roll ice-cream balls in chips to cover completely. Refreeze, until ready to serve.

In small heavy saucepan, put ½ cup chocolate chips, 2 tablespoons heavy cream, and 3 tablespoons water.

Simmer over low heat and stir well until chocolate melts into a thick smooth sauce. Keep sauce warm. You will have ½ cup.

Whip remaining heavy cream until thick. Divide cream evenly on 4 dessert plates. Place *tartufo* in center of whipped cream. Drizzle with warm chocolate sauce.

Serves 4

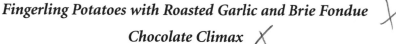

A Dinner for Epicurus

Pickled Shrimp in Rice Vinegar

Bay-Smoked Chateaubriand with Truffle Oil, Truffle-Roasted Salt X

Fingerling Potatoes with Roasted Garlic and Brie Fondue X

Chocolate Climax X

12 ingredients

Hedonism, the seeking of pleasure above all other values, is often a good thing . . . especially around dinnertime. To my way of thinking, an epicure is a hedonist with a drink in his hand.

Epicurus, the Greek philosopher who lived long ago, was no doubt a fancier of bay leaves, also known as laurel. In ancient Greece, a crown of these prized leaves was a symbol of wisdom and glory and not a bad way to cook a roast.

Bay leaves, although slightly bitter when fresh, sweeten as they dry, thereby perfuming a hunk of meat as it cooks — leaving this entrée, you might say, roasting on its laurels.

The meal becomes more hedonistic as it approaches its end, "climaxing" in dessert — a stupendous three-ingredient puddle of chocolate that resolves itself into an urbane cake.

But back to Epicurus: Let's raise a glass to the man who first promoted the business of pleasure.

GRAPENOTE

Were he a sherry drinker, Epicurus would consider nutty Manzanilla a pleasurable match with the first course. With the main course, he would splurge on a great Pauillac like Les Forts de la Tour. (There's no telling what he'd have with dessert. . . .)

PICKLED SHRIMP IN RICE VINEGAR

48 uncooked medium shrimp (1½ pounds), in their shells
6 tablespoons rice-wine vinegar
2 tablespoons pickling spice

In heavy medium pot with cover, put unpeeled shrimp. Add 4 tablespoons rice-wine vinegar, pickling spice, 1½ cups water, 25 black peppercorns, and 2 teaspoons kosher salt.

Cover pot and bring to a boil. When shrimp are just beginning to turn pink and lose their translucence, about 2 minutes, turn off the heat.

Cover and let shrimp cool in the liquid. Refrigerate until very cold.

Add remaining 2 tablespoons rice-wine vinegar to shrimp and toss. Add salt to taste.

Remove shrimp from liquid with a slotted spoon and transfer to 6 chilled flat soup plates. Place liquid in small ramekins for dunking. Serve with plenty of napkins.

Optional garnish: Toast an additional tablespoon of pickling spice over low heat in small nonstick skillet until fragrant. Grind in spice grinder until fine and sprinkle over shrimp.

Serves 6

BAY-SMOKED CHATEAUBRIAND WITH TRUFFLE OIL, TRUFFLE-ROASTED SALT

2¾ pounds "trimmed weight" fillet of beef, tied in 1½-inch intervals
2 or 3 tablespoons truffle oil*
18 California bay leaves

Preheat oven to 400°.

Coat fillet of beef with 1 to 2 teaspoons truffle oil using your hands. Make sure the entire fillet is lightly coated. Grind black pepper all over fillet.

In heavy shallow roasting pan, scatter 15 bay leaves in center of pan. Place fillet on top. Tuck 3 bay leaves on top of fillet, under strings.

Roast for 30 minutes. Turn meat over and roast 5 to 6 minutes longer, or until internal temperature is between 125° and 130° for rare or higher for medium-rare. Remove from oven. Allow to stand 10 minutes before carving. Lightly salt the roast.

To make truffle-roasted salt: Mix 2 tablespoons coarse French sea salt with ¼ teaspoon truffle oil. Place in small nonstick skillet and toast over medium heat, stirring constantly. Remove when salt begins to brown. Cool on paper towel.

Carve meat in ½-inch-thick slices. Drizzle each slice with a little truffle oil, and serve little mounds of truffle-roasted salt with the meat.

Serves 6 to 8

---

* Truffle oil is available in specialty-food shops, or you may use store-bought or homemade Garlic Oil (see page 8) or extra-virgin olive oil.

✕ FINGERLING POTATOES WITH ROASTED GARLIC AND BRIE FONDUE

1 very large head garlic
2 pounds (about 24) fingerling potatoes
12 ounces Brie cheese

Prepare roasted garlic before you cook the chateaubriand (see the preceding recipe). Preheat oven to 400°. Wrap garlic loosely in aluminum foil. Place on pie tin and bake for 1 hour. Allow to cool.

Prepare potatoes 25 minutes before you're going to serve them. Scrub potatoes, but do not peel. Place in large pot of salted water and bring to a boil. Lower heat and cook for 15 to 20 minutes, or until tender when pierced with a sharp knife. Drain in colander.

Cut rind off cheese and cut cheese into small cubes. Put in small heavy saucepan over low heat with 1 tablespoon water. Stir constantly until cheese melts.

Cut roasted garlic in half through center of head to expose all cloves. Squeeze each half of garlic head to extract softened garlic pulp. You will have 2 to 3 tablespoons. Add to melted Brie and mix well.

Cut warm potatoes in half lengthwise. Place on platter or in shallow casserole, and spoon hot brie and garlic sauce over top. You may briefly place in oven at 400° to keep potatoes warm before serving.

Serves 6

CHOCOLATE CLIMAX

1¼ pounds excellent-quality semisweet chocolate
2½ sticks cold unsalted butter
8 extra-large eggs, at room temperature

Preheat oven to 425°.

Butter a 10-inch, removable-bottom cake pan and line the bottom and sides with waxed paper. Make sure your pan fits tightly; it will sit in a water bath, and you don't want any leakage. Cover the bottom and outside of pan with a single large sheet of aluminum foil for assurance.

Chop chocolate into small pieces. Cut butter into cubes. Place in large bowl over pot of simmering water until melted and completely smooth, stirring frequently. The bottom of the bowl should not touch the water. Remove from heat and let cool 5 minutes.

Meanwhile, warm bowl of electric mixer in hot water. Dry completely. Add eggs, one at a time, beating constantly. Add pinch of salt and continue to beat for 6 to 7 minutes, until soft peaks are formed.

Fold half the eggs into the melted chocolate, mix well, then fold in remaining eggs.

Pour batter into cake pan and cover pan with buttered foil, buttered side down. Place cake pan in a large, deep pan and add enough boiling water to reach the level of batter. Bake for 5 minutes, remove top foil, and bake 12 minutes longer.

Remove cake carefully from water bath and let cool 3 to 4 hours before serving. Cake will continue to set as it cools. You may serve at this point or refrigerate for later use. Let come to room temperature before serving.

Serves 12

■ ■ ■

Keeping Company

Onion, Wild Mushroom, and Brie Soup ✕

Stuffed Tenderloin with Black Olives and Sun-Dried Tomatoes

Roasted Garlic Flan ✕

Spinach and Celery Puree

Fresh Fruit en Papillote

15 ingredients

Simplicity, combined with perfection of raw ingredients, delivers the gastronomic equivalent of "less is more" — a theme that pervades this book. The "more" of this particular menu is depth of flavor.

You'll find this uncommonly felicitous for entertaining because so much is prepared early: Soup can be made days ahead, adding cheese to finish; tenderloin is stuffed well before dinner hour; garlic flans can be prepared at leisure, then rewarmed in a water bath alongside the roast.

Even the hot dessert can be preassembled, then popped in the oven as main course dishes are cleared.

As befits every good party giver, this menu enables you to have your own good time, even before company arrives.

GRAPENOTE

The assertive soup needs an assertive wine, a heavily wooded white, like the white Rioja from Muga. The robust flavors of the main course call for a Châteauneuf-du-Pape, a Barolo, or the terrific Bordeaux-style blend from BV in California called Tapestry.

ONION, WILD MUSHROOM, AND BRIE SOUP

¾ ounce (⅔ cup) dried mushrooms
1¼ pounds yellow onions
9 ounces Brie cheese, chilled

Place mushrooms in a bowl. Pour 3 cups boiling water over mushrooms and let soak for 30 minutes.

Meanwhile peel onions and slice very thin. Place onions in large nonstick skillet and cook over medium-high heat for 15 minutes, or until onions are dark brown.

Transfer onions to a medium pot. Pour in soaking liquid from mushrooms through a coffee filter or a double layer of cheesecloth, and add 2 cups water. Bring to a boil. Cover, lower heat, and cook for 45 minutes. Chop mushrooms and reserve for later.

Remove rind from cheese with a sharp knife. Cut into small pieces and add to soup. Stir until melted, but do not boil. Add half the chopped mushrooms or more to taste. Flavor and intensity will depend on type of mushrooms. Add salt and freshly ground white pepper to taste. Stir well and heat gently before serving.

Serves 6 (makes 5¼ cups)

STUFFED TENDERLOIN WITH BLACK OLIVES AND SUN-DRIED TOMATOES

1 trimmed beef tenderloin (about 2½ pounds), without tail
1 cup pitted oil-cured black olives
1 cup sun-dried tomatoes in oil

Preheat oven to 400°.

Using the handle of a large wooden spoon, poke a hole through the length of the tenderloin, creating a tunnel hole that is ¾ inch to 1 inch in diameter.

Drain oil from tomatoes and set aside. In a food processor, puree olives and sun-dried tomatoes with freshly ground black pepper until a coarse paste is formed.

Using a pastry bag with a large tip, pipe olive filling into the tunnel. If you do not have a pastry bag, pack filling into tunnel using the handle of a wooden spoon.

Season tenderloin lightly with salt and place in shallow roasting pan. Drizzle 2 tablespoons reserved tomato oil over meat. Roast for 40 to 45 minutes, depending on diameter. Meat thermometer should read 125° to 130° for rare.

Remove from oven. Let rest 5 minutes before slicing. Serve with any natural juices.

If there is any filling left, form into small quenelle shapes and serve alongside meat.

Serves 6

ROASTED GARLIC FLAN

2 large heads garlic
1½ cups heavy cream
3 extra-large eggs

Preheat oven to 400°.

Wrap garlic in a foil packet. Place in a pie tin. Bake for 1 hour. Let cool.

Lower oven temperature to 350°.

Cut garlic heads in half, exposing all cloves. Squeeze pulp from skins. Place in food processor and puree until a smooth paste is formed. Add cream, eggs, 1 teaspoon salt, and freshly ground white pepper, and process again until smooth. Do not overprocess, or cream will thicken.

Ladle mixture into 6 ½-cup custard cups or rame-kins. Place cups or ramekins in deep baking dish. Pour boiling water into dish to come two-thirds of the way up sides of molds.

Bake for 35 to 40 minutes, or until custard is set. Do not overcook. Let sit 5 minutes and turn out. These can be made ahead of time and refrigerated in their baking molds. They should be warmed in a hot-water bath, covered, for 10 minutes at 400°.

Serves 6

SPINACH AND CELERY PUREE

1 pound (½ large bunch) celery, with leaves
12 ounces fresh curly spinach leaves
2 tablespoons unsalted butter, chilled

Wash celery well. Remove leaves and set aside for later use. Wash spinach and remove any stems.

Cut celery into 1-inch pieces. Place in a medium pot with water just to cover. Cook 15 to 18 minutes over medium heat, or until celery is soft.

Add spinach and cook over high heat for 2 minutes, stirring constantly. Spinach will wilt.

Drain celery-spinach mixture in a colander. Place in a blender or food processor and puree until very smooth. Mixture will be bright green. Add butter, cut into small pieces, and process again. Add salt and freshly ground black pepper to taste.

Transfer to a platter and garnish with celery leaves. Serve immediately.

Serves 6

FRESH FRUIT *EN PAPILLOTE*

3 small to medium bananas
6 juice oranges
18 large ripe strawberries, at least 6 with stems

Preheat oven to 450°.

Tear off 6 pieces aluminum foil, 30 inches long. Fold in half so each piece is 15 inches long.

Wash berries and dry. Reserve 6 strawberries with stems.

To make each papillotte: Cut an unpeeled banana in half lengthwise. Place on foil. Using a vegetable peeler, remove 2 strips of orange rind from one orange, about 1½ inches long by ½ inch wide. Set aside. Next, remove the remaining rind and pith from the orange, using a sharp knife. Slice orange into 3 thick slices. Place overlapping slices next to banana. Tuck 2 strips of orange rind in between oranges and banana. Remove stems from 2 strawberries and cut berries in half lengthwise. Place around fruit.

Fold foil in half to make a package. Crimp the edges of the packet by making little folds, to make an airtight package. You may assemble these just before dinner and bake at the last minute. Place *papillottes* on baking sheets. Bake for 8 minutes, or until packets are fully puffed. Remove from oven.

Slice packets open and top fruit with a strawberry with stem, cut into a fan (see page 17). You may serve the fruit in the packet on a large flat plate while warm, or remove the fruit and all the juices and place in large flat soup plates and serve at room temperature.

Serves 6

■ ■ ■

English-Style Holiday Dinner

Smoked Salmon Tartare, Dill Mousse

Salt-and-Pepper Prime Rib with Horseradish Sauce and Yorkshire Pudding

Brussels Sprouts and Tangerine Beurre Noisette

Oven-Roasted Pears with Stilton, Warm Honey Syrup

15 ingredients

This meal has a bit of Dickens about it, but Ebenezer Scrooge no doubt would balk at the rather considerable outlay required.

The menu's structure and its elements are "terribly English" — smoked salmon, prime rib, Yorkshire pud, brussels sprouts, Stilton, and pears; the very sort of holiday dinner you might find some night in Claridge's or Simpsons-in-the-Strand, or perhaps even on Grub Street, where my English publisher is situated.

When Recipes 1-2-3 was published in Great Britain, I was flattered by some lovely endorsements, one of which read "inspiring and reassuring, without gimmickry or tricksiness." "Tricksiness"? I love that!

So here it is, an unflaggingly English din-din without tricksiness.

GRAPENOTE

Because the English love old sparklers, start with an aged champagne like Bollinger RD. Then on to a festive claret like good vintages of Château Ducru-Beaucaillou or Château Pape-Clement, or Francis Ford Coppola's velvety red called claret. Yes, port with dessert would be most congenial.

SMOKED SALMON TARTARE, DILL MOUSSE

1 pound best-quality smoked salmon, sliced ⅛ inch thick
2 large bunches fresh dill
4 tablespoons olive oil

Meticulously cut smoked salmon into small dice (between ⅛ and ¼ inch). Place in a medium bowl. Wash dill and dry. Add ¼ cup finely chopped fresh dill and freshly ground black pepper. Mix gently and cover. Chill until ready to use.

To make dill mousse: Reserve some dill sprigs for garnish. Cut remaining dill to get 1 cup packed leaves with a little of the stems attached to the leaves. Chop coarsely and place in a blender. Puree dill on high speed, slowly adding 4 tablespoons olive oil and 2 tablespoons cold water. Add ⅛ teaspoon

kosher salt, and puree until thick and smooth. You will have ½ cup.

To serve, pack smoked salmon mixture into 4 rings so that each "cake" is about 2¾ inches in diameter by 1 inch high. Place in center of 4 large plates. Spoon mousse on top of each cake to cover. Garnish with tiny sprigs of fresh dill. Spoon any remaining mousse decoratively around tartare.

Serves 4 *

---

* This recipe is easily increased by 50 percent for 6 servings or doubled for 8 servings.

SALT-AND-PEPPER PRIME RIB WITH HORSERADISH SAUCE AND YORKSHIRE PUDDING

3-rib prime rib roast (about 5½ pounds), trimmed well
1 cup heavy cream
5 tablespoons prepared white horseradish

YORKSHIRE PUDDING

2 cups milk
4 extra-large eggs
2 cups self-rising flour

Preheat oven to 300°.

Make sure rib roast is at room temperature before roasting.

Mix together 2 tablespoons kosher salt and 1 teaspoon butcher-grind black pepper. Rub well into fat on top of the roast, covering thoroughly. Place in shallow roasting pan, fatty side up, and roast for 1 hour and 50 minutes, or approximately 20 minutes per pound for rare.

Meanwhile, whip cream with electric mixer until thick. Gently mix in horseradish, salt, and freshly ground white pepper to taste. You will have 2½ cups. Refrigerate until ready to use.

Fifteen minutes before roast is finished, increase oven temperature to 450°.

During the last 15 minutes of cooking the roast, prepare Yorkshire pudding: Beat milk and eggs together in bowl of electric mixer. Add ¾ teaspoon salt and flour and beat until a smooth, thick batter is formed.

Remove roast from oven when internal temperature is between 120° and 125°. Place on cutting board and let sit, covered loosely with foil, for 20 minutes, or until Yorkshire pudding is done. Save ⅓ cup drippings from roast and place them in a 9-by-11-inch shallow casserole.

Pour in pudding batter and bake at 450° for 20 to 22 minutes.

Remove pudding from oven and let rest 5 minutes while you cut the roast. Cut the meat away from the bone in one piece. You will have approximately 3½ pounds of meat. Carve into thin or thick slices, as desired. Cut through the bones and serve separately. You will have 3 meaty ribs. (If too rare, you can put the bones under the broiler for 1 minute.)

Serve roast with any pan juices, warm Yorkshire pudding, optional bones, and cold horseradish sauce.

Serves 6 or more

BRUSSELS SPROUTS AND TANGERINE *BEURRE NOISETTE*

3 tangerines
1 pound brussels sprouts
3 tablespoons unsalted butter

Grate zest of 2 tangerines so that you have ½ teaspoon. Set aside.

Peel 2 tangerines and cut away as much white pith as possible, using a small sharp knife. Cut into segments along membranes.

Bring a pot of salted water to a boil. Wash and trim brussels sprouts and remove any dark outer leaves. Add brussels sprouts to water and boil for 8 minutes. Drain in colander. Cut brussels sprouts in half through the core.

In a large nonstick skillet melt 1 tablespoon butter. Add halved brussels sprouts, tangerine segments, and grated zest. Cook over medium heat for 5 minutes. Cut remaining tangerine in half and squeeze juice of a tangerine half into pan with brussels sprouts. Cook over high heat for 1 minute, adding salt and freshly ground black pepper to taste. Keep brussels sprouts warm.

In a small nonstick skillet, melt remaining 2 tablespoons butter and cook over medium heat until browned and you can smell a faint nutty odor. Be careful not to burn. Squeeze in juice of remaining tangerine half. Cook 30 seconds and pour over cooked brussels sprouts. Serve immediately.

Serves 4 or more

OVEN-ROASTED PEARS WITH STILTON, WARM HONEY SYRUP

4 large firm Anjou pears (2 pounds), with stems
6 ounces Stilton cheese, at room temperature
½ cup honey

Preheat oven to 350°.

Wash pears and cut in half lengthwise. Remove the core and any seeds. Place pears, cut side down, on metal baking sheet. Bake 20 minutes. Turn pears over. Bake another 20 minutes, turn pears again, and bake 10 minutes longer. Pears should be golden brown and soft. Remove from oven. Let come to room temperature.

Meanwhile, cut cheese into 8 chunks. Using 2 small spoons, make 8 quenelles, or oval shapes. Set aside.

In heavy small saucepan, put honey and ½ cup water. Bring just to a boil, stirring until honey is dis-solved. Lower heat to a simmer and cook 10 minutes, until syrup thickens. You should have ½ cup. Let cool 10 minutes.

To serve, put pears in warm oven (from cooking the Salt-and-Pepper Prime Rib with Horseradish Sauce and Yorkshire Pudding, page 291), just to warm through. Place 2 pear halves on each plate with cut side up. Place a cheese quenelle on each. Spoon 1 tablespoon warm honey syrup over each pear half. Serve immediately.

*Serves 4 **

* If serving 6 or 8, you have the option of serving one pear half or increasing the recipe proportionately.

4

More Magical Menus

You can use this book to construct myriads of satisfying and creative menus — for with modest knowledge and superb ingredients, even the most simple meal can be made magical.

The following thirty-two menus, all using recipes in this book, speak to many of our basic needs: There are easy soup-salad-sandwich lunches, picnics, brunches, and menus that require no cooking! Nothing shows off the stunning simplicity of quality ingredients more than dishes that require only a bit of prep and are not altered in any way by heat. These menus are especially suited for lighter meals and warmer weather.

Also included are complete two-course dinners, each with only six ingredients; an afternoon tea; a cocktail party; a sumptuous wedding supper; and a traditional New Year's Day celebration called the Vodka Table.

These themes and variations illustrate only some of the possible menus you can create to provide beautifully harmonious meals — morning, noon, and night.

Morning

SHORT-ORDER COOK

Smoked Salmon Quesadillas (page 17)
Scrambled Eggs and Onions (page 52)
Tiny Melons Filled with Raspberries and
Framboise (page 37)
9 ingredients

VILLA D'ESTE

Zucchini Flan (page 153)
Homemade Focaccia (page 148)
Fresh Figs, Bitter Orange Mascarpone (page 44)
9 ingredients

A "NO-COOK" BREAKFAST

Home-Cured Gravlax (page 22)
Endive and Grapefruit Salad (page 151)
Strawberries in Cassis, Crème Fraîche (page 274)
9 ingredients

SOUTHERN HOSPITALITY

Country-Style Ham and Eggs, Redeye Gravy (page 31)
Buttermilk Grits Soufflé (page 49)
Spicy Stewed Red Plums (page 19)
9 ingredients

"MED-RIM" MORNING

Chilled Sliced Oranges with Rosewater and
Dates (page 260)
Turkish Eggplant Flan (page 198)
Whole Wheat Pita Bread (page 246)
Poached Prunes with Cardamom Yogurt (page 200)
12 ingredients

LITTLE A.M. MEALS
6 ingredients each

Warm Cheese Scones (page 42)
Fresh Fruit *en Papillote* (page 288)

***

Tostones: Fried Plantains and Fresh Lime (page 125)
Oranges and Strawberries *en Gelée* (page 24)

***

Souffléed Ricotta Terrine (page 37)
Fresh Cherry Soup (page 77)

***

Almond "Toast" (page 20)
Almond Milk with *Orzata* and Coffee Ice
Cubes (page 59)

***

Halvah and Golden Raisin Turnovers (page 58)
Breakfast Chocolate (page 35)

Noon

A "NO-COOK" CHAMPAGNE BRUNCH

Oysters with "Champagne" Mignonette, substituting champagne vinegar for the malt vinegar in the recipe (page 134)

Smoked Salmon Tartare, Dill Mousse (page 290)

Strawberries in Cassis, Crème Fraîche (page 274)

9 ingredients

SOUP AND SANDWICH

Tomato-Mascarpone Soup, Basil Chiffonade (page 72)

Bel Paese and Prosciutto *Bruschetta* (page 46)

Brutti ma Buoni (Ugly but Good) Cookies (page 257)

9 ingredients

***

Zucchini Vichyssoise (page 240)

Canadian Bacon and Dill Tostadas (page 39)

Lemon-Curd Yogurt Tarts (page 220)

9 ingredients

SOUP AND SALAD

Sweet Corn Soup with Scallion Butter (page 107)

Salad of Watercress, Orange, and Chorizo (page 90)

Black Grapes and Rum Raisins, Black Grape Granita (page 180)

9 ingredients

AT THE BEACH

Lemony Tuna Salad, Tuna-Tahina Dressing (page 80)

Sweet Pepper Green Beans (page 80)

Homemade Focaccia (page 148)

Fruit Salad *Vino Cotto* (page 81)

12 ingredients

BACKYARD PICNIC

Country Garlic Bread (page 91)

Jumbo Lump Crab, Avocado Sauce (page 191)

Cabbage "Cream" Slaw (page 131)

Old-Fashioned Rice Pudding (page 136)

12 ingredients

"NO-COOK" LUNCHES

Roquefort Mousse and Celery Crudités (page 94)

Chilled Tomato-Orange Soup with Tarragon (page 194)

Margarita Sorbet, Sugared Raspberries (page 125)

9 ingredients

***

Home-Cured Gravlax (page 22)

Mâche and Granny Smith Salad, Apple Vinaigrette (page 76)

Tiny Melons Filled with Raspberries and Framboise (page 37)

9 ingredients

***

Fennel and Orange Salad (page 231)

Bresaola and Mango, Parmesan Shards (page 161)

Anisette Espresso Coupe (page 224)

9 ingredients

FOUR O'CLOCK TEA

Warm Buttermilk Biscuits, made in miniature (page 31)
Fresh Strawberries, Gingered Yogurt (page 17)
Brown Sugar Shortbread (page 78)
Chocolate Climax, cut into slivers (page 283)
12 ingredients

NEW YEAR'S DAY: THE VODKA TABLE

A salmon duet: Home-Cured Gravlax (page 22) and
Pickled Fresh Salmon (page 52)
Pickled Shrimp in Rice Vinegar (page 280)
Horseradish Potato Salad (page 108)
A Simple Strudel (page 209)
15 ingredients

Night

THE COCKTAIL HOUR

Tiny Clams with Wasabi and Pickled Ginger (page 111)
Pithiviers of Smoked Ham and Port Salut, hors d'oeuvre
size (page 75)
Scallops-in-Shiitakes (page 178)
Roquefort Mousse and Celery Crudités (page 94)
Tequila Melon (page 140)
15 ingredients

A COLORFUL SUMMER SUPPER

A Rainbow of Roasted Tomatoes in Peppers (page 166)
Pavé of Cod, *Herbes de Provence* (page 162)
Fresh Spinach and Lemon Oil (page 158)
Oranges and Strawberries *en Gelée* (page 24)
12 ingredients

DINNERS IN TWO COURSES
6 ingredients each

WINTER
Pot-au-Feu: Chicken, Beef Shin, and Leeks (page 182)
Oven-Roasted Pears with Stilton, Warm Honey
Syrup (page 293)

SPRING
Veal Roast with Caramelized Soup Greens, Vegetable
Jus (page 232)
Rhubarb Compote and Sour Cream Ice Cream,
Rhubarb-Pepper Syrup (page 176)

SUMMER
Cornish Hens with Tarragon Rice, served
cold (page 203)
Strawberry Gratin à la Sabayon (page 243)

FALL
Crisped Duck with Roasted Turnips, Port Wine
Reduction (page 208)
Apples *Talibur* in Puff Pastry, Apple Confit (page 184)

A VEGETARIAN FEAST

Roasted Beet Soup with Pickled Beet Greens (page 217)

Portobello Mushroom Melt (page 226)

Curried Couscous with Currants (page 260)

Smooth and Chunky Turnip Puree, Caramelized
Shallots (page 212)

Gingersnap Baked Apples (page 117)

15 ingredients

SUPPER AT THE KITCHEN TABLE

Mamaliga: Rumanian Cornmeal Porridge (page 26)

Pickled Fresh Salmon (page 52)

Cabbage "Cream" Slaw (page 131)

Warm Apple Kissel, Apple Chips (page 132)

12 ingredients

NEW YEAR'S EVE

Spinach and Smoked Salmon Terrine Lutèce (page 202)

Scallops-in-Shiitakes (page 178)

Bay-Smoked Chateaubriand with Truffle Oil, Truffle-
Roasted Salt (page 281)

Savoy Cabbage with Lardons and Champagne
Vinegar (page 163)

Chocolate *Dacquoise* (page 154)

15 ingredients

WEDDING SUPPER

Sweet Corn Soup with Scallion Butter (page 107)   ✗

Smoked Salmon Quesadillas (page 17)

Stuffed Tenderloin with Black Olives and Sun-Dried
Tomatoes (page 286)

Potato Silk (page 96)

Gelato d'Arancina, Candied Orange Peel (page 159)

15 ingredients

5

Menus from the Healthy Kitchen

Using the following lists of healthful recipes, you can compose menus based on many of the principles outlined in this book.

There are twenty-seven fat-free recipes with one gram of fat or less per serving.

Low-fat recipes are defined as having five grams of fat or less per serving for appetizers, side dishes, and desserts and under ten grams of fat for main courses.

Low-calorie recipes contain fewer than 165 calories per serving for appetizers, side dishes, and desserts and under 350 calories for main courses.

You will be astonished at the depth of flavor and the generous portion size of each of these dishes.

In addition, there are twelve "Healthy Kitchen" menus, making you feel not only like a culinary virtuoso but also virtuous.

Fat-Free Recipes

1 gram of fat or less per serving

Morning

Spicy Stewed Red Plums (page 19)

Oranges and Strawberries *en Gélee* (page 24)

Egyptian Carrot Jam (page 29)

Candied Tomatoes (page 32)

Quince-Glazed Fresh Fruit Kabobs (page 34)

Tiny Melons Filled with Raspberries and Framboise (page 37)

Two-Melon Soup (page 40)

Morning Granita: Grapefruit-Campari (page 47)

Mangoes, Prunes, and Pomegranates (page 53)

Warm Pear and Cranberry Compote, Cranberry Syrup (page 56)

Noon

Salade de Tomates with *Verjus* (page 65)

Amaretto Granita (page 70)

Fresh Cherry Soup (page 77)

Margarita Sorbet, Sugared Raspberries (page 125)

Warm Apple Kissel, Apple Chips (page 132)

Tequila Melon (page 140)

Fruit Salad *Vino Cotto* (page 81)

Poached Oranges in Lemon Syrup, Citrus Granita (page 88)

Almond Water Ice with Fresh Cherry Salad, Cherry Syrup (page 97)

Night

Chilled Tomato-Orange Soup with Tarragon (page 194)

Chickpea Soup with Cilantro (page 250)

Ruby Cranberries with Sun-Dried Cherries: Relish and Compote (page 214)

Pears in White Wine Caramel (page 149)

Pear-Poire-Pepper Sorbet (page 168)

Chilled Sliced Oranges with Rosewater and Dates (page 260)

Fresh Fruit *en Papillote* (page 288)

Desserts

Spicy Stewed Red Plums (page 19)

Oranges and Strawberries *en Gelée* (page 24)

Quince-Glazed Fresh Fruit Kabobs (page 34)

Tiny Melons Filled with Raspberries and Framboise (page 37)

Two-Melon Soup (page 40)

Morning Granita: Grapefruit-Campari (page 47)

Mangoes, Prunes, and Pomegranates (page 53)

Amaretto Granita (page 70)

Pear-Poire-Pepper Sorbet (page 168)

Fresh Cherry Soup (page 77)

Margarita Sorbet, Sugared Raspberries (page 125)

Warm Apple Kissel, Apple Chips (page 132)

Tequila Melon (page 140)

Fruit Salad *Vino Cotto* (page 81)

Poached Oranges in Lemon Syrup, Citrus Granita (page 88)

Almond Water Ice with Fresh Cherry Salad, Cherry Syrup (page 97)

Pears in White Wine Caramel (page 149)

Chilled Sliced Oranges with Rosewater and Dates (page 260)

Fresh Fruit *en Papillote* (page 288)

Low-Calorie Recipes

165 calories or less per serving for first course, side dish, or dessert
350 calories or less per serving for main course

Morning

Irish Oatmeal with Buttermilk and Poppy Seeds (page 19)

Baked Eggs Splendido (page 46)

Scrambled Eggs and Onions (page 52)

Buttermilk Eggs in Tomato Shells (page 39)

Fresh Strawberries, Gingered Yogurt (page 17)

Spicy Stewed Red Plums (page 19)

Oranges and Strawberries *en Gelée* (page 24)

Raspberry "Borscht" (page 26)

Egyptian Carrot Jam (2 tablespoons) (page 29)

Quince-Glazed Fresh Fruit Kabobs (page 34)

Tiny Melons Filled with Raspberries and Framboise (page 37)

Two-Melon Soup (page 40)

Peaches Flamed in Southern Comfort (page 50)

Noon

Salade de Tomates with *Verjus* (page 65)

Immune Soup (page 127)

Roquefort Mousse and Celery Crudités (based on 6 servings) (page 94)

Tiny Clams with Wasabi and Pickled Ginger (page 111)

Oysters with "Malted" Mignonette (page 134)

Mâche and Granny Smith Salad, Apple Vinaigrette (page 76)

Polenta "Lasagne" with Smoked Mozzarella (page 69)

Blasted Green Beans with Niçoise Olives (page 70)

Lemon Yellow Beans (page 132)

Sweet Pepper Green Beans (page 80)

Courgettes with Basil (page 100)

Horseradish Potato Salad (page 108)

Cremini Mushrooms, Sherry-Pepper Cream (page 135)

Fresh Cherry Soup (page 77)

Tequila Melon (page 140)

Pink Grapefruit Sherbet, Pink Grapefruit Syrup (page 92)

Brown Sugar Shortbread (1 piece) (page 78)

Night

A Rainbow of Roasted Tomatoes in Peppers (page 166)

Chilled Tomato-Orange Soup with Tarragon (page 194)

Roasted Beet Soup with Pickled Beet Greens (page 217)

Pickled Shrimp in Rice Vinegar (page 280)

Salmon Prunier with Tomato Julienne and Mint (page 152)

Pavé of Cod, *Herbes de Provence* (page 162)

Chicken Paillards, Adobo Style (page 191)

Manchego Chicken with Prosciutto (page 194)

Portobello Mushroom Melt (as a main course) (page 226)

Fresh Artichokes with Mint (page 171)

Sugar Snaps with Diced Bacon and Radishes (page 175)

Warm Onion Gratin (page 179)

Simple Green Beans (page 180)

Pepper Confit with Sherry Vinegar (page 195)

Belgian Endive and Blue Cheese Gratin (page 204)

Smooth and Chunky Turnip Puree, Caramelized Shallots (page 212)

Slow-Cooked Zucchini with Thyme (page 224)

Sautéed Red Swiss Chard (page 237)

Watercress Sauté with Garlic Chips (page 242)

Green Beans and Potatoes in Pesto (page 257)

Braised Eggplant, Balsamic Syrup (page 264)

Spinach and Celery Puree (page 287)

Brussels Sprouts and Tangerine *Beurre Noisette* (page 292)

Brutti ma Buoni (Ugly but Good) Cookies (2 cookies) (page 257)

Chilled Sliced Oranges with Rosewater and Dates (page 260)

Low-Fat Recipes

5 grams of fat or less per serving for first course, side dish, or dessert
10 grams of fat or less per serving for main course

Morning

Irish Oatmeal with Buttermilk and Poppy Seeds (page 19)

Buttermilk Eggs in Tomato Shells (page 39)

Baked Eggs Splendido (page 46)

Fresh Strawberries, Gingered Yogurt (page 17)

Raspberry "Borscht" (page 26)

Noon

Immune Soup (page 127)

Oysters with "Malted" Mignonette (page 134)

Tiny Clams with Wasabi and Pickled Ginger (page 111)

Bay Scallops with Parsley Puree (page 86)

Tubetti with Zucchini (page 84)

Courgettes with Basil (page 100)

Horseradish Potato Salad (page 108)

Gingersnap Baked Apples (page 117)

Lychee Sorbet and Almond Cookie Dessert (page 129)

Pink Grapefruit Sherbet, Pink Grapefruit Syrup (page 92)

Red, White, and Blueberries (page 109)

Night

Roasted Beet Soup with Pickled Beet Greens (page 217)

Pickled Shrimp in Rice Vinegar (page 280)

Portobello Mushroom Melt (as a main course) (page 226)

Salmon Prunier with Tomato Julienne and Mint (page 152)

Barbecued Tuna, London-Broil Style (page 179)

Chicken Paillards, Adobo Style (page 191)

Smooth and Chunky Turnip Puree, Caramelized Shallots (page 212)

Curried Couscous with Currants (page 260)

Brown Rice with Sun-Dried Cherries (page 268)

Spinach and Celery Puree (page 287)

Fig Confit with Sesame and Honey (page 248)

Brutti ma Buoni (Ugly but Good) Cookies (1 cookie) (page 257)

Turkish Grapes with Wild-Thyme Honey and Yogurt (page 253)

"Healthy Kitchen" Menus

Morning

ALMOST FAT-FREE BREAKFAST

Whole Wheat Pita Bread (page 246)

Egyptian Carrot Jam (page 29)

Fresh Fruit *en Papillote* (page 288)

9 ingredients

LOW-FAT BREAKFASTS

Irish Oatmeal with Buttermilk and Poppy Seeds (page 19)

Warm Pear and Cranberry Compote, Cranberry Syrup (page 56)

6 ingredients

***

Fruit Salad *Vino Cotto* (page 81)

Baked Eggs Splendido (page 46)

Morning Granita: Grapefruit-Campari (page 47)

9 ingredients

Noon

ALMOST FAT-FREE LUNCH

Salade de Tomates with *Verjus* (page 65)

Chickpea Soup with Cilantro (page 250)

Whole Wheat Pita Bread (page 246)

Poached Oranges in Lemon Syrup, Citrus Granita (page 88)

12 ingredients

REDUCED-FAT LUNCHES

Tiny Clams with Wasabi and Pickled Ginger (page 111)

Salmon Prunier with Tomato Julienne and Mint (page 152)

Spinach and Celery Puree (page 287)

Almond Water Ice with Fresh Cherry Salad, Cherry Syrup (page 97)

12 ingredients

***

Tubetti with Zucchini (page 84)
Bay Scallops with Parsley Puree (page 86)
Courgettes with Basil (page 100)
Pink Grapefruit Sherbet, Pink Grapefruit
Syrup (page 92)
12 ingredients

***

Chilled Tomato-Orange Soup with Tarragon (page 194)
Barbecued Tuna, London-Broil Style (page 179)
Horseradish Potato Salad (page 108)
Fresh Strawberries, Gingered Yogurt (page 17)
12 ingredients

UNDER-650-CALORIE LUNCHES

Polenta "Lasagne" with Smoked Mozzarella (page 69)
Slow-Cooked Zucchini with Thyme (page 224)
Tiny Melons Filled with Raspberries and
Framboise (page 37)
9 ingredients

Chicken Paillards, Adobo Style (page 191)
Cremini Mushrooms, Sherry-Pepper Cream (page 135)
Two-Melon Soup (page 40)
9 ingredients

Night

A 625-CALORIE SUPPER

Baked Eggs Splendido (page 46)
Blasted Green Beans with Niçoise Olives (page 70)
Braised Eggplant, Balsamic Syrup (page 264)
Two-Melon Soup (page 40)
12 ingredients

UNDER-650-CALORIE DINNERS

Pepper Confit with Sherry Vinegar (page 195)
Manchego Chicken with Prosciutto (page 194)
Warm Onion Gratin (page 179)
Quince-Glazed Fresh Fruit Kabobs (page 34)
12 ingredients

***

Immune Soup (page 127)
Pavé of Cod, Herbes de Provence (page 162)
Belgian Endive and Blue Cheese Gratin (page 204)
Pink Grapefruit Sherbet, Pink Grapefruit
Syrup (page 92)
12 ingredients

Index

Açorda (Garlic Bread Pudding), 195
almond(s):
    Cookie and Lychee Sorbet Dessert, 129
    Milk with *Orzata* and Coffee Ice Cubes, 59
    "Toast," 20
    Toasted, Coffee Ice Cream with Prune Syrup and, 84
    Water Ice with Fresh Cherry Salad and Cherry Syrup, 97
amaretto:
    Granita, 70
    Syrup and Cream, Roasted Nectarines with, 172
anchovies, in "Pasta @ Noon," 72
Anisette Espresso Coupe, 224
apple(s):
    Gingersnap Baked, 117
    Granny Smith, and Mâche Salad with Apple Vinaigrette, 76
    Kissel with Apple Chips, 132
    Strudel, Simple, 209
    Talibur in Puff Pastry with Apple Confit, 184
Arepas with Butter and *Queso Blanco*, 35
artichokes:
    Fresh, with Mint, 171
    Globe, Stuffed with Sun-Dried Tomato Couscous, 147
Arugula Salad with Sweet Garlic Dressing, 255
Asiago-Pepper Roulades, 222

asparagus:
    and Eggs Georges Blanc, 23
    Roasted, and Provolone Salad, 146
Avocado Sauce, Jumbo Lump Crab with, 191

banana(s):
    Fresh Fruit *en Papillote,* 288
    Quince-Glazed Fresh Fruit Kabobs, 34
    Tarts, Warm, 189
Barley with Dates, 248
bean(s):
    Ful Mudammas with Lemon, 28
    Smoky Pink, and Rice, 192
    White, and Shrimp in Pesto Broth, 156
    White, Puree, Truffled, 237
    Yellow, Lemon, 132
    see also green beans
beef:
    Bresaola and Mango with Parmesan Shards, 161
    Chateaubriand, Bay-Smoked, with Truffle Oil and Truffle-Roasted Salt, 281
    Chuck Braised for Hours with Orange Essence, 272
    Prime Rib, Salt-and-Pepper, with Horseradish Sauce and Yorkshire Pudding, 291
    Rib Steak, Gorgonzola-Grappa, 276

    Shin, Chicken, and Leeks (Pot-au-Feu), 182
    Short Ribs, Wine-Dark, 268
    Skirt Steak with *Salsa Verde* and Raw and Roasted Garlic, 138
    Steak, Skillet Chopped, with Scallions and Soy, 134
    Tenderloin Stuffed with Black Olives and Sun-Dried Tomatoes, 286
beet(s):
    Baby, with Roquefort Cheese and Hazelnut Oil, 271
    and *Frisée* Salad with Goat Cheese Dressing, 186
    Roasted, Soup with Pickled Beet Greens, 217
Belgian Endive and Blue Cheese Gratin, 204
Bel Paese and Prosciutto *Bruschetta,* 46
Beurre Blanc, Mustard, 157
beverages:
    Almond Milk with *Orzata* and Coffee Ice Cubes, 59
    Café Cantata, 56
    Chocolate, Breakfast, 35
Biscotti, Chocolate Terrine, 229
Biscuits, Warm Buttermilk, 31
Blueberries, Red, White and, 109
blue cheese:
    and Belgian Endive Gratin, 204
    see also Roquefort
"Borscht," Raspberry, 26

bread(s):
    Almond "Toast," 20
    Buttermilk Biscuits, Warm, 31
    Cheese Scones, Warm, 42
    Focaccia, Homemade, 148
    Garlic, Country, 91
    Garlic, Pudding (*Açorda*), 195
    Pita, Whole Wheat, 246
breakfast and brunch fare, 13–59
    Almond Milk with *Orzata* and Coffee Ice Cubes, 59
    Almond "Toast," 20
    Arepas with Butter and *Queso Blanco*, 35
    Bel Paese and Prosciutto *Bruschetta,* 46
    Buttermilk Biscuits, Warm, 31
    Buttermilk Grits Soufflé, 49
    Café Cantata, 56
    Canadian Bacon and Dill Tostadas, 39
    Carrot Jam, Egyptian, 29
    Cheese Scones, Warm, 42
    Chocolate, 35
    Chocolate-Raspberry Turnovers, 58
    Feta Cheese–Olives–Grilled Pita, 29
    Figs with Bitter Orange Mascarpone, 44
    Ful Mudammas with Lemon, 28
    Grapefruit-Campari Granita, 47
    Gravlax, Home-Cured, 22
    Halvah and Golden Raisin Turnovers, 58

breakfast and brunch fare (*cont.*)
Labaneh in Olive Oil with Cucumbers, 28
Mamaliga (Rumanian Cornmeal Porridge), 26
Mangoes, Prunes, and Pomegranates, 53
Melons, Tiny, Filled with Raspberries and Framboise, 37
Melon Soup, 40
Oatmeal, Irish, with Buttermilk and Poppy Seeds, 19
Oranges and Strawberries *en Gelée*, 24
Panettone French Toast, 55
Peaches Flamed in Southern Comfort, 50
Pear and Cranberry Compote with Cranberry Syrup, 56
Plums, Spicy Stewed Red, 19
Quince-Glazed Fresh Fruit Kabobs, 34
Raspberry "Borscht," 26
Salmon, Pickled Fresh, 52
Smoked Salmon Quesadillas, 17
Souffléed Ricotta Terrine, 37
Strawberries and Gingered Yogurt, 17
Tomatoes, Candied, 32
Tomatoes, Fried Red, 43
see also egg(s)
Bresaola and Mango with Parmesan Shards, 161
Brie:
Fondue, Fingerling Potatoes with Roasted Garlic and, 282
Onion, and Wild Mushroom Soup, 285
Broccoli Florets, Polenta with, 273
Brown Rice with Sun-Dried Cherries, 268
Brown Sugar Shortbread, 78
brunch. *See* breakfast and brunch fare
Bruschetta, Bel Paese and Prosciutto, 46
Brussels Sprouts and Tangerine *Beurre Noisette*, 292
Brutti ma Buoni (Ugly but Good) Cookies, 257
Bulgur Wheat with Caramelized Onions, 252
buttermilk:
Biscuits, Warm, 31
Eggs in Tomato Shells, 39
Grits Soufflé, 49
Butternut Squash Soup with Leek Cream, 267

cabbage:
"Cream" Slaw, 131
Savoy, with Lardons and Champagne Vinegar, 163
Café Cantata, 56
Calf's Liver, Venetian Style, 263
Campari-Grapefruit Granita, 47
Canadian Bacon and Dill Tostadas, 39
Carrot Jam, Egyptian, 29
celery:
Crudités, Roquefort Mousse and, 94
Salad with French Black Olives and Truffle Oil, 104
and Spinach Puree, 287
Celery Root Gratin, 188
cereals:
Mamaliga (Rumanian Cornmeal Porridge), 26
Oatmeal, Irish, with Buttermilk and Poppy Seeds, 19
Chateaubriand, Bay-Smoked, with Truffle Oil and Truffle-Roasted Salt, 281
Cheddar–Sweet Potato Gratin, 213
cheese:
Scones, Warm, 42
see also specific cheeses
cherry(ies):
Fresh, Salad, Almond Water Ice with Cherry Syrup and, 97
Fresh, Soup, 77
Sun-Dried, Ruby Cranberries with (Relish and Compote), 214
chicken:
Beef Shin, and Leeks (Pot-au-Feu), 182
Breasts in Walnut and Pomegranate Sauce (*Fesenjune*), 199
Chipotle with Red Onions, 124
Fricassee with Pearl Onions and Lardons, 187
Liver Royale with Red Onions and Bacon, 235
Manchego, with Prosciutto, 194
Paillards, Adobo Style, 191
with Preserved Lemons and Green Olives, Moroccan, 120
Roulades with Roasted Peppers and Soppressata, 116
wings, in Immune Soup, 127
chickpea(s):
Soup with Cilantro, 250
Warm Salad of Pasta and, 146
Chili-Cooked Garlic Spareribs with Cilantro, 128
Chili Oil, 9

chocolate:
Biscotti Terrine, 229
Breakfast, 35
Chocolate *Tartufo,* 278
Climax, 283
Crema, Baked, 196
Dacquoise, 154
Raspberry Turnovers, 58
"Seeds," Watermelon Granita with, 101
Semifreddo, 265
Chorizo, Salad of Watercress, Orange and, 90
Citrus Granita, Poached Oranges in Lemon Syrup with, 88
Clams, Tiny, with Wasabi and Pickled Ginger, 111
Coconut Ice Cream with Blue Curaçao, 192
cod:
Pavé of, with *Herbes de Provence,* 162
with Potato Flakes, Crispy, 100
coffee:
Amaretto Granita, 70
Anisette Espresso Coupe, 224
Café Cantata, 56
Ice Cream with Toasted Almonds and Prune Syrup, 84
Ice Cubes, Almond Milk with *Orzata* and, 59
condiments:
Carrot Jam, Egyptian, 29
Chili Oil, 9
Garlic Oil, 8
Rosemary Oil, 9
Salt-Preserved Lemons, 10
Tapenade, 10
Consommé with Marrow, 182
cookies:
Brown Sugar Shortbread, 78
Brutti ma Buoni (Ugly but Good), 257
corn:
Skillet-Roasted, Sour Cream Mashed Potatoes with, 139
Sweet, Soup with Scallion Butter, 107
Cornish Hens with Tarragon Rice, 203
cornmeal:
Arepas with Butter and *Queso Blanco,* 35
Porridge, Rumanian (*Mamaliga*), 26
see also polenta
Courgettes with Basil, 100
couscous:
with Currants, Curried, 260

Sun-Dried Tomato, Globe Artichokes Stuffed with, 147
Crab, Jumbo Lump, with Avocado Sauce, 191
cranberry(ies):
and Pear Compote with Cranberry Syrup, 56
Ruby, with Sun-Dried Cherries (Relish and Compote), 214
Crema, Chocolate, Baked, 196
Crème Brûlée, 205
Cremini Mushrooms with Sherry-Pepper Cream, 135
Cucumbers, *Labaneh* in Olive Oil with, 28

Dacquoise, Chocolate, 154
desserts:
Almond Water Ice with Fresh Cherry Salad and Cherry Syrup, 97
Apple Kissel with Apple Chips, 132
Apples *Talibur* in Puff Pastry with Apple Confit, 184
Banana Tarts, Warm, 189
Black Grapes and Rum Raisins with Black Grape Granita, 180
Brown Sugar Shortbread, 78
Brutti ma Buoni (Ugly but Good) Cookies, 257
Cherry, Fresh, Soup, 77
Chocolate, *Dacquoise,* 154
Chocolate Biscotti Terrine, 229
Chocolate Climax, 283
Chocolate *Crema,* Baked, 196
Chocolate *Semifreddo,* 265
Crème Brûlée, 205
Fig Confit with Sesame and Honey, 248
Fruit *en Papillote,* 288
Fruit Salad *Vino Cotto,* 81
Gingersnap Baked Apples, 117
Grapefruit, Pink, Sherbet with Pink Grapefruit Syrup, 92
Grapes with Wild-Thyme Honey and Yogurt, Turkish, 253
Lemon-Curd Yogurt Tarts, 220
Limoncello Zabaglione, 233
Nectarines, Roasted, with Amaretto Syrup and Amaretto Cream, 172
Oranges, Chilled Sliced, with Rosewater and Dates, 260
Oranges, Poached, in Lemon Syrup with Citrus Granita, 88
Panna Cotta with Amber Crystals, 164

Pears, Marsala-Poached, with Crushed Amaretti, 73
Pears, Oven-Roasted, with Stilton and Warm Honey Syrup, 293
Pears in White Wine Caramel, 149
Pineapple Flan, 113
Plums, Purple, with Mascarpone and Brown Sugar, 66
Polenta with Sugar and Oranges, 105
Profiteroles, Valrhona, 269
Prunes, Poached, with Cardamom Yogurt, 200
Pumpkin-Eggnog Flan with Custard Sauce, 215
Red, White, and Blueberries, 109
Rhubarb Compote and Sour Cream Ice Cream with Rhubarb-Pepper Syrup, 176
Rice Pudding, Old-Fashioned, 136
Strawberries in Cassis with Crème Fraîche, 274
Strawberry Gratin à la Sabayon, 243
Strudel, Simple, 209
Tequila Melon, 140
see also granita; ice cream; sorbet
duck:
Crisped, with Roasted Turnips and Port Wine Reduction, 208
Liver Salad, Warm, 207

Eggnog-Pumpkin Flan with Custard Sauce, 215
eggplant(s):
Braised, with Balsamic Syrup, 264
Flan, Turkish, 198
Japanese, with Roasted Garlic and Sun-Dried Tomatoes, 68
eggs:
and Asparagus Georges Blanc, 23
Baked, Splendido, 46
Buttermilk, in Tomato Shells, 39
Buttermilk Grits Soufflé, 49
Frittata with Pancetta and Mint, 43
Ham and, with Redeye Gravy, Country-Style, 31
Panettone French Toast, 55
Poached, Fennel Wafers with, 174
Poached, with Lime Hollandaise, 16
Scrambled, and Onions, 52
endive:
Belgian, and Blue Cheese Gratin, 204
and Grapefruit Salad, 151
Espresso Anisette Coupe, 224

fennel:
and Orange Salad, 231
Wafers with Poached Eggs, 174
Fesenjune (Chicken Breasts in Walnut and Pomegranate Sauce), 199
feta cheese:
–Olives–Grilled Pita, 29
and Roasted Red Onion Salad, 99
Warm, and Cherry Tomato Compote, 119
Fettuccine, Spinach, with Ricotta and Parmesan, 65
fig(s):
with Bitter Orange Mascarpone, 44
Confit with Sesame and Honey, 248
first courses:
Asiago-Pepper Roulades, 222
Beets, Baby, with Roquefort Cheese and Hazelnut Oil, 271
Bresaola and Mango with Parmesan Shards, 161
Chicken Liver Royale with Red Onions and Bacon, 235
Clams, Tiny, with Wasabi and Pickled Ginger, 111
Crab, Jumbo Lump, with Avocado Sauce, 191
Eggplant Flan, Turkish, 198
Eggplants, Japanese, with Roasted Garlic and Sun-Dried Tomatoes, 68
Fennel Wafers with Poached Eggs, 174
Feta Cheese, Warm, and Cherry Tomato Compote, 119
Fusilli Cacio e Pepe, 170
Gravlax, Home-Cured, 22
Jalapeño and Pepperoni Tortilla Flat, 128
Labaneh-Stuffed Tomatoes with Olive Oil, 245
Oysters with "Malted" Mignonette, 134
Pepper, Roasted, "Sandwiches," 86
Portobello Mushroom Melt, 226
Roquefort Mousse and Celery Crudités, 94
Salmon, Smoked, Tartare with Dill Mousse, 290
Scallops-in-Shiitakes, 178
Shrimp, Pickled, in Rice Vinegar, 280
Shrimp Sticks, Prosciutto-Wrapped, 276

Spinach and Smoked Salmon Terrine Lutèce, 202
Tomatoes, Roasted Rainbow of, in Peppers, 166
Tomato Polenta, 262
see also salads; soups
fish:
Cod, Pavé of, with Herbes de Provence, 162
Cod with Potato Flakes, Crispy, 100
Halibut Baked with Sour Cream and Parmesan, 166
Sardines Baked in Grape Leaves with Tomato Reduction, 83
Sea Bass in Cartoccio with Black Olive Tapenade and Oranges, 170
Sea Bass Steamed in Lettuce with Rosemary Oil, 95
Swordfish, Pan-Grilled, with Pepper-Lime Sauce, 111
Swordfish Stuffed with Watercress, Braised, 175
Tuna, Barbecued, London-Broil Style, 179
Tuna Salad, Lemony, with Tuna-Tahina Dressing, 80
Turbot, Gougonettes of, in Chickpea Flour, 103
see also salmon; shellfish; shrimp
flan:
Eggplant, Turkish, 198
Garlic, Roasted, 287
Pineapple, 113
Pumpkin-Eggnog, with Custard Sauce, 215
Zucchini, 153
Focaccia, Homemade, 148
Framboise, Tiny Melons Filled with Raspberries and, 37
French Toast, Panettone, 55
Frisée and Beet Salad with Goat Cheese Dressing, 186
Frittata with Pancetta and Mint, 43
fruit:
Fresh, en Papillote, 288
Kabobs, Quince-Glazed, 34
Salad Vino Cotto, 81
see also specific fruits
Ful Mudammas with Lemon, 28
Fusilli Cacio e Pepe, 170

garlic:
Bread, Country, 91
Bread Pudding (Açorda), 195
Oil, 8
Roasted, Flan, 287

Gelato d'Arancina with Candied Orange Peel, 159
Gingersnap Baked Apples, 117
Ginger Sugar, 11
goat cheese:
Dressing, Frisée and Beet Salad with, 186
Warm, with Fresh Mint Salad, 259
Gorgonzola-Grappa Rib Steak, 276
Gouda, Aged, Dutch Noodles with, 117
granita:
Amaretto, 70
Black Grape, Black Grapes with Rum Raisins and, 180
Citrus, Poached Oranges in Lemon Syrup with, 88
Grapefruit-Campari, 47
Watermelon, with Chocolate "Seeds," 101
grapefruit(s):
Campari Granita, 47
and Endive Salad, 151
Fruit Salad Vino Cotto, 81
Pink, Sherbet with Pink Grapefruit Syrup, 92
grapes:
Black, and Rum Raisins with Black Grape Granita, 180
with Wild-Thyme Honey and Yogurt, Turkish, 253
gratins:
Belgian Endive and Blue Cheese, 204
Celery Root, 188
Onion, Warm, 179
Sweet Potato–Cheddar, 213
Gravlax, Home-Cured, 22
green bean(s):
with Niçoise Olives, 70
and Potatoes in Pesto, 257
Simple, 180
Soup, Chilled, with Sour Cream Dollop, 123
Sweet Pepper, 80
Grits Soufflé, Buttermilk, 49

Halibut with Sour Cream and Parmesan, Baked, 166
Halvah and Golden Raisin Turnovers, 58
ham:
and Eggs with Redeye Gravy, Country-Style, 31
Smoked, Pithiviers of Port Salut and, 75
hazelnuts, in Brutti ma Buoni (Ugly but Good) Cookies, 257

Ice, Almond Water, with Fresh
    Cherry Salad and Cherry
    Syrup, 97
ice cream:
    Anisette Espresso Coupe, 224
    Chocolate-Chocolate *Tartufo,* 278
    Coconut, with Blue Curaçao, 192
    Coffee, with Toasted Almonds
        and Prune Syrup, 84
    Sour Cream, with Rhubarb
        Compote and Rhubarb-Pepper
        Syrup, 176
    Spumoni, 238
    Valrhona Profiteroles, 269
    Vanilla Bean, with Orange-
        Flower Water and Pistachios,
        121
Immune Soup, 127
ingredients, 6

Jalapeño and Pepperoni Tortilla
    Flat, 138

Kissel, Apple, with Apple Chips,
    132

labaneh:
    in Olive Oil with Cucumbers, 28
    -Stuffed Tomatoes with Olive Oil,
        245
lamb:
    Bombay Leg of, with Yogurt and
        Lime, 259
    Chops with Goat Cheese and
        Lavender, 241
    Riblets, Mustard-Molasses, 131
    Shish Kebabs with Onions and
        Pomegranate Molasses, 247
    Shoulder with Comté and Rose-
        mary, Roast, 256
    Stew with Cumin and Fresh
        Tomato, Oven-Braised, 251
Lavash, Pilaf Baked in, 121
lemon(s):
    Curd Yogurt Tarts, 220
    Salt-Preserved, 10
Limoncello Zabaglione, 233
Lychee Sorbet and Almond Cookie
    Dessert, 129

Mâche and Granny Smith Salad
    with Apple Vinaigrette, 76
main courses:
    Calf's Liver, Venetian Style, 263
    Cornish Hens with Tarragon
        Rice, 203
    Duck, Crisped, with Roasted
        Turnips and Port Wine Reduc-
        tion, 208

Mussels, Steamed, *Crema di
    Salsa,* 91
Pasta and Chickpeas, Warm
    Salad of, 146
"Pasta @ Noon," 72
Pithiviers of Smoked Ham and
    Port Salut, 75
Polenta "Lasagne" with Smoked
    Mozzarella, 146
Pork Loin and "Packed Rack"
    with Dried Fruit and Fennel
    Sausage, 218
Scallops, Bay, with Parsley Puree,
    86
Spareribs, Chili-Cooked Garlic,
    with Cilantro, 128
Spinach Fettuccine with Ricotta
    and Parmesan, 65
Turkey Breast, Brine-Cured, with
    Turkey Bacon and Roasted
    Pears with Roasted Pear
    "Gravy," 211
see also beef; chicken; fish; lamb;
    salmon; veal
Mamaliga (Rumanian Cornmeal
    Porridge), 26
mango(es):
    and *Bresaola* with Parmesan
        Shards, 161
    Prunes, and Pomegranates, 53
Margarita Sorbet with Sugared
    Raspberries, 125
mascarpone:
    Bitter Orange, Fresh Figs with,
        44
    Purple Plums with Brown Sugar
        and, 66
    Tomato Soup with Basil Chiffon-
        ade, 72
melon(s):
    Tequila, 140
    Tiny, Filled with Raspberries and
        Framboise, 37
    Two-, Soup, 40
Mint Salad, Warm Goat Cheese
    with, 259
mozzarella:
    Portobello Mushroom Melt, 226
    Smoked, Polenta "Lasagne" with,
        146
mushroom(s):
    Cremini, with Sherry-Pepper
        Cream, 135
    Portobello, Melt, 226
    Shiitakes, Scallops-in-, 178
    Wild, Onion, and Brie Soup, 285
Mussels, Steamed, *Crema di Salsa,*
    91
Mustard Beurre Blanc, 157

Nectarines, Roasted, with Amaretto
    Syrup and Amaretto Cream,
    172
Noodles with Aged Gouda, Dutch,
    117

Oatmeal, Irish, with Buttermilk and
    Poppy Seeds, 19
oils:
    Chili, 9
    Garlic, 8
    Rosemary, 9
olives:
    –Feta Cheese–Grilled Pita, 29
    French Black, Celery Salad with
        Truffle Oil and, 104
    Niçoise, Blasted Green Beans
        with, 70
    "Pasta @ Noon," 72
    Tapenade, 11
onion(s):
    Caramelized, Bulgur Wheat with,
        252
    Disguised as Marrow Bones, 219
    Gratin, Warm, 179
    Roasted Red, and Feta Salad, 99
    Scrambled Eggs and, 52
    Tomatoes and, "Short-Stack,"
        242
    Wild Mushroom, and Brie Soup,
        285
orange(s):
    Bitter, Mascarpone, Fresh Figs
        with, 44
    Chilled Sliced, with Rosewater
        and Dates, 260
    and Fennel Salad, 231
    Fresh Fruit *en Papillote,* 288
    Gelato d'Arancina with Candied
        Orange Peel, 159
    Poached, in Lemon Syrup with
        Citrus Granita, 88
    Polenta with Sugar and, 105
    Salad of Watercress, Chorizo and,
        90
    and Strawberries *en Gelée,* 24
    Tomato Soup with Tarragon,
        Chilled, 194
Orzata, Almond Milk with Coffee
    Ice Cubes and, 59
Orzo, Toasted, with Rice, 200
Oysters with "Malted" Mignonette,
    134

Pancetta, Frittata with Mint and, 43
Panettone French Toast, 55
Panna Cotta with Amber Crystals,
    164
pantry, minimalist, 8–11

Parmesan:
    Shards, *Bresaola* and Mango
        with, 161
    Spinach Fettuccine with Ricotta
        and, 65
pasta:
    Fusilli Cacio e Pepe, 170
    "Pasta @ Noon," 72
    Spinach Fettuccine with Ricotta
        and Parmesan, 65
    Tubetti with Zucchini, 84
    Twirl of, with Parsley-Garlic
        Sauce, 167
    Warm Salad of Chickpeas and,
        146
pastry(ies):
    Banana Tarts, Warm, 189
    Chocolate-Raspberry Turnovers,
        58
    Halvah and Golden Raisin Turn-
        overs, 58
    Lemon-Curd Yogurt Tarts, 220
    Pithiviers of Smoked Ham and
        Port Salut, 75
    Profiteroles, Valrhona, 269
    Puff, Apples *Talibur* in, with
        Apple Confit, 184
    Strudel, Simple, 209
pea(s):
    Sugar Snaps with Diced Bacon
        and Radishes, 175
    Yellow, Soup with Dill, 115
Peaches Flamed in Southern Com-
    fort, 50
pear(s):
    and Cranberry Compote with
        Cranberry Syrup, 56
    Marsala-Poached, with Crushed
        Amaretti, 73
    Oven-Roasted, with Stilton and
        Warm Honey Syrup, 293
    -Poire-Pepper Sorbet, 168
    in White Wine Caramel, 149
pepper(s):
    Asiago Roulades, 222
    Confit with Sherry Vinegar, 195
    Rainbow of Roasted Tomatoes in,
        166
    Red, Potato Cakes, 228
    Roasted, "Sandwiches," 86
    Sweet, Green Beans, 80
Pepperoni and Jalapeño Tortilla
    Flat, 138
pesto:
    Broth, White Beans and Shrimp
        in, 156
    Green Beans and Potatoes in, 257
Pilaf Baked in Lavash, 121
Pineapple Flan, 113

pita:
Bread, Whole Wheat, 246
Grilled, Feta Cheese–Olives–, 29
Pithiviers of Smoked Ham and Port
Salut, 75
Plantains, Fried, and Fresh Lime
(*Tostones*), 125
plums:
Purple, with Mascarpone and
Brown Sugar, 66
Spicy Stewed Red, 19
Poire-Pear-Pepper Sorbet, 168
polenta:
"Lasagne" with Smoked Mozza-
rella, 69
with Sugar and Oranges, 105
with Tiny Broccoli Florets, 273
Tomato, 262
Pomegranates, Mangoes, and
Prunes, 53
pork:
Loin and "Packed Rack" with
Dried Fruit and Fennel Sau-
sage, 218
Spareribs, Chili-Cooked Garlic,
with Cilantro, 128
Portobello Mushroom Melt, 226
Port Salut, *Pithiviers* of Smoked
Ham and, 75
potato(es):
Boiled, with Caper Vinaigrette,
183
Fingerling, with Roasted Garlic
and Brie Fondue, 282
Green Beans and, in Pesto, 257
Pan-Fried Sage, 277
Red Pepper Cakes, 228
Salad, with Horseradish, 108
Silk, 96
Sour Cream Mashed, with Skil-
let-Roasted Corn, 139
Pot-au-Feu (Chicken, Beef Shin,
and Leeks), 182
Prime Rib, Salt-and-Pepper, with
Horseradish Sauce and York-
shire Pudding, 291
Profiteroles, Valrhona, 269
prosciutto:
and Bel Paese *Bruschetta*, 46
-Wrapped Shrimp Sticks, 276
Provolone and Roasted Asparagus
Salad, 146
prune(s):
Mangoes, and Pomegranates,
53
Poached, with Cardamom
Yogurt, 200
Syrup, Coffee Ice Cream with
Toasted Almonds and, 84

puddings:
Garlic Bread (*Açorda*), 195
Rice, Old-Fashioned, 136
Yorkshire, 291
Pumpkin-Eggnog Flan with Cus-
tard Sauce, 215

Quesadillas, Smoked Salmon, 17
Queso Blanco, Arepas with Butter
and, 35
Quince-Glazed Fresh Fruit Kabobs,
34

raisin(s):
Golden, and Halvah Turnovers,
58
Rum, Black Grapes with Black
Grape Granita and, 180
raspberry(ies):
"Borscht," 26
Chocolate Turnovers, 58
Pear-Poire-Pepper Sorbet, 168
Red, White, and Blueberries, 109
Sugared, Margarita Sorbet with,
125
Tiny Melons Filled with Fram-
boise and, 37
reduction theory, 7
Rhubarb Compote and Sour Cream
Ice Cream with Rhubarb-Pep-
per Syrup, 176
Rib Steak, Gorgonzola-Grappa, 276
rice:
Brown, with Sun-Dried Cherries,
268
Jasmine, and Poppy Seeds, 112
Pilaf Baked in Lavash, 121
Pudding, Old-Fashioned, 136
Smoky Pink Beans and, 192
Toasted Orzo with, 200
with Water Chestnuts and
Sesame Oil, 129
ricotta:
Spinach Fettuccine with Parme-
san and, 65
Terrine, Souffléed, 37
Roquefort:
Baby Beets with Hazelnut Oil
and, 271
Mousse and Celery Crudités, 94
Rosemary Oil, 9

Sabayon, Strawberry Gratin à la, 243
salads:
Arugula, with Sweet Garlic
Dressing, 255
Asparagus, Roasted, and Provo-
lone, 146
Cabbage "Cream" Slaw, 131

Celery, with French Black Olives
and Truffle Oil, 104
Duck Liver, Warm, 207
Endive and Grapefruit, 151
Fennel and Orange, 231
Frisée and Beet, with Goat Cheese
Dressing, 186
Fruit, *Vino Cotto*, 81
Mâche and Granny Smith, with
Apple Vinaigrette, 76
Mint, Warm Goat Cheese with,
259
Onion, Roasted Red, and Feta,
99
of Pasta and Chickpeas, Warm,
146
Potato, with Horseradish, 108
Salade de Tomates with *Verjus*,
65
Tuna, Lemony, with Tuna-Tah-
ina Dressing, 80
of Watercress, Orange, and Cho-
rizo, 90
salmon:
Gravlax, Home-Cured, 22
"Osso Buco" of, 157
Pickled Fresh, 52
Prunier with Tomato Julienne
and Mint, 152
Smoked, and Spinach Terrine
Lutèce, 202
Smoked, Quesadillas, 17
Smoked, Tartare with Dill
Mousse, 290
Steak, Seared, with Cornichon
Vinaigrette, 108
Sardines Baked in Grape Leaves
with Tomato Reduction, 83
scallops:
Bay, with Parsley Puree, 86
-in-Shiitakes, 178
Scones, Warm Cheese, 42
sea bass:
in Cartoccio with Black Olive Ta-
penade and Oranges, 170
Steamed in Lettuce with Rose-
mary Oil, 95
Semifreddo, Chocolate, 265
shellfish:
Clams, Tiny, with Wasabi and
Pickled Ginger, 111
Crab, Jumbo Lump, with Avo-
cado Sauce, 191
Mussels, Steamed, *Crema di
Salsa*, 91
Oysters with "Malted" Mignon-
ette, 134
Scallops, Bay, with Parsley Puree,
86

Scallops-in-Shiitakes, 178
see also shrimp
Sherbet, Pink Grapefruit, with Pink
Grapefruit Syrup, 92
Shiitakes, Scallops-in-, 178
Shish Kebabs with Onions and
Pomegranate Molasses, 247
Shortbread, Brown Sugar, 78
Short Ribs, Wine-Dark, 268
shrimp:
Pickled, in Rice Vinegar, 280
Prosciutto-Wrapped, Sticks, 276
and White Beans in Pesto Broth,
156
side dishes:
Açorda (Garlic Bread Pudding),
195
Artichokes, Fresh, with Mint, 171
Artichokes, Globe, Stuffed with
Sun-Dried Tomato Couscous,
147
Barley with Dates, 248
Beans, Lemon Yellow, 132
Beans, Smoky Pink, and Rice, 192
Belgian Endive and Blue Cheese
Gratin, 204
Brown Rice with Sun-Dried
Cherries, 268
Brussels Sprouts and Tangerine
Beurre Noisette, 292
Bulgur Wheat with Caramelized
Onions, 252
Cabbage, Savoy, with Lardons
and Champagne Vinegar, 163
Cabbage "Cream" Slaw, 131
Celery Root Gratin, 188
Celery Salad with French Black
Olives and Truffle Oil, 104
Courgettes with Basil, 100
Couscous with Currants, Cur-
ried, 260
Cranberries, Ruby, with Sun-
Dried Cherries (Relish and
Compote), 214
Cremini Mushrooms with
Sherry-Pepper Cream, 135
Eggplant, Braised, with Balsamic
Syrup, 264
Focaccia, Homemade, 148
Garlic, Roasted, Flan, 287
Garlic Bread, Country, 91
Green Beans, Simple, 180
Green Beans, Sweet Pepper, 80
Green Beans and Potatoes in
Pesto, 257
Green Beans with Niçoise Olives,
70
Mâche and Granny Smith Salad
with Apple Vinaigrette, 76

side dishes (*cont.*)
  Noodles with Aged Gouda, Dutch, 117
  Onion Gratin, Warm, 179
  Onions Disguised as Marrow Bones, 219
  Orzo, Toasted, with Rice, 200
  Pasta, Twirl of, with Parsley-Garlic Sauce, 167
  Pepper Confit with Sherry Vinegar, 195
  Pilaf Baked in Lavash, 121
  Pita Bread, Whole Wheat, 246
  Polenta with Tiny Broccoli Florets, 273
  Red Pepper–Potato Cakes, 228
  Rice, Jasmine, and Poppy Seeds, 112
  Rice with Water Chestnuts and Sesame Oil, 129
  Spinach, Fresh, and Lemon Oil, 158
  Spinach and Celery Puree, 287
  Sugar Snaps with Diced Bacon and Radishes, 175
  Sweet Potato–Cheddar Gratin, 213
  Swiss Chard, Red, Sautéed, 237
  Tomatoes and Onions, "Short-Stack," 242
  Tomatoes Provençale, 87
  Tostones (Fried Plantains and Fresh Lime), 125
  Tubetti with Zucchini, 84
  Turnip Puree, Smooth and Chunky, with Caramelized Shallots, 212
  Watercress Sauté with Garlic Chips, 242
  White Bean Puree, Truffled, 237
  Yorkshire Pudding, 291
  Zucchini, Slow-Cooked, with Thyme, 224
  Zucchini Flan, 153
  see also potato(es)
Slaw, Cabbage "Cream," 131
sorbet:
  Lychee, and Almond Cookie Dessert, 129
  Margarita, with Sugared Raspberries, 125
  Pear-Poire-Pepper, 168
Soufflé(ed):
  Buttermilk Grits, 49
  Ricotta Terrine, 37
soups:
  Beet, with Pickled Beet Greens, 217

  Butternut Squash, with Leek Cream, 267
  Cherry, Fresh, 77
  Chickpea, with Cilantro, 250
  Consommé with Marrow, 182
  Corn, Sweet, with Scallion Butter, 107
  Green Bean, Chilled, with Sour Cream Dollop, 123
  Immune, 127
  Melon, 40
  Onion, Wild Mushroom, and Brie, 285
  Pea, Yellow, with Dill, 115
  Raspberry "Borscht," 26
  Tomato-Mascarpone, with Basil Chiffonade, 72
  Tomato-Orange, with Tarragon, Chilled, 194
  White Beans and Shrimp in Pesto Broth, 156
  Zucchini Vichyssoise, 240
Sour Cream Ice Cream, Rhubarb Compote with Rhubarb-Pepper Syrup and, 176
Spareribs, Chili-Cooked Garlic, with Cilantro, 128
spinach:
  and Celery Puree, 287
  Fettuccine with Ricotta and Parmesan, 65
  Fresh, and Lemon Oil, 158
  and Smoked Salmon Terrine Lutèce, 202
Spumoni, 238
Stilton, Oven-Roasted Pears with Warm Honey Syrup and, 293
strawberry(ies):
  in Cassis with Crème Fraîche, 274
  Fresh, and Gingered Yogurt, 17
  Fresh Fruit *en Papillote,* 288
  Fruit Salad *Vino Cotto,* 81
  Gratin à la Sabayon, 243
  and Oranges *en Gelée,* 24
  Quince-Glazed Fresh Fruit Kabobs, 34
Strudel, Simple, 209
sugar:
  Ginger, 11
  Vanilla, 11
Sugar Snaps with Diced Bacon and Radishes, 175
Sweet Potato–Cheddar Gratin, 213
Swiss Chard, Red, Sautéed, 237

swordfish:
  Braised, Stuffed with Watercress, 175
  Pan-Grilled, with Pepper-Lime Sauce, 111

Tapenade, 10
tarts:
  Banana, Warm, 189
  Lemon-Curd Yogurt, 220
  Tartufo, Chocolate-Chocolate, 278
Tequila Melon, 140
toast:
  Almond, 20
  Panettone French, 55
tomato(es):
  Candied, 32
  Cherry, Compote and Warm Feta Cheese, 119
  Fried Red, 43
  Labaneh-Stuffed, with Olive Oil, 245
  Mascarpone Soup with Basil Chiffonade, 72
  and Onions, "Short-Stack," 242
  Orange Soup with Tarragon, Chilled, 194
  Polenta, 262
  Provençale, 87
  Roasted Rainbow of, in Peppers, 166
  Salade de Tomates with *Verjus,* 65
  Shells, Buttermilk Eggs in, 39
  Tortilla Flat, Jalapeño and Pepperoni, 138
  Tostadas, Canadian Bacon and Dill, 39
  Tostones (Fried Plantains and Fresh Lime), 125
  Tubetti with Zucchini, 84
tuna:
  Barbecued, London-Broil Style, 179
  Salad, Lemony, with Tuna-Tahina Dressing, 80
Turbot, *Gougonettes* of, in Chickpea Flour, 103
Turkey Breast, Brine-Cured, with Turkey Bacon and Roasted Pears with Roasted Pear "Gravy," 211
Turnip Puree, Smooth and Chunky, with Caramelized Shallots, 212
turnovers:
  Chocolate-Raspberry, 58
  Halvah and Golden Raisin, 58

utensils, 6–7

vanilla:
  Bean Ice Cream with Orange-Flower Water and Pistachios, 121
  Sugar, 11
veal:
  Chops with Lemon and Basil, 227
  Pan-Roasted Breast of, Marcella Hazan, 223
  Roast with Caramelized Soup Greens and Vegetable Jus, 232
  Shanks with Forty Cloves of Garlic and Pinot Noir Reduction, 236
Vichyssoise, Zucchini, 240

Water Chestnuts, Rice with Sesame Oil and, 129
watercress:
  Salad of Orange, Chorizo and, 90
  Sauté with Garlic Chips, 242
Watermelon Granita with Chocolate "Seeds," 101
white bean(s):
  Puree, Truffled, 237
  and Shrimp in Pesto Broth, 156
White Wine Caramel, Pears in, 149
wine selection, 5

yogurt:
  Cardamom, Poached Prunes with, 200
  Gingered, Fresh Strawberries and, 17
  Labaneh in Olive Oil with Cucumbers, 28
  Labaneh-Stuffed Tomatoes with Olive Oil, 245
  Lemon-Curd, Tarts, 220
  Red, White, and Blueberries, 109
  Turkish Grapes with Wild-Thyme Honey and, 253
Yorkshire Pudding, 291

Zabaglione, *Limoncello,* 233
zucchini:
  Courgettes with Basil, 100
  Flan, 153
  Slow-Cooked, with Thyme, 224
  Tubetti with, 84
  Vichyssoise, 240